The Coordination of Public Sector Organizations

Public Sector Organizations

Editors: **B. Guy Peters**, Maurice Falk Professor of Government, Pittsburgh University, USA, and **Geert Bouckaert**, Professor at the Public Management Institute, Katholieke Universiteit Leuven, Belgium

Organizations are the building blocks of governments. The role of organizations, formal and informal, is most readily apparent in public bureaucracy, but all the institutions of the public sector are composed of organizations, or have some organizational characteristics that affect their performance. Therefore, if scholars want to understand how governments work, a very good place to start is at the level of the organizations involved in delivering services. Likewise, if practitioners want to understand how to be effective in the public sector, they would be well-advised to consider examining the role of organizations and how to make the organizations more effective.

This series will publish research-based books concerned with organizations in the public sector and will cover such issues as: the autonomy of public sector organizations, networks and network analysis; bureaucratic politics; organizational change and leadership; and methodology for studying organizations.

Titles include:

Geert Bouckaert, B. Guy Peters and Koen Verhoest
THE COORDINATION OF PUBLIC SECTOR ORGANIZATIONS
Shifting Patterns of Public Management

Koen Verhoest, Paul G. Roness, Bram Verschuere, Kristin Rubecksen and Muiris MacCarthaigh
AUTONOMY AND CONTROL OF STATE AGENCIES
Comparing States and Agencies

Forthcoming title:

Amanda Smullen
TRANSLATING AGENCY REFORM
Rhetoric and Culture in Comparative Perspective

Public Sector Organizations Series
Series Standing Order ISBN 978-0-230-22034-8 (Hardback)
978-0-230-22035-5 (Paperback)
(outside North America only)

You can receive future titles in this series as they are published by placing a standing order. Please contact your bookseller or, in case of difficulty, write to us at the address below with your name and address, the title of the series and the ISBNs quoted above.

Customer Services Department, Macmillan Distribution Ltd, Houndmills, Basingstoke, Hampshire RG21 6XS, England

The Coordination of Public Sector Organizations

Shifting Patterns of Public Management

Geert Bouckaert
Professor of Public Management, Catholic University of Leuven, Belgium

B. Guy Peters
Maurice Falk Professor of Government, University of Pittsburgh, USA

and

Koen Verhoest
Assistant Professor and Research Manager, Public Management Institute, Catholic University of Leuven, Belgium

First published 2010 by
PALGRAVE MACMILLAN

Palgrave Macmillan in the UK is an imprint of Macmillan Publishers Limited, registered in England, company number 785998, of Houndmills, Basingstoke, Hampshire RG21 6XS.

Palgrave Macmillan in the US is a division of St Martin's Press LLC, 175 Fifth Avenue, New York, NY 10010.

Palgrave Macmillan is the global academic imprint of the above companies and has companies and representatives throughout the world.

Palgrave® and Macmillan® are registered trademarks in the United States, the United Kingdom, Europe and other countries

ISBN 978–0–230–24015–5   hardback

This book is printed on paper suitable for recycling and made from fully managed and sustained forest sources. Logging, pulping and manufacturing processes are expected to conform to the environmental regulations of the country of origin.

A catalogue record for this book is available from the British Library.

A catalog record for this book is available from the Library of Congress.

Printed and bound in Great Britain by
CPI Antony Rowe, Chippenham and Eastbourne

Contents

List of Figures

List of Tables

Appendix

Notes on Authors

Geert Bouckaert is Professor of Public Management, Director of the Public Management Institute at the Katholieke Universiteit Leuven, and President of the European Group of Public Administration. He has published on issues of performance measurement and management reform.

B. Guy Peters is Maurice Falk Professor of American Government at the University of Pittsburgh, and also holds honorary appointments at several universities around the world. His most recent publications include the *Handbook of Public Administration* and the *Handbook of Public Policy (both edited with Jon Pierre)* and *Institutional Theory in Political Science* (2nd edn).

Koen Verhoest is Assistant Professor at the Public Management Institute at the Katholieke Universiteit Leuven where he specializes in research on government control, organization, marketization and governance, including relationships between the State, agencies and private-sector organizations. He has published several book chapters and articles on these issues in, among others, *Governance, Public Administration and Development, Public Organization Review, International Review of Administrative Sciences* and *Policy Studies Journal*.

Acknowledgements

We would like to thank Eva Beuselinck for her thorough research on the case of the United Kingdom, as well as for the writing up of that country chapter. We are thankful to Amaury Legrain, Wim Pierlé and Ann Wauters for their involvement in related earlier research and data-gathering, which resulted in the basis material for most of the country chapters. Also Oliver James, Bob Gregory, Jonathan Boston, Claude Rochet, Jon Pierre, Jan-Eric Furubo, Sandra Van Thiel, Kutsal Yesilkagit and Maarten Mookhoek must be thanked for their comments on the detailed analytical schemes of their own countries. Moreover, we thank Tom Christensen and all the participants of the 2006 session of the 'EGPA Study Group on Governance of Public Sector Organizations' for most valuable comments on an earlier version of the concluding chapter. Last but not least, we thank the anynomous reviewer of the book manuscript for his feedback.

List of Abbreviations

AAI	Independent Administrative Authorities (France)
ACE	Autonomous Crown Entities (New Zealand)
Ad Hoc Com	Ad hoc Commissions (Sweden)
BUD	Ministry of Budget and Finances (Belgium)
Cab Off	Cabinet Office (Sweden)
CBO	Congressional Budget Office (USA)
CEO	Chief executive officer
CIATER	Comité Interministériel de l'administration territoriale
CIM	Interministerial Committees (France)
CISI	Comité interministériel pour la société de l'information
CSG	Committee of the Secretary General (Belgium)
DIRE	Délégation interministérielle à la Réforme de l'Etat
DPMC	Department of Prime Minister and Cabinet (New Zealand)
EPN	Etablissements Publics Nationaux – National Public Bodies (France)
EU	European Union
FIN	Department of Finance (Sweden)
FTE	full-time employee
GAO	General Accounting Office (USA)
GDP	gross domestic product
Gen Aff	Department of General Affairs (The Netherlands)
HRM	human resource management
ICE	Independent Crown Entities (New Zealand)
ICG	Inter-Cabinet Groups (Belgium)

IMC	Interministerial Committees (The Netherlands; Belgium)
Int Aff	Ministry of Internal Affairs (Belgium)
MP	Minister-President (The Netherlands)
NDPB	Non-departmental Public Body (United Kingdom)
NHS	National Health Service (United Kingdom)
NPM	New Public Management
NSC	National Security Council (USA)
OECD	Organization for Economic Cooperation and Development
OMB	Office of Management and Budget (USA)
PBO	Performance Based Organizations (USA)
PM	Prime Minister
PMD	Prime Minister's Department
PM Off	Prime Ministers' Office (Sweden; Belgium)
Pub Adm	Department of Public Administration (Sweden)
Pub Corp	Public Corporations (Sweden)
RIM	Réunions Interministerielles (France)
SOE	State-owned enterprises
SMC	Strategic Management Committee
SSC	State Service Commission (New Zealand)
TR	Treasury
WHO	White House Office (USA)
ZBO	Public law bodies and private law bodies ('Zelfstandige Bestuursorganen' – The Netherlands)

Part 1
Concepts, Theories and Methodology

1
The Main Argument – Specialization without Coordination is Centrifugal

In 2000, the new New Zealand Minister of State Services, Trevor Mallard (2000), commented in one of his speeches on the current state of the New Zealand state sector:

> Let me outline the three overall areas where I think we need to see change in the State sector.
>
> Area one is fragmentation. Today we have 38 Public Service departments and more than 100 major Crown entities. And that doesn't take into account the defence and police forces, much of the education sector, and local government. That's a large number of State agencies for a country of fewer than four million people. In the major agencies – in the Public Service departments and the Crown entities – the results of that fragmentation are apparent. For example, in the labour market, departments compete against each other to hire the same staff, sometimes to the detriment of the Government overall. Some sectors – say education – require major co-ordination from the centre that soaks up resources. There's an absence of full-loop learning – feedback on whether policies actually work – because the policy advisors work in a department other than the delivery one and the connections between operations and advice aren't established.
>
> Area two is the role of the centre: that's the three central agencies – the SSC, the Treasury, and DPMC, plus the political executive – the Cabinet. Not surprisingly, in a fragmented system, the centre needs to be relatively strong. But – paradoxically – I think the centre has been struggling for definition in the last ten years or so.
>
> Area three is 'style' or 'culture'. Part of the problem here is the vertical, linear nature of purchase. That's the process by which

departments and Crown entities 'sell' their services to Ministers. It's a good system in that it makes it clear what is being produced, and at what cost. But we have taken it too far. Has anybody here seen a departmental purchase agreement that included a statement of values and behaviours that the department should apply on behalf of the Government? I bet you haven't ... but as I have just said, values and behaviour are one of the defining characteristics of the State sector. (Mallard 2000, quoted in Boston and Eichbaum 2005, footnote 5)

Shortly after this announcement, several new reforms were introduced, which addressed these concerns and stressed the 'whole-of-government' capability for effective service delivery. For the New Zealand administrative apparatus, that was at least a shift in emphasis, given that during the past two decades New Zealand had been 'the most radical, comprehensive and innovative' example of 'new public management' (Boston and Eichbaum 2005). From 1984 onwards, and based on public choice and neo-institutional economical thinking, a large number of new semi-autonomous, single-objective agencies was created in order to decouple advisory, delivery, regulatory and commercial functions. Departments and agencies were controlled by output-oriented contracts, with ministers as being purchasers and being underpinned by equally output-oriented financial and human resources management systems.

Scholars see this shift of emphasis in New Zealand as being exemplary of a new – some say, post-New Public Management (NPM) (Richards and Smith 2006) – trend in several OECD countries, and as a reaction to a previous trend with respect to public sector organization. This first trend was the breaking up of large multi-objective bureaucracies in many small, mostly single-objective organizations, such as agencies and other autonomous bodies. As a consequence of NPM dynamics, this specialization movement has been launched in many countries of the OECD. Recently, a renewed emphasis on coordination of policy and management seems noticeable in many of these countries (6 et al. 2002; Gregory 2006; Halligan 2006; Bogdanor 2005; Richards and Smith 2006). 'Whole-of-government' initiatives like 'Joined-up government' (UK), 'Horizontalism' (Canada), similar initiatives in Australia, and 'Reviewing the Centre' (New Zealand) that contained an increased focus on horizontal collaboration and integrated service delivery between public organizations and governmental levels, as well as mergers of departments and reintegration and standardization of agencies, are interpreted as manifestations of this new trend (Christensen and Laegreid 2006a).

An increasing number of scholars argue that these two trends are interrelated as cause and consequence (Christensen and Laegreid 2006c; Pollitt and Bouckaert 2004; Pollitt 2003; Verhoest and Bouckaert 2005; Boston and Eichbaum 2005; Gregory 2006; Halligan 2006):

> These 'Whole of Government' trends can therefore be seen as a reaction to the 'siloization' or 'pillarization' of the public sector that seems to be typical for the NPM reforms. The principle of 'single-purpose organisations', with many specialised and nonoverlapping roles and functions, may have produced too much fragmentation, self-centred authorities and lack of co-operation and co-ordination, hence hampering effectiveness and efficiency. (Christensen and Laegreid 2006b: 15)

Thus, the specialization trend appeared to be a fragmentation which sometimes was so significant that existing, new and renewed mechanisms of coordination had to be (re-) established. This shift demonstrates a basic assertion of organization theory that specialization and differentiation increases the need for coordination (Thompson 1967; Mintzberg 1979). But to what extent does reality reflect this pattern of specialization, followed by increased coordination? Is this pattern only visible in countries which vigorously applied the NPM paradigm of separating policy implementation from design by creating single-objective agencies? Is this an overall pattern in OECD countries from different politico-administrative cultures, or are there different trajectories? Is specialization, and the perceived fragmentation stemming from it, the only or main driver for a renewed emphasis on coordination? What do these coordination strategies look like? Are coordination instruments other than traditional hierarchical mechanisms used? Do these new coordination strategies turn back agentification or other forms of organizational proliferation or do they rather co-exist with high degrees of specialization (Christensen and Laegreid 2006a: concluding chapter)?

In this book we assess the validity of this scholarly argument by analysing specialization and coordination strategies in seven OECD countries. The focus is on central government, including the three levels of politics, ministries and their related autonomous entities. This research analysed evolution over a period of about 25 years, from 1980 to 2005. The selected countries have different politico-administrative cultures and are known for a different level of adherence to the NPM doctrines of administrative reform (Pollitt and Bouckaert 2004):

- Anglo-American countries: New Zealand and the UK as high-profile NPM reformers, and the USA as an example of a reluctant reformer.
- Nordic European: Sweden as a Scandinavian country with a moderate NPM profile.
- Continental European: The Netherlands, which is clearly influenced by the NPM doctrine.
- Latin European: Belgium and France, both known to be rather low profile with respect to NPM-based administrative reforms.

For that purpose, we have developed a classification of coordination mechanisms and instruments, based on hierarchy, market and network as fundamental coordination mechanisms (based on Thompson et al. 1991; Peters 1998, 2003; Verhoest et al. 2003). Also, a systematic methodology for mapping these instruments has been designed (cf. Verhoest and Bouckaert 2005). These operationalizations help us in describing and analysing changes at a general macro level in a systematic way.

1.1   The structure of this book

As we develop the argument about specialization and coordination we first discuss our initial hypothesis on the trajectory of specialization and coordination, which we assumed to be standard for OECD countries. In Chapter 2 the concept of 'coordination' is defined, along with related concepts such as specialization, and factors which increase the need for coordination are pointed out. Chapter 3 elaborates on the mechanisms and resources for coordination, resulting in a typology of coordination mechanisms – 'hierarchy-type' mechanisms (HTM), 'network-type' mechanisms (NTM) and 'market-type' mechanisms (MTM). In the subsequent methodological chapters we outline a comparative static method that enables us to analyse schematically evolutions in specialization and coordination in OECD countries over a period of 25 years.

The empirical component of the book begins with an in-depth analysis of specialization and coordination in New Zealand in order to see if the assumed consequence and causality of increased specialization and increased coordination indeed matches reality. Six other countries are subsequently studied, each in one chapter and using the same methodology. In the last empirical chapter we make some cross-country comparisons from various angles. In a final section we frame our observations about similarities and dissimilarities in countries theoretically and point at some possible explanations. Hypotheses for further explanatory research are also framed.

1.2 The basic argument of this book

The general hypothesis motivating our research is shown in Figure 1.1 (Verhoest and Bouckaert 2005). We assume, as is commonly accepted in organization theory, that specialization results in efficiency gains. This efficiency is apparent for single tasks as well as for broader clusters and departments within organizations. According to New Public Management theory this logic also applies to families of organizations at a particular level of government. Following this logic major monolithic organizations have been dismantled into smaller parts, each granted a level of autonomy. As well as an increase of decentralization and devolution, a clear expansion of the number of autonomous 'agencies'

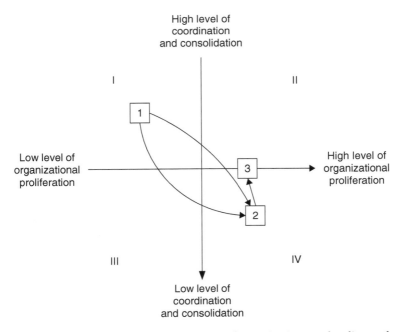

Figure 1.1 Specialization and coordination of organizations and policy cycles: assumed general trajectory in OECD countries
Sources: Verhoest and Bouckaert 2005; Verhoest et al. 2007.

has been visible in the public sector. This resulted in a fragmentation of public organizations which was perceived as proliferation getting out of control. This movement was combined with two other traditional shifts in the public sector. First, there was the familiar split between politics and administration, and second, there is the split between policy design and implementation. This double shift is cyclical.

In the early part of the twentieth century scientific management favoured a politics/administration split. As part of a 'Government for the Efficient' it was necessary for the politicians to focus on the political issues, and for the administration to the focus on the administrative issues. This split for reasons of efficiency was supposed also to benefit responsibility and accountability. Later, these positions were weakened, and a mutual influence was considered to have some benefits (Appleby 1940). Contemporary New Public Management again supports the split between politics and administration for the same reasons as at the beginning of the twentieth century. Ministers become 'purchasers' and administrations become 'providers', and there is a quasi-market pattern between these two parties resulting in a contract, as is the case in New Zealand.

The split or merger of policy design and implementation has always been cyclical. The classical model keeps these two major components of the cycle together since implementation should follow the logic of its design. Design also should take into account the strengths and weaknesses of implementation. Locating these functions as organizational proxies should facilitate their interaction because of the possibility of intra-organizational communication. On the other hand, a focus on checks and balances, redefining responsibilities and accountabilities for different functions, has encouraged experimentation with a policy cycle split. Design is in one organization, and implementation could be in another, private or public. In the United Kingdom, for example, HM Prison Service is developing a prison policy and its implementation is contracted to public or private services. Again, the most common coordination is through contracting, with or without tenders. In New Public Management, as an extreme type of public management reform, there was a clear preference for this split. This policy resulted in the separation of policy design in small ministries, with implementation through a separate agency (public or private, subject to competitive tendering), and finally evaluated by still another entity. The policy cycle evolved from a consolidated to a decoupled cycle, and decoupling was supposed to generate efficiency gains through specialization.

There is an initial position of a monolithic traditional administration, a bureaucracy, which is in charge of a consolidated policy cycle. Quadrant I of Figure 1.1 refers to an integrated concept of the three levels (political level L1, department level L2, and level of quasi-autonomous agencies L3). In this starting position coordination is mainly carried out by using hierarchy-type mechanisms (such as input control by central agencies and direct control by ministers).

This starting position evolved to a broad range of specialized and autonomous organizations which have divided the work, including the disconnected parts of the policy cycle. This combined movement should result in better performance because of the possibility of 'managers to manage', to 'make' them manage or to 'let' them manage. They have their own budget which they can spend with some degree of freedom, including on personnel. There is *ex post* evaluation of performance as agreed upon in a contract instead of an *ex ante* input and resource control system.

Figure 1.1 shows a summary of the hypothesized trajectories in this research.

Although the mechanisms reallocating responsibility and redesigning accountability appeared quite satisfactory, there was an 'unforeseen' major dysfunction of having too developed or unconditional autonomy and decoupling (quadrant IV in Figure 1.1). Allocating autonomy in a disconnected organizational framework, which is only linked through contracts, triggers centrifugal forces in which autonomy is further expanding, responsibility becomes rhetorical, and accountability becomes symbolic. There was a general loss of macro control over the global system of the public sector.

This level of disconnection resulted in corrective reactions which could mean, theoretically, first reducing the organizational proliferation, second, reconsolidating the policy cycle, or third, combinations of reducing organizational proliferation and policy re-consolidation. To some extent (see below) all three of these responses have been tried.

Specialization resulted in two mechanisms for organizational proliferation. The number of autonomous organizations increased, and hence the corrective measure has been to decrease that number by re-integrating them into the 'mother-organization'. A second mechanism was the acceleration of the heterogeneity and diversity of organizations by reducing the standardization and uniformity of management practices. The corrective measure in this case has been to re-standardize, sometimes at the level of creating holding organizations, and abolishing *ad hoc* solutions. On the vertical consolidation-decoupling axis there could be an emphasis on

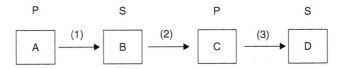

Comparative static analytical framework

P: Problem; S: Solution

(1) Maintain, modernize, marketize, minimize (4 Ms)
(2) Dysfunctional pressure, dysfunctional specialization
(3) Correcting mechanisms (HTM, NTM, MTM)

Figure 1.2 Simple stimulus–response scheme regarding specialization and coordination
Sources: Verhoest and Bouckaert 2005; Verhoest et al. 2007.

intra-policy cycle consolidation or coordination (that is, of policy design, implementation and evaluation). A second pattern could be across policy fields (inter-policy coordination or consolidation). Obviously, increased decoupling has put pressure on a homogeneous policy culture.

It is clear that these adjustments in the public sector have been based on an action–reaction pattern where the solution to a problem turns into a problem itself which then needs to be solved, as shown in Figure 1.2. An initial situation is perceived as a problem. Since the 1980s the reactions of countries have been to maintain, modernize, marketize or minimize their public sectors (Pollitt and Bouckaert 2004). This resulted in a range of acceptable 'solutions' to the perceived problems. However, as described above, these solutions became too extreme or too dysfunctional because of loss of control. In general the set of solutions that were developed to solve the second generation of problems could be based on mechanisms (and their related instruments) of hierarchy, markets and networks. Specifically, market-type mechanisms and network-type mechanisms can be assumed to have been used to a great extent because of their higher level of compatibility with organizational autonomy.

Figure 1.3 provides the substance of the scheme shown in Figure 1.2. There existed perceived problems of guaranteeing performance, taking and allocating responsibility, substantiating accountability, keeping, or even enhancing, transparency, making functional control, and keeping a sufficient policy capacity. As a 'solution', agencies were created, autonomy was granted, specialization was increased, and single policy capacity was developed. However, these reforms resulted in dysfunctional levels of autonomy, centrifugal organizations, a

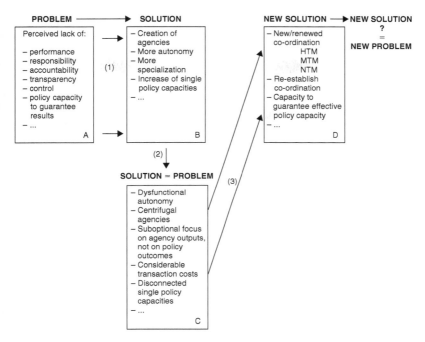

Figure 1.3   Refined stimulus–response scheme regarding specialization and coordination
Sources: Verhoest and Bouckaert 2005; Verhoest et al. 2007.

suboptimal focus on agency outputs rather than on policy outcomes, considerable transaction costs between the components of the policy cycle and between agencies, and disconnected policy capacity which was too specialized and lacked critical mass. This problem triggered new 'solutions' which were based on re-establishing coordination by using renewed hierarchy-type mechanisms, as well as new market-type mechanisms and network-type mechanisms. A key question is whether these solutions will generate new problems.

As a general picture in OECD countries, one could *hypothesize* that in the early 1980s monolithic ministries tried to include all aspects of a policy cycle and remained in quadrant I (position 1), although some non-departmental bodies already existed. In the 1980s and the early 1990s there is a combined evolution of organizational proliferation based on the creation of autonomous or quasi-autonomous agencies, devolution, and decentralization on the one hand, and separating stages of the policy cycle on the other hand (towards quadrant IV [position 2]). From the mid-1990s, OECD countries strengthened their coordination capacity using both renewed and new HTM, NTM and (to a lesser extent) MTM. This coordination capacity resulted in a recoupling of the policy cycle and in some cases in a small decrease of organizational proliferation (quadrant II [position 3]).

The central research questions in this book are:

To what extent have countries increased the coordination of management and policy as a reaction to excessive high levels of specialization and its centrifugal fragmentation?

To what extent have countries introduced new coordination mechanisms (more markets and networks rather than hierarchies) to cope with the negative consequences of increased specialization?

The central hypotheses in this book are:

1 *Following NPM doctrines, OECD countries have increased levels of specialization within their public sector (quadrant IV [position 2] in Figure 1.1).*
2 *Fragmentation of management and policies increases because of higher levels of specialization.*
3 *Fragmentation is reduced by increasing the levels of coordination and introducing new coordination mechanisms (quadrant II [position 3]).*
4 *New coordination mechanisms based on NTM and MTM, rather than strict HTM, were introduced to match the new state structure and to combine some merits of specialization and autonomy with the benefits of coordination.*

When analysing OECD countries we would expect a generic evolution of more specialization followed by more coordination. This sequence is not a coincidence. Specialization, introduced as a solution to certain problems, generated new problems for which the new and renewed coordination mechanisms were supposed to provide solutions. The crucial issue is that the underlying and resulting problems are related to a loss of governments' policy capacity.

2
Coordination: What Is It and Why Should We Have It?

This part of the book discusses the concept of coordination, related concepts like specialization and their operationalization in research, drawing from several theories and other research. Needs, resources and mechanisms for coordination will be elaborated, resulting in a clustering in MTM (market-type mechanisms), HTM (hierarchy-type mechanisms), and NTM (network-type mechanisms).

2.1   The coordination problem

Coordination is one of the oldest problems facing the public sector. As soon as government was sufficiently differentiated to have several organizations providing different services, or providing the same service in different ways (an army and a navy, for example), coordination became an issue. So long as government remained relatively small and under the control of a monarch or other central figure, coordination could be handled relatively easily. A monarch such as Henry VIII, or his Wolsey, might be able to manage the affairs of state themselves and might know what was happening in all the relevant policy areas and be able to ensure that there was some degree of coherence in policy.[1] Even in those primitive governing systems, however, there might be problems with coordination, and public offices were created to ensure that there was some common policy throughout the territory governed by the monarch.[2]

As government became involved in an increasing range of activities, and attempted to impose its rule over larger geographical spaces, coordination quickly evolved as a 'philosopher's stone' for government (Seidman 1998; Jennings and Krane, 1994; Webb 1991; Anderson 1996; 6 et al. 2002). That is, the more the public sector has evolved and expanded the more that incoherence and the failure to be capable of encouraging, or coercing, programmes to work together have come to be seen as among the more crucial root causes of the numerous perceived failures of government. Governments are inherently multi-organizational. The specialization reflected in its multi-organizational nature often affects the quality of public decisions. Further, specialization is importantly politically for government because it provides a clear locus for the identification and activities of client groups within society.

Despite those virtues, the many organizations existing in government create problems of coordination and coherence, and those coordination problems are very troubling for political leaders. As Davis (1996: 131) argued in relation to government:

> An elective official confronted with a state which simultaneously encompasses internal conflicts, competing external imperatives, contested boundaries, unclear jurisdictions, policy lacunae and interest capture is likely to desire some form of coordination.

Often one organization within the public sector does not appear even to have the most basic information about what other parts are doing, and the individuals involved appear to care little about the actions of their counterparts elsewhere. Further, coordination failures are particularly vexing to leaders in the public sector (and also to citizens) because they appear so fundamental. No matter how numerous they may have become, the programmes that are not coordinated adequately are all part of the same government, and therefore should be capable of operating together toward a common public purpose.

The search for the philosopher's stone, although it proved to be futile in the past, seems to have become again a major focus of several OECD governments in recent 'whole of government' initiatives (Christensen and Laegreid 2006b; OECD 1996). Decisions made in earlier decades have intensified the need for effective coordination, just as the increased emphasis on policy performance among the public has done. The search may remain futile, but there are too many political reasons for that basic goal not to be pursued.

2.2 The meaning of coordination

We have been discussing coordination as if we knew what the term meant, and as if there is a single definition of a single type of problem that is undermining the capacity of government to deliver integrated and effective services to the public. That is not the case and although coordination has a commonsense meaning in the context of government it has a number of other facets and complexities that need to be considered. For example, coordination is both a process through which decisions are brought together and an outcome of that process (Alexander 1995). In addition, a number of other terms are often used as virtual synonyms for coordination – cooperation, coherence, collaboration and integration. Therefore, before we can proceed any further in the analysis we will need to define the term, and the coordination problem, and then discuss various types of failures in coordination and their possible consequences for government.

Although it is in many ways a commonsense term, there is a need for a clear definition of coordination. Two of the most direct and most generally applicable definitions of coordination in the policy and administration literature is that coordination (see Alexander 1995 for an extensive discussion of coordination in interorganizational context):

> . . . is the extent to which organizations attempt to ensure that their activities take into account those of other organizations (Hall et al. 1976: 459)

> . . . is mutual adjustment between actors or a more deliberate interaction produces positive outcomes to the participants and avoids negative consequences (Lindblom 1965: 23, 154)

In many ways both Hall's and Lindblom's definitions are deceptively simple. All governments have to do is to have their programmes and organizations identify the means of taking into consideration the actions of other organizations and programmes, and consider in advance the consequences of their decisions. These definitions do not take into account explicitly, although they certainly do implicitly, the numerous different causes of coordination problems, and the barriers that exist in almost all political systems to effective coordination. Moreover, there is a *wide range* of available coordination instruments and mechanisms, which are not all as purposeful as they appear in these definitions. Markets, for example, may be conceptualized as coordinating organizations by an invisible hand. Common cultures, values and norms may implicitly enhance alignment of actions. Finally, there are various *levels* of coordination that can be achieved through various investments of resources, or simply because some programmes are easier to coordinate than others, while some civil service systems may promote coordination

Table 2.1   Levels of coordination as an outcome (Metcalfe 1994)

9	Government strategy
8	Establishing central priorities
7	Setting limits on ministerial action or actions of organizations
6	Arbitration of policy differences
5	Search for agreement among ministers/organizations
4	Avoiding divergences among ministers/organizations
3	Consultation with other ministers/organizations (feedback)
2	Communication with other ministers/organizations (information exchange)
1	Independent decision-making by ministers/organizations

Source: Based on Metcalf (2004).

more explicitly than do others. Les Metcalfe (1994; see Table 2.1) has presented a scale of coordination within the public sector that extends from independent decisions by organizations as the lowest level of coordination (or in this case almost total absence of coordination) of activities among public programmes up to a very high level of cooperation and coherence indicated by a coherent government strategy encompassing all areas of the public sector.[3] Thus, coordination at one level may be achieved, while coordination at a higher level may not be achieved. The question, then, is: What is the level of aspiration of the participants in the process for the coherence of the outcomes (see also Kassim et al. 1999)?

In this book we mainly focus on coordination as a *process* and the strategies and instruments governments use to coordinate organizations or programmes within the public sector. In this book, coordination in a public sector interorganizational context is considered to be *the instruments and mechanisms that aim to enhance the voluntary or forced alignment of tasks and efforts of organizations within the public sector. These mechanisms are used in order to create a greater coherence, and to reduce redundancy, lancunae and contradictions within and between policies, implementation or management* (Metcalfe 1994; Peters 1998, Alexander 1995; Thompson 1967).

2.3   Coordination and affiliated concepts

Coordination is a familiar term but a number of other terms have been applied to the same general area in the literature on public management. One of the earliest differentiations made in the organizational literature (Schermerhorn, 1975; Rogers and Whetten 1985: 12–13) was between cooperation and coordination. The former was deemed to be a more temporary and informal means of creating relationships among organizations for mutual benefit, while the latter was conceptualized as more formal structures and procedures designed to impose greater coordination among individuals and organizations.

The literature on managing social programmes in particular has discussed 'collaboration' as a mode of interaction among organizations (see Huxham and Vangen 2005; Hudson et al. 2002). For example, Bardach (1996; 1998; Bardach and Lesser 1996) has written a great deal on collaboration and the deceptively simple aspects of 'managerial craftsmanship' required to get agencies to work together. In this book, we will deal with collaboration as a subset of coordination, in which cooperation and 'working together' is voluntary and based on normative agreements. This approach to collaboration is valuable but, as will become very evident throughout this book, a good deal of coordination is not produced by agreement but rather is the result either of coercion[4] or the use of incentives. It is certainly more pleasant if the coordination can be based on common norms, but governments do not wait for that agreement to arise naturally.

Jan Kooiman has discussed collaboration and cooperation in a somewhat different manner. He argued (2003) for a difference between these two terms, with the former representing something more fleeting in terms of agreements among organizations to work together, while the latter represented more enduring patterns of working together, and perhaps (although Kooiman is far from clear on this point) something approaching the level of policy integration mentioned above. Kooiman is interested in all these forms of interorganizational working as means of achieving his more general concern of 'governance', meaning some level of coordination not only within the public sector but also between the public and private sectors.

In organization theory, coordination as a concept is very much related, or even equivalent to, the issue of integration. Here, we refer to integration as a process rather than a result (see our discussion of policy integration above). Integration is one basic principle in organizing, as a counterweight to differentiation, which is in turn a consequence of specialization (Lawrence and Lorsch 1967; March and Simon 1958; Mintzberg 1979). In organization theory, integrating organizational parts is achieved through installing coordination mechanisms (Mintzberg 1979; Galbraith 1977). However, in interorganizational perspective, integration is sometimes considered to be more radical than coordination. For example, in the perspective of Perri 6 (6 2004; 6 et al. 2002: 33–4),[5] the distinction between coordination (for example, information exchange, dialogue and joint planning) and integration (for example, joint working, joint ventures, mergers) refers both to the preparation and actual implementation of joint actions, as well as more modest forms of interorganizational collaboration versus more radical forms. As we will elaborate further in the next chapter, we consider the integration of working practices and organizations as particular instruments within coordination strategies, rather than a distinct theoretical concept.

Practitioners, especially those in the United Kingdom, have also been using terms such as 'joined-up government' and 'holistic government' to address the fundamental issue of coordination and coherence in governing (6 2004; Bogdanor 2005; Pollitt 2003). These terms were designed to be political terms as much or more than to provide analytic leverage for scholars, but they do describe tasks and styles of coordination within the political system. The Blair government began early in its existence to talk about joined-up government (Bogdanor 2005), reflecting in part the fragmented government they had inherited from the previous Tory administration.[6] That government had decentralized substantially, but even without this policy there would have been more general problems of coordination that are endemic to all governments. The creation of joined-up government by the Blair administration was, however, superseded by a concern to create 'holistic' government, meaning that not only did they attempt to get programmes to work together more effectively, but they had the further ambition to have programmes with more consistent goals and greater coherence across the public sector.

Joined-up government has been defined by Pollitt, based on a review of relevant UK governmental sources, as denoting the aspiration to achieve horizontally and vertically coordinating thinking and action (Pollitt 2003). It clearly aims at the coordination of policies and implementation in an interorganizational setting, across departments, agencies and, by extension, relevant private and voluntary bodies (Bogdanor 2005: 1–2). Benefits are seen in addressing complex social problems in a comprehensive, integrated way, the elimination of mutually undermining policies, better use of scarce resources, the creation of synergies by bringing together different key stakeholders in a policy field or network, and providing citizens with seamless access to a set of related services (Pollitt 2003; Bogdanor 2005). *Holistic government* is, according to Perri 6 et al. (2002; see also 6 2004), an even more ambitious quest. Whereas joining-up only refers to *consistency* between organizational arrangements of programmes, policies or agencies, holistic government aims at establishing clear and *mutually reinforcing* sets of objectives, which are framed in terms of outcomes and which are translated into mutually reinforcing means and instruments.

More broadly, all these initiatives are referred to as *whole-of-government* (WoG) (Christensen and Lægreid 2006b), which, according to some scholars (see Ling 2002), is not to be seen as a coherent set of ideas and tools but rather as 'an umbrella term describing a set of responses to the problem of increased fragmentation of the public sector and public services and a wish to increase co-ordination' (Christensen and Lægreid 2006b; Richards and Kavanagh 2000; Gregory 2006; Halligan 2006). The trend towards WoG is considered to be a post-NPM reform ideology, and is enabled by, among other things, the progress in ICT technologies, rising expectations of consumers for integrated services, and ongoing concerns about efficiency and budgetary pressure (Mulgan 2005; Christensen and Lægreid 2006b).

Related to these changes is also an emphasis on *strengthening the role of the centre* (political level and core administration) in building coherence in policies and implementation (OECD 1996; Halligan 2006; Gregory 2006; Richards and Smith 2006). The role of the centre is crucial when studying coordination within central government and is a central issue in the empirical country studies in this book. The centre here refers to the political level of the cabinet, but also to the 'central agencies'. Central agencies (Campbell and Szablowski 1965) are organizations such as ministries of the Prime Minister, of finance or the civil service that provide few if any services directly to citizens but rather are concerned primarily with providing horizontal services, with regulating and coordinating, within the public sector. Although the WoG reforms stress horizontal coordination and voluntary collaboration to a high extent, the emphasis on the reassertion of the centre points to the inherently vertical and top-down dimensions of such reforms (Christensen and Laegreid 2006a: concluding chapter).

2.4 Different dimensions of coordination and the focus of the book

There are several dimensions of coordination covered in our analysis of practices in various OECD countries. First, we discuss some dimensions related to the *intention* or *content* of coordination initiatives. Then we look at the *locus* or direction of coordination.

Positive and negative

Implied in the definition of coordination given above is the notion that programmes and organizations should work together to achieve ends that are not attainable through their individual actions. This is a reasonable reading of ideas of coordination, but a minimalist form of coordination can be attained without even that very basic degree of collaboration. *Negative coordination* involves only the agreement, even if tacit, of the actors that they will not harm each other's programmes or operations. Fritz Scharpf (1994), for example, has discussed negative coordination in his discussion of governance, noting that it is a minimum condition for governing. This principle is often enshrined in law and practice, as in the *Ressortsprinzip* in German government that each minister has the right to control policy and administration in his/her own area.

One can also focus on the *positive* aspects of coordination, and how coordination can build coherence, rather than just minimize conflict. This positive conception of coordination is much more difficult to achieve than is negative coordination. Positive coordination may require the actors involved to give up some policy goals, and almost certainly some of their preferred ways of achieving those goals, in order to attain greater overall performance by government. Requiring that self-denial may be asking a great deal of organizations that have developed their goals and procedures in the sincere belief that what they are doing already serves the public. If these organizations are correct in that belief, as they generally are, then expecting them to jettison some aspects of those programmes in favour of some vague benefits achieved through coordination is asking a great deal. This is all the more true given that contemporary managerialism in the public sector tends to focus on the performance of single organizations (see below).

In this book, this distinction between positive and negative forms of coordination will not be a central focus of analysis since the quality of our data does not allow us to judge that aspect of coordination in the countries we study. However, one may assume more emphasis on positive forms of coordination, since we focus explicitly on the instruments used for enhancing coordination.

Policy, administration or management

One of the most fundamental issues in the analysis of coordination is the strategic question of whether policy-makers should focus more on policy ('joined-up policy design') or on administration ('joined-up policy implementation') from a policy coordination point of view (Pollitt 2003: 37). Like most interesting, important and difficult questions about governing there are good reasons for choosing either answer. This debate to some extent mirrors the 'top-down' versus 'bottom-up' issues in the analysis of implementation (Sabatier and Jenkins-Smith 1993; Linder and

Peters 1987; Winter 2003). The fundamental question then is whether it is possible to design policies sufficiently well at the top of government to produce the desired outcomes in the field, or whether the policy-maker needs to depend more on the local knowledge existing with the policy implementers at the bottom to produce viable programmes and coordination.

The first option is to coordinate policy design from the top, and be sure that the policy is coherent, with the assumption that if the underlying policies are consistent then their implementation will by necessity be compatible. The argument supporting this view of coordination is that if policies are fundamentally compatible, then the administration can proceed along normal functional lines and still produce outcomes that will be coherent. Further, this style of coordination, if it can actually be achieved, is likely to be more efficient than one that depends upon local bargaining. This is especially true if there is a strong desire for uniformity of implementation in the field. Relying on coordination in the field means that there will be numerous local bargains and hence potentially broad differences in the policies implemented.

However, one could argue that so many aspects of policy can go amiss between the centre and the field and that even the most compatible policies in the centre may well diverge once they are implemented. Phrased in the language of economics, there is a danger of loss of agency (Jensen and Meckling 1976; Pratt and Zeckhauser 1991; Waterman and Meier 1998), with administrators making their own decisions about good policy and the intention of legislation that may be different from the intentions of the 'formators' (see Lane 1983; Lipsky 1980). Further, the investment of political effort and time in policy-making may not constitute an efficient means of producing coherence when difficult issues, and individual cases, will still have to be worked out at the level of implementation. Therefore, the better approach is to focus on making the bottom of government, and the administrative process, better coordinated; then there will be a better chance of getting the policies right.

The choice between these two strategies often is a political one, given that the design of policies may be the result of political decisions in a legislature or in the political executive. At times those political leaders may not wish to face the political battles necessary to coordinate effectively (see below) and will simply leave it up to their officials to confront the problems in the field. That choice, in turn, provides the political leaders with the opportunity to blame any resulting failures in coordination on the failings of the notorious 'bureaucracy'. This abdication of responsibility is by far the easiest political strategy, but it is one that obviously may produce suboptimal results for citizens and for bureaucrats. Pollitt argues that the 'joined-up government' initiative by the UK political leadership acknowledges explicitly the need for coordination of both policy and administration (Pollitt 2003: 37; Cabinet Office 2000: 3–4).

However, coordination issues in government are not only related to the design and implementation of externally oriented policies. Governments also invest enormous amounts of energy in the coordination of management practices within the public sector, in order to increase the uniformity or convergence of 'management'. We can refer to standard rules on HRM and financial management, or to harmonization of management systems with respect to ICT or quality assurance across public-sector organizations. Related to this is the coordination of administrative reform processes. In this 'coordination of management', central ministries (finance, the civil service) will normally play a central leading role.

In our empirical analysis of coordination strategies in seven countries, our focus on coordination is broad. It encompasses coordination of policy design, policy implementation, and of management,[7] although we do not explicitly distinguish between them in all instances. Since we analyse the coordination strategies of countries by looking to the coordination instruments that are deployed, the emphasis of our analysis is more on forms and modes of coordination, rather then on the content of coordination strategies.

Policy-specific or systemic/whole-of-government goals

Most of the coordination efforts within government are devoted to the coordination of specific policies and problems, but some coordination efforts are directed at the policies and behaviour of the politico-administrative system more broadly. Two prominent examples of these coordination dimensions have been environmental and gender and race issues. These dimensions of policy have supplemented the financial and budgetary considerations that have long been systemic issues that have guided policy-making in government. What these concerns with both environment and with gender and race issues do is to impose additional cross-cutting criteria on programmes, ensuring that they are coordinated not only with each other but also with other government-wide priorities.

In our analysis, the dominant focus is on coordination initiatives that pursue WOG or systemic goals. This is not to say, however, that initiatives oriented towards specific policy sectors are not important, but we include them in our analysis to the extent that they involve or affect several policy sectors and have a generic aspect. For example, the introduction of quasi-markets in the health and education sectors in the United Kingdom in the late 1980s represents an example of a shift towards more market-oriented-type mechanisms of coordination. One drawback of this approach is that, with our aim of mapping evolutions in overall coordination strategies, we do not give full accounts of what happened in individual policy sectors in these countries. Obviously, one could debate to what extent coordination strategies in individual policy sectors do converge towards one another and if in all policy sectors the same evolutions are observable as in the overall coordination strategies. We now turn to some other dimensions which refer to the *locus* of coordination. By discussing these, we will make clear the levels on which we will analyse coordination efforts in the seven countries.

Inside and outside

The bulk of the discussion on coordination within the public sector is concerned with the behaviours of multiple public-sector organizations. This is reasonable given that these organizations might be expected to be playing on the same team and cooperating to produce better services for citizens. Although the focus in this book will be on coordination within the public sector, we acknowledge that there is also a clear and growing need and trend for organizations in the public sector to coordinate with organizations in society, whether these are for-profit or not-for-profit organizations. This need for working across the boundary of state and society has always been there, but is becoming more clearly defined as 'governance' and begins to be a paradigm for the public sector and its management (see Peters and Pierre 2000). As Salamon (2002) and others have pointed out, many if not most major initiatives of government now have some elements of partnerships between the public and private sectors, and therefore thinking about coordination across that permeable boundary between state and society becomes all the more important. Recently, this trend has been referred to as 'joined-up governance', as distinct from 'joined-up government', initiatives which are mainly oriented towards cooperation between public-sector organizations (Pollitt 2003: 38).

Vertical and horizontal

The conceptual distinction between vertical and horizontal coordination is particularly important in the context of this book. Horizontal coordination refers to forms of coordination between organizations or units on the same hierarchical tier within government, for example, between ministers, between departments or between agencies. By contrast, vertical coordination is the coordination by a higher-level organization or unit of lower-level actors' actions. One could think of vertical coordination *between* levels of government, such as central governments, which harmonize the activities of local authorities, or vertical coordination *within* one level of government, such as the coordination of several agencies' actions by one parent department. Issues of vertical coordination *between* levels of government are becoming more important as 'multi-level governance' (Bache and Flinders 2004) becomes a more common challenge for contemporary governments.

In our analysis we focus on both horizontal and vertical coordination strategies within one level of government, that is, the public sector at national level. Vertical coordination by national public bodies of lower governmental levels (regional or local authorities) is in principal not a subject of study. Neither is the coordination by supra-national governments (such as the EU) of national authorities. However, we do refer to the coordination by national-level bodies of their policy input to the EU because this is an issue of interorganizational coordination within central government.

In horizontal coordination, no actor can impose decisions on another actor by recourse to hierarchical authority. Therefore, horizontal coordination will have a predominantly voluntary nature, in contrast to vertical coordination. However, analytically this distinction is not necessarily straightforward. A minister may force two agencies to negotiate and exchange information in order to achieve more integrated service delivery. As such, analytically one would observe horizontal linkages between the agencies, but ones that are not based on pure voluntary initiatives. This mix of horizontal and vertical coordination was seen in 'joined-up government' programmes in the United Kingdom. Somewhat similarly one can distinguish between top-down and bottom-up policy coordination in governments (OECD 1996: 31). When bottom-up coordination prevails, ministries negotiate among themselves in order to achieve programme delivery that is better adapted to the needs of clients.

Political and administrative

This dimension of coordination is closely related to the dimension of policy and administration discussed above. In both cases there is a focus on the capacity to make programmes work together once they have been adopted and are implemented. It requires focus on the behaviours of the political actors responsible for the formulation and management of programmes, rather than a focus on the actions of the administrators who are involved in the day-to-day process of implementation.

The logic of approaching coordination as a political rather than administrative activity is that the legitimacy and political power necessary to push and prod organizations out of their established patterns of delivering policies through 'silos' is vested largely in political leaders rather than in administrators. Producing effective, coordinated policy action requires making government go against many ingrained patterns of making decisions and managing programmes, and most administrative officials will have few incentives to engage in that type of battle. Therefore, political leaders may need to utilize their legitimate power in government to change such ingrained patterns.

Relying even on politicians with responsibilities for a particular ministry may not be effective in producing the type of horizontal coordination that may be required for effective governance. To be effective as the leader of an individual ministry or agency the political leader will need to defend that organization and its programmes against threats at the cabinet table and in budget hearings, and in other settings in which the resources and political power of organizations are tested against each other. Acknowledging the important role played by the locus of coordination, we will study coordination initiatives within national government at and between the political and administrative levels, initiatives that consist of a central and a more peripherical part:

1 The political tier of the cabinet (or Council of Ministers), ministers and their political secretariats;
2 The (inter)departmental tier, consisting of central and functional departments and their relations, and;
3 The tier of (semi-)autonomous agencies, public enterprises and other autonomous public sector bodies.

2.5 Specialization and other grounds for coordination problems

Having some sense of the meaning of coordination, it should be clear that this single term covers a number of different, if related, problems in the public sector. Each of these problems involves the interaction or absence of interaction of multiple public organizations. The roots of the problems we observe are political, administrative and organizational.

Individuals and organizations may be pursuing specific policy and political goals, and do not want to cooperate for fear of reducing their chances of reaching those goals. Likewise, administrative routines and even legal mandates for implementation may be undermined by attempts to achieve greater coherence in governing, and, finally, organizations (whether public or private) tend to maintain their own patterns and may not cooperate because of self-interest or simply routine.

A basis of coordination problems lies in specialization, and in the division of governments along both horizontal and vertical dimensions. In organization and management theory, specialization (or work division, or differentiation) (Gulick and Urwick 1937) and coordination are seen as closely related, even complementary, matters (Mintzberg 1979; Heffron 1989). Specialization as an organizational-theoretical concept refers to *the definition of which tasks and relations can be grouped together and coordinated and which can be separated* (Christensen and Laegreid 2006c). One can structure tasks and organizations based on different specialization principles: geographical territory, function, process and client (Gulick 1937). Specialization leads to differentiation within and across organizations (Lawrence and Lorsch 1967).

In a public-sector context, specialization could be defined as the creation of new public-sector organizations, with limited objectives and specific tasks, out of traditional core administrations which have many tasks and different, sometimes conflicting, objectives (Pollitt and Bouckaert 2004; Hood and Dunsire 1981). It may emerge in two forms (cf. Heffron 1989[8]): 1) *horizontal specialization*, or 'the splitting of organisations at the same administrative and hierarchical level [...] and assigning tasks and authority to them' (for example, splitting one departement into two);[9] 2) *vertical specialization*, or the 'differentiation of responsibility on hierarchical levels, describing how political and administrative tasks and authority are allocated between forms of affiliation' (Laegreid et al. 2003). The level of vertical specialization depends upon the extent to which tasks and policy-cycle stages are transferred from the core administration to the more peripheral parts of the public sector. This transfer has been labelled as decentralization, devolution, delegation, agencification (Pollitt et al. 2001; Greve et al. 1999), outsourcing and even privatization (Savas 2000).

Through horizontal and vertical specialization, autonomous organizations are created with smaller fields of competencies, to the extent of being single-purpose agencies or task-homogeneous bodies. Moreover, within a policy (sub)domain, the different stages of the policy cycle (policy design, development and preparation, policy implementation, policy evaluation and audit) are separated and assigned as specific tasks to different organizations. Splitting up sometimes closely connected policy stages within an administration is an outcome of specialization. In classical economic theory it is assumed that specialization leads to units having a comparative advantage over others, leading to innovation and market dominance. In the NPM doctrine, which is strongly based on these theories, specialization as such is considered a key mechanism for enhancing performance improvement in the public sector (Hood 1991; Massey 1997).

Specialization provides a number of important benefits to government, but it also creates a number of problems. Organizations that are structured around particular purposes, and that have clearly defined policy goals, will tend to organize themselves in a rather linear, top-down manner that will focus attention on the delivery of that service. In the simplest form this organizational format would lead to a clear, hierarchical focus on achieving a single purpose within the department. The manifest purpose of the organization,[10] and the structures developed around it, may constitute a set of blinders that will make it difficult for members of the organization to find common cause with other organizations and with other policy proposals.

Specialization inherently brings about new coordination needs. Structuring organizations according to one specialization principle, such as function, enhances expertise in relation to this function; however, at the same time it makes it harder to deliver integrated services to one locality (geographical territory), or to a specific group of clients, or achieve economies of scale for certain processes. Establishing specific coordination instruments on a specialized organizational structure may overcome the potential problems of specialization, such as fragmentation, redundancy, contradictions or lacunae in service delivery. As such, specialization – and the resulting single-objective organizational divisions – produces numerous benefits for government as well as many for the clients of government programmes. However, specialization is also the source of numerous problems. At the same time that specialization focuses expertise on a public problem or the needs of clients, it tends to segment (often artificially) those problems and those clients rather than presenting a more integrated conception of the causes and possible remedies for the difficulties. The benefits of specialization in public tasks must be balanced against the benefits that could be obtained from a more unified and holistic approach to governing. This more unified conception of governing and service delivery can provide services to the 'whole client', while potentially also saving government money by eliminating redundant and conflicting programmes.

As stated by several scholars, 'there is no simple trade-off between specialization and coordination' (6 2004: 107; Pollitt and Bouckaert 2004). Specialization and coordination may coexist and be mutually reinforcing: for example, one could hive off operational tasks from parent departments to autonomous agencies, and enhance the coordination at the centre. Alternatively, central governments could shift competencies to local authorities in order to enhance local coordination of fragmented central policy directives.

The coordination problem is actually several problems, each resulting from failures to align one public programme with others. Government programmes sometimes overlap and duplicate, or even contradict, each other. Reporting, inspection and licensing requirements are often cited as examples of public-sector programmes that overlap and duplicate each other. For example, the Canadian government in the late 1990s and the early part of the 21st century engaged in an effort to eliminate the duplications found in food inspections and licensing. Prior to that time inspections were done by both the federal and provincial governments, and by several organizations within each.

Ordinary citizens also feel the impact of poor coordination when they must cope with government. The emphasis in management reforms on the 'one-stop shop' for social services and for small businesses is one indication of the demands of the public for reduced duplication. Even then, however, the individual may have to fill out multiple forms containing the same information to obtain the range of services desired – the only difference will be the ability to do so at a single location. The more desirable outcome of a coordination process would be to have common forms for a range of allied services or licences so that so much redundancy would not occur.[11] Centrepoint in Australia is an attempt to produce coordination of that sort for the clients of social services and labour-market programmes.

Although duplication of programmes does demonstrate problems in coordination, coordination problems leading to direct contradictions are even more troublesome. One commonly cited example of programmes that contradict each other is the tobacco policy, or policies, of the United States. On the one hand the US Department of Health and Human Services spends millions of dollars attempting to reduce or eliminate smoking in the United States. At the same time the US Department of Agriculture spends millions of dollars subsidizing tobacco growers. Likewise, it spends money supporting the export of tobacco to many parts of the world. An even more rationalist government such as that in France finds that on the one hand it is promoting the consumption of (French) wine but also extremely concerned about the level of drink driving (Sciolino 2004). These different policy emphases are explicable in terms of the commitment of different departments and ministries to particular constituencies and to their own policy missions, but the outcome is nonetheless inconsistent, and wasteful of public money.

The above example of inconsistency and conflict among programme goals is costly but produces little direct harm to citizens, except in terms of their capacity as taxpayers. Other examples of inconsistency and incompatibility of programmes may have more tangible negative consequences for citizens. One such set of inconsistences has been the 'poverty trap' that existed in the United Kingdom and other countries for years, as a result of the failure to coordinate means-tested social benefits and taxation. This lack of effective coordination meant that as low-income individuals earned more money there would be points along the earnings scale at which their net income would reduce for the marginal pound earned, given that benefits were lost or taxes began to be levied. While the most extreme cases of this problem have been eliminated, tax and benefit programmes are rarely well-coordinated and low-income families tend to bear the burden of those programmatic inconsistencies.

In other instances government programmes may have major gaps so that necessary services are not available to the public, or to specific segments of the population. These service gaps often occur in social services where some categories of people with particular characteristics are excluded from receiving services. Some of the more egregious cases of coordination failures producing service gaps have come to light as a result of the events of September 11, 2001. It became clear as the causes of that disaster were considered that there were massive coordination failures that played no small part in permitting the disaster to occur. Each of the major security services in the United States – the Central Intelligence Agency, the Federal Bureau of Investigation and the National Security Agency – as well as other organizations such as the Immigration and Naturalization Service, played a part in the picture, but no one had been able to 'connect the dots'.[12]

The lack of adequate policy coordination may also result in something as simple as lost opportunities for effective cooperation among organizations charged with delivering public services and programmes. Very few public services can be as effective as they might be without the involvement of other services, but coordination is more often seen as a real cost to the organization rather than a potential benefit. The calculus in which organizations and their leaders engage is rather predictable; the benefits of cooperation and coordination are uncertain and remote while the costs are clear and immediate. Further, it is not clear to what extent each organization involved in a cooperative effort would be rewarded for their involvement. In such a situation the rational manager or political leader might well decline to participate.

These coordination problems may be particularly visible in the public sector, since there are several additional barriers to effective coordination. First of all, one barrier is simple pigheadedness, or simply a lack of interest in coordinating. Coordination requires some flexibility and some willingness to think about policy and administration in less conventional ways, and hence individuals and organizations operating in the stereotypical, path-dependent manner usually ascribed to 'bureaucracy' may be unwilling to move away from existing patterns. A similarly obvious problem is ignorance and a shortage of shared information about the function of other governmental bodies that may inhibit joint working. Moreover, there are often strong incentives for maintaining secrecy, and hence poor coordination, in government. Information is power for organizations (public or private), and organizations are often reluctant to share information because they will lose their bargaining position with other organizations, or with political leaders. One standard bargaining scenario in governing is when organizations are willing to trade the information they have for that held by others or, more commonly, exchange it for budgetary concessions or programmatic latitude with politicians or with central agencies such as ministries of finance.[13]

Partisan politics also can present major barriers to policy entrepreneurs seeking to achieve necessary coordination. These political problems often appear in coalition governments in which there are ministers from different political parties responsible for different policy areas (Döring 1995). Such political differences within a government may produce different policy priorities that will make creating policy coherence difficult. In addition, the political differences may simply make cooperation less likely among the participants in Cabinet, with each minister potentially being unwilling to help the other. Partisan politics may hamper coordination within coalitions, but also between governmental levels and organizations, as well as over time.

In addition to different partisan ideologies, the commitment of individuals and organizations to beliefs about what constitutes good policy in their area of concern is one of the more difficult barriers to effective coordination. Organizations have ideologies, or more exactly the members of organizations have ideologies about policy, and those belief patterns shape their approach to the policy (Chan and Clegg 2002; Campbell 2001). Further, organizational ideologies or differing professional values often make it difficult for organizations to cooperate, since they begin with fundamentally different conceptions of a problem.

Time is also a barrier. While coordinating programmes at those single points in time is certainly an important issue for public management, and is the most common format of cooperation among organizations, there are also problems that emerge because organizations and programmes must work together across broader spans of time. Governments often make successive decisions about an issue, and those decisions must be compatible and consistent if the desired outcomes for the society are to be produced. This coordination problem extending across time may be even more difficult to manage than the conventional issues because the organizations involved may not be in immediate contact with each other, and hence they may not recognize the manner in which decisions interact. One of the most compelling examples of the role of time in coordination is food safety and regulation. Citizens in industrialized countries have come to expect a safe food supply but numerous incidents during the 1990s and the early part of the 21st century – dioxin in chickens and the perception of contaminated cola drinks in Belgium, *listeria* in cheese in Britain, salmonella in eggs in any number of countries, and *E. coli* in ground beef in the United States, to name some of the more notable cases – have made it clear that guaranteeing that safety is difficult. The process by which animals and plants move from farms to the consumers' shopping carts and then to their tables is a long and complex one, and often involves a number of government departments, often at different levels of government (see Dyckman 2004), that regulate food production, food processing and the distribution of food. That regulatory process has become all the more difficult, given the amount of food that now moves across international borders (Coleman 2005) and there is a need to track and regulate those foodstuffs at all stages of the process.

The final barrier to effective policy coordination to be discussed here is far from the least important. Accountability is always a crucial question in a democratic government, and it can also constitute a major barrier to coordination among public organizations. In order for administrative accountability to function effectively there must be clear patterns of responsibility for action, and identifiable purposes for which public funds are spent. Coordination can cloud some of these authoritative relationships, and make it more difficult to trace the sources of legal power and the uses of public money. For example, at one point the Department of the Environment designed urban programmes in the United Kingdom that required merging funds from several ministries, and from several programmes within the same ministry. These urban programmes soon ran afoul of the Treasury that wanted to be certain that it could trace all the money being spent, and provide a full accounting of those funds. It is not just financial accountability than can be threatened by attempts to coordinate programmes. As already noted, performance management programmes attempt to hold managers and their organizations accountable for meeting predetermined performance targets. There can be performance systems that work across departments and programmes and even government-wide systems of performance indicators,[14] but since no organization really 'owns' these indicators or can be directly responsible for the outcomes according to the indicator, then none of them is really accountable for the outcomes. Achieving these system-wide goals may be desirable, especially for the centre of government (presidents and prime ministers), but the level of commitment of any individual programme manager to achieving those broad goals is likely to be less than it is for the individual programmes for which he or she, and the associated organization, is responsible. The manager is judged on the basis of, and his or her career may depend upon, the performance of the single programme and hence there may be little real interest in the performance of the cross-cutting programmes.

2.6   Concluding summary

Coordination has been a central concern in public administration for centuries, but the emphasis on coordination has been increasing over the past several decades. Despite the importance of coordination in contemporary public management there is relatively little systematic knowledge about how it is managed in different political systems, or about how coordination programmes have developed across time. This volume will address that gap in the literature by providing systematic evidence across several decades and seven countries. Further, the countries selected represent a range of different types of administrative systems and state traditions, and thus enable us to test a range of hypotheses about coordination more effectively.

In addition to the comparative information that will be developed in this volume, we will attempt to understand coordination, and the dynamics of coordination and specialization, in a more theoretical manner. We conceptualize the range of coordination instruments somewhat more broadly than have most scholars. In addition, we have developed a set of hypotheses about changes over time that we can test with our qualitative data. This volume therefore attempts to make a significant contribution to the way in which scholars of public administration and public policy interpret coordination. It may also provide some practical guidance[15] for practitioners faced with the task of enhancing coordination within their own governments.

3
Resources, Mechanisms and Instruments for Coordination

3.1 Mechanisms of coordination

Coordination is not a simple political and administrative problem. It can imply a wide range of problems within the public sector, and the need for cooperation may arise for a variety of administrative and political reasons. It is not surprising therefore that scholars have advanced theoretical approaches to understanding this subject through social science theory, nor that practitioners have tried a variety of methods to achieve coordination. The theoretical approaches to the range of coordination problems are in most instances the same as those utilized in many other areas of inquiry in political science. Probing their applicability for understanding coordination, however, enables us to understand better how coordination can be brought about, and helps us gain an idea of the range of possible solutions to the common problem of achieving cooperation.

In addition to the three dominant theoretical approaches – hierarchy, markets and networks – we will attempt to identify the fundamental social processes that are involved in making coordination work, within and among organizations. The underlying argument here (based on Hedström and Swedberg 1998) is that to understand social and political dynamics it is necessary to identify the basic processes and resources, such as bargaining, cooptation and coercion, that are required to make coordination (or other organizational processes) function effectively. These basic processes are authority, power, information, bargaining, mutual cooptation and norms (Peters 2003).

We thus discern three alternative theoretical approaches to coordination in the public sector. Each of these approaches has something to contribute to understanding the causes of coordination problems, the gains to be achieved through coordination, and the mechanisms through which better coordination can be achieved. The distinction between hierarchies, markets and networks as three fundamental mechanisms of coordination in social life is widely accepted in the literature (Thompson et al. 1991; O'Toole 1997; Kaufmann et al. 1986). Table 3.1 presents their basic features. Within hierarchical institutional arrangements the central pattern of interaction is authority, operationalized in administrative orders, rules and planning on the one hand and dominance and authority as the basic control system on the other. Markets as coordinating institutions are based on competition, bargaining and exchange between actors. The price mechanism, incentives and the self-interest of actors coordinate the activities of the different actors by creating an 'invisible hand'. Coordination within networks takes the

Table 3.1 The features of hierarchies, markets and networks

	Hierarchy	Market	Network
Base of interaction	Authority and dominance	Exchange and competition	Cooperation and solidarity
Purpose	Consciously designed and controlled goals	Spontaneously created results	Consciously designed purposes or spontaneously created results
Guidance, control and evaluation	Top-down norms and standards, routines, supervision, inspection, intervention	Supply and demand, price mechanism, self-interest, profit and losses as evaluation, courts, invisible hand	Shared values, common problem analyses, consensus, loyalty, reciprocity, trust, informal evaluation – reputation
Role of government	Top-down rule-maker and steerer; dependent actors are controlled by rules	Creator and guardian of markets, purchaser of goods; actors are independent	Network enabler, network manager and network participant
Resources needed	Authority Power	Bargaining Information Power	Mutual cooptation Trust
Theoretical basis	Weberian bureaucracy	Neo-institutional economics	Network theory

Sources: Based on Thompson et al. (1991); O'Toole (1997); Kaufmann et al. (1986); Peters (2003).

form of cooperation between actors whose interorganizational relations are ruled by the acknowledgement of mutual interdependencies, trust and the responsibilities of each actor.

In our opinion these three mechanisms provide a useful typology for analysing coordination efforts within the public sector.[1] This typology matches the classification made by Alexander (1995: 36–40; see also Mulford and Rogers 1982: 17–31) in which he ranks coordination strategies by their level of voluntarism/coerciveness. He distinguishes between control strategies, based on authority, structural changes (hierarchy) or competition (market) on the one hand, and cooperative strategies, based on mutual exchange of resources, cooptation and information (network/s). Similarly, besides hierarchical and market-based interorganizational coordination structures and systems, he distinguishes coordination structures and systems based on solidarity–association, which builds on trust-based consensus or agreement (Alexander 1995: 55, see also Hegner 1986: 415–23). The hierarchy–market–network typology proves to be a powerful analytical tool, at least at a generic level, as it has been used by several scholars at different levels. Hegner (1986), for example, applies an analogous typology to different levels of social interaction (society, organizational fields, organization, group, individuals). Ouchi's basic forms for control within organizations (bureaucratic, market and social mechanism) reflect the same triology (Ouchi 1980; Vosselman 1996). Others develop future scenarios for local governance based on the triology of hierarchy, market and networks (Bouckaert et al. 2002). Van Heffen and Klok (2000) use it to distinguish different models of the State. Interorganizational relations and partnerships between government, public and private organizations are analysed by Osborne (2002), as well as by Lowndes and Skelcher (2002).

We will look to each of these mechanisms in more detail by elaborating on their basic characteristics, the specific way they manifest themselves in more specific coordination instruments, and by referring to the processes and resources that they most draw upon. The differences between these three coordination mechanisms lie in the extent to which they need these specific kinds of processes and resources.

Hierarchy as a coordination mechanism

Hierarchy is the most familiar mechanism used to produce coordination between programmes and organizations within the public sector. The use of hierarchy to coordinate within the public sector is theoretically framed in the bureaucratic theory of Weber (1947) with its emphasis on division of labour on the one hand and on rules, procedures and authority as coordination instruments on the other hand. The hierarchical coordination mechanism draws primarily on authority and power as fundamental processes and resources. Without labouring the point, authority implies legitimacy and the 'ability to get things done without opposition'.[2] In other words, if there is authority a government can govern simply by expressing its belief in the appropriateness of certain behaviours, including the coordination of programmes. If a government does not have authority it may have to utilize power to achieve its purposes. That is, governments may be able to overcome resistance to their expressed desires through the use of law, budgets and, if absolutely necessary, legitimate coercion.

For management and control within public organizations the use of hierarchy can have two aspects: *bureaucratic hierarchical control* and *political hierarchical control*. The first is based on the assumption that public organizations remain basic bureaucracies that are controlled by rules and internal authority. While the numerous administrative reforms of the past decade might easily lead one to question this assumption (Pollitt and Bouckaert 2004; Christensen and Laegreid 2001), there is still a pronounced element of legalism and formalism in government. To some extent the nature of the public sector requires that there must be some formal rules that guide the behaviour of participants in the governing process and specify the rights and obligations of citizens and administrators.

The alternative conception of hierarchy in the public sector is more political. In this view public-sector organizations and their behaviour are ultimately controlled by political leaders. Control exercised by those politicians is often imperfect, and hence the bureaucratic elements of hierarchy may actually dominate, but there are nevertheless attempts by politicians to rule. Therefore, many of the hierarchical methods of control discussed here depend heavily upon the willingness of politicians to assert their formal powers.

Hierarchy-type coordination could be considered as a control strategy for coordinating organizations' behaviour 'by biasing their decisions to produce action which they might otherwise not have taken' (Alexander 1995: 37). Hierarchy-based coordination efforts may exist in a variety of forms within the public sector, ranging from issuing *legislation and other mandates* to structure patterns of coordination within the public sector, to control efforts, to more procedural mechanisms. Basically, these means involve the *mandated* change of division of labour between public-sector organizations, the autonomy, function and domain of these organizations, and their legitimacy and positioning in relation to other organizations, based on command and control. Several of them refer to what Alexander calls coordination by 'structural positioning' (1995: 38) or what has elsewhere been called 'coordination by architecture' (Hood 2005).

A first means is (the right/power of cabinet, ministers or senior management) *to reallocate and change the division of labour* within the public sector by merging or splitting organizations. Shifts of competencies and tasks between departments or agencies may bring related activities within the same organization, and as such internalize and, ultimately, reduce needs for coordination between organizations. Related activities could be brought together by centralizing or merging them in one organization (Hult 1987). However, even decentralization may enhance coordination of related policy fields under certain conditions. One can devolve more operational competencies to an agency or regional body in order to facilitate coordination of strategic issues at the remaining and smaller centre. Reorganizing the governmental apparatus by changing the basic principle of specialization, such as from a function-based organization to a clientele- or an area-based organization (see Gulick 1937), involves shifts of competencies and tasks between public organizations, and is mostly aimed at improving the coordination of activities applying to the same target group or area.

Establishing and changing lines of control is another structural, hierarchical way for achieving better coordination (Alexander 1995: 39). Hierarchical superiors in the executive branch of government – prime ministers and their associates, ministries of finance, and other central departments such as those managing government staff issues and budgets – may issue specific orders to individual subordinate organizations about their objectives, tasks and operations. At a lower level, ministers can use their own authority and lines of control to ensure congruous behaviours within their own departments. As such, organizations are forced to align their activities more closely with adjacent organizations, to avoid duplications or gaps. Alternatively, subordinate organizations can be pressed to coordinate their activities in line with the goals of the government of the day. Another means would be to enhance coordination by establishing cross-cutting lines of control, through the introduction of lateral management systems (project and matrix management). Similarly, governments may create a specific coordinating functionary or unit responsible for the guidance and monitoring of some plan or objective, such as the prime minister as coordinator within the cabinet, coordinating ministers in the Netherlands, coordinating units in the Cabinet Office in the UK, or the *préfet* in France. In all these instances, political or administrative control is imposed over bureaucratic organizations, even though those organizations may have the capacity to govern a particular policy area effectively on their own.

As well, *planning and budgeting processes* within government may be used in a hierarchical way. Planning and strategic management systems may formulate government-wide and organization-specific objectives from the top down, leaving little room for negotiation with or input from subordinate organizations. More broadly, in a bureaucracy, the discretion for organizations to use their resources (such as personnel or finances) as they see fit is very restricted, as many rules and regulations impose strict controls by central departments. These strict controls foster uniformity between organizations and may, for example, enhance the mobility of personnel between public organizations. The traditional input-oriented financial management system, comprising budget, accounting and audit subsystems, stipulates clearly and in great detail which resources should be spent on what. In such a financial management system, budgetary savings are expressed as unilateral demands, which all organizations have to comply with. More modern output-oriented financial management systems allow for more management autonomy and attenuate the hierarchical dimension to some extent (for the changing role of central departments, see Hart 1998).

As well as the direct application of authority to produce coordination, governments may also develop *procedural mechanisms or routines* to achieve the same purposes. Standard operating procedures (Mintzberg 1979) may enhance the standardization of similar or related processes in different organizations. In some instances these mechanisms may simply require one programme informing another of their actions (Davis 1996). More explicit forms include mandated consultation or review systems, and forced points of passage during the preparation of policy initiatives, such as the requirement for new policy proposals to be commented on by all the various departments before submission to the Cabinet (OECD 1996). In other instances procedures have placed individual programmes into larger *strategic assemblies of programmes*, and have created comprehensive approaches to major public problems (see Ministry of Finance, Finland 2001). The feature common to all these expressions of the hierarchical coordination mechanism is that authority and power are used to make coordination more or less automatic among organizations and programmes, or at least are used to impose coordination on organizations and individuals. Public organizations' activities are coordinated by the direct control by the government of individual public organizations (see Figure 3.1).

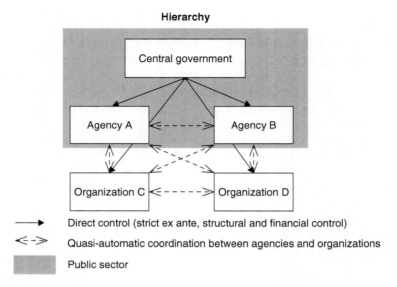

Figure 3.1   Coordination by hierarchy-type mechanisms (HTM)

While hierarchy is the conventional means of coping with coordination and most other problems of governing, it is a far from foolproof means of achieving its ends (see Chisholm 1989). All governments require some delegation of authority (Huber and Shipan 2002) in order to be able to govern efficiently, and this delegation in the case of more or less autonomous public organizations is in practice quite extensive. Even in the decentralized, reformed structures that have become central formats for governing in many contemporary political systems, there are important hierarchical elements that may contribute to problems of coordination. For example, even reforms such as the creation of autonomous and quasi-autonomous organizations within government (Pollitt et al. 2005) tend to retain some forms of hierarchical control for leaders in the public sector. Indeed, the notion of autonomy in the public sector is often over-sold in both analytic and practical terms (see Verhoest et al. 2004). The real question to be tackled in understanding autonomy and control is: What forms of control remain and how are they imposed on the presumably autonomous organizations? The management difficulty then lies in finding means to balance the rightful autonomy of public organizations with the need to govern in a more coherent and coordinated manner.

Markets as coordination mechanisms

Markets constitute the second basic mechanism for coordination, with exchange among actors being central in producing the desired outcomes. In their most basic form markets are inherently a means of coordination, bringing together buyers and sellers, and equilibrating supply and demand through a price mechanism. Without the creation of markets, through laws establishing property rights and providing for the enforcement of contracts, buying and selling would be very difficult and expensive. Once established and functioning properly, markets are able to rather effortlessly coordinate the actions of buyers and sellers, using the price mechanism as a means of finding an appropriate level at which buyers and sellers can both be satisfied. The use of markets as coordination mechanisms builds mainly on bargaining as basic process and resource. Moreover, market forms of coordination also involve some elements of both information and power. Bargaining among programmes may be dependent upon the availability of information about the programmes, and making the negotiation system effective may require backing with power (or authority) (Peters 2003).

Markets perform their coordination function most optimally when there are enough purchasers and providers, when providers can enter and exit the market without incurring high costs, when there is full transparency as to information about prices and quality of services (Le Grand and Bartlett 1993; Plug et al. 2003: 14). Competition is a basic mechanism for 'controlling' the behaviour of the organizations in the market. According to Alexander (1995: 57), markets as a coordination mechanism need no formal links between member organizations: 'coordinated decisions are the systemic result of partisan mutual adjustment of each unit in the market to its perceived environment.' Organizations react to the perceived signals of price, offer and demand and the strategies of competitors. As such, the coordination of actions is done by the 'invisible hand' of the market.

This neoclassical conception of the market may work well for economic exchanges but does not apply directly to decision-making situations within government (see, for another viewpoint, Alexander 1995: 57). Given that markets are relatively indeterminate, the incentives available to the actors must be structured by some central authority in order to produce the outcomes that government would want. However, relationships analogous to markets can be created within the public sector. The idea of market-type coordination within government finds a strong theoretical basis in public choice theory (Niskanen 1971) and economic neo-institutionalism, like property rights and agency theory

(Furubotn and Pejovich 1974; Jensen and Meckling 1976; Pratt and Zeckhauser 1991). These theoretical frameworks emphasize the importance of competition, result-oriented contracts and performance-related incentives as instruments for controlling public-sector organizations in an efficient way.

Market-type coordination mechanisms in the public sector can take several forms. Within the public sector, regulated quasi-markets and economic incentives can be used to create the incentives for actors to coordinate, and to enhance their collective performance (for example, the 'common resource pool' of Ostrom 1990). Some of the more prominent examples of programmes using market-type mechanisms for coordination have been found in the health sector. Quasi-markets have been used to bring together purchasers and providers through contracts. The primary intention of these programmes has been to lower costs and enhance the efficient allocation of resources (Jerome-Forget et al. 1995). Internal markets have also been used in areas such as elderly care, housing and child care (Le Grand and Bartlett 1993; OECD 1993). Whereas network coordination could involve both policy development and implementation, market-type mechanisms are generally reserved for matters of policy implementation (with experiments in New Zealand as an exception). When operating in a well-regulated market, a public-service provider will get clear signals as to what extent the quality and level of their services can be adjusted both to the demand of its users and to the supply by other service providers, through changes in the level of income the public service provider yields from selling its services, as well as through changes in market shares. In that respect, a kind of automatic coordination occurs between services provided by public organizations and other organizations that provide similar services. As well, price and contracts ensure coordination of activities between public organizations as purchasers and public organizations as providers.

When creating such markets, the government must ensure at least two conditions: 1) there must be a clear link between the service of a public organization and the price that reflects the (fluctuating) value of the service on the market, and; 2) there must be competition between providing organizations and freedom of choice for the users of the service. Therefore, government must regulate (or deregulate) such things as market entry and exit, price formation, and set minimum standards for quality, safety and guarantees of accessibility for each kind of user. The government has to monitor the market, avoid monopolies or monopsonies, and to sanction non-compliant organizations. In this respect government acts as the 'midwife' of markets (Plug et al. 2003;

Walsh 1995). So, government can deliberately construct, regulate and shape markets that involve public-sector organizations. Moreover, market creation has been explicitly enhanced by EU liberalization policies, such as in the field of telecommunications, public transport, postal services and energy.

The use of contracting within the public sector can be considered a central element in the introduction of market-type coordination.[3] This is particularly the case if the contracts stress clear objectives, targets and harsh sanctions in case of contract failure (in contrast with the more 'relational' type of contracting – see Williamson 1985; Davis and Walker 1998). Contracts imply – at least rhetorically – the element of reciprocal relations between equal partners which bargain for the exchange of products for financial return. Per definition, in contractual relations, the hierarchical element is diminished.[4] Contracts exist between political principals and public-sector bodies and between public purchasers and providers within internal and quasi-markets.

Within such markets and contracts, incentives to increase organizational performance through linking funding to performance are crucial. More broadly, the financial management systems within government can have a strong market orientation. For example, one can think of a result-oriented financial management system in which the organizational funding is linked to the expected or past performance (p^*q) of the organizations and in which financial sanctions are applied in case of underperformance. Such budgeting is a precondition for creating (quasi-)markets. In such systems, budgets, accounts and audits will be geared towards organizational performance.

Figure 3.2 shows the optimal operation of coordination through market-type mechanisms. The coordination of public organizations is mainly 'horizontal' self-coordination induced by the forces of price, competition, supply and demand. Relations between public organizations are mainly based on contractual exchange. The government mainly acts as a market creator and regulator. To the extent that government controls public providers, this control is mainly indirect and ex-post in nature.

Networks as coordination mechanisms

Networks are the third of the fundamental modes of explanation of coordination in the public sector. In many ways thinking about the utilization of networks in the public sector should be a natural part of analysing coordination, and indeed a certain amount of coordination – leading to networks – always takes place with or without conscious design

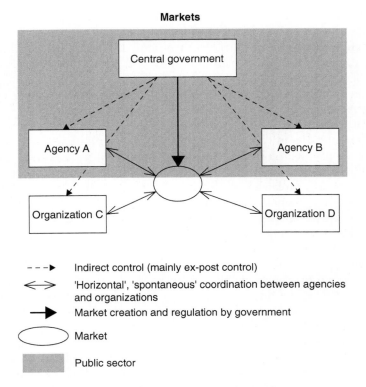

Figure 3.2   Coordination by market-type mechanisms (MTM)

by government officials. Networks are here considered as an alternative form of governance and coordination, and depend more on voluntary collaborative actions by and solidarity between relevant organizations (Kooiman 1993; Börzel 1998; Powell 1991). A general definition of networks would be: '(more or less) stable patterns of cooperative interaction between mutually dependent actors around specific issues of policy (or management)' (based on Kickert et al. 1997: 6; Klijn and Koppenjan 2000).

Rather than having coordination imposed 'vertically' from above and depending primarily on authority to achieve its purposes, horizontal coordination in network-type arrangements tends to depend upon bargaining, negotiation and mutual cooptation among the participants (Peters 2003). In the first instance, the members of the networks develop some reciprocal trust so that they can accept each others' actions in good faith and also believe that any bargain struck will be effective. Coordination using authority may be achieved relatively quickly if the participants in the process accept the legitimacy of the central actors, but coordination through networks will require some time and some interactions in order to be sufficiently reliable. There should be some information-sharing among the organizations so that a minimum basis for coordination and coherence can be satisfied.

Within the existing literature on coordination through inter-organizational systems there has been a gradual evolution of conceptual models. Initially the inter-organizational literature that developed within the sociology and management literatures identified the interdependence of organizations and the need to structure their interaction. In political science the literature on inter-organizational analysis grew out of studies of policy implementation (such as Pressman and Wildavsky 1974; Metcalfe 1976). This literature tends to focus on the individual organization and its placement in a web of interconnections with other organizations operating in its 'field'. Inevitably this approach involves some of the logic of networks of organizations, but the primary emphasis is on the individual organizations. As the literature has evolved, the more contemporary network literature provides a development of and to some extent a complementary perspective on the interaction of multiple organizations as a means of reaching some collective goals.

What forms may network-type coordination take? Alexander (1995: 36–7) refers to different strategies for coordination that may be relevant in this context. Cooperative strategies involve voluntary interaction and collaboration through bargaining and resource exchange, co-sponsorship and cooptation. Communicative strategies, information-based and persuasive strategies build on mutual awareness of interdependence and common interests, on common values or partisanship. And cultural strategies depend on compatibility between goals or core values of organizations (see also Sharpe 1985).

One important early analysis of inter-organizational relations involved in coordination (Rogers and Whetten 1982: 19) argued that there were three alternative strategies for managing coordination, all within this broader approach to inter-agency relations. First, the 'mutual adjustment model' in the inter-organizational approach refers to interactions that are loosely structured and depend upon creating informal norms and modifying agency goals. The intermediate level in this taxonomy of interorganizational relations is described as the 'alliance model', in which there are negotiated rules and a mixture of collective and agency (organizational) goals. This alliance model implies that organizations are at once pursuing their own goals and using the inter-organizational environment in which they function as a means of pursuing those goals. At the same time they must recognize that they are members of the collectivity of organizations and that there are some collective goals (if only incoherent ones at times) that can only be achieved through cooperation. The negotiation among the various organizations will define the collective goals and each partners' contribution. At the other end of the spectrum, the 'corporate strategy model' was said to be a highly formalized and centralized pattern of interactions among the participants, regulating the interactions of the actors involved through formal rules. As the name implies this approach is very much in the vein of traditional management within private-sector corporations and relates closely to hierarchy-type mechanisms. Building on this framework, we distinguish different levels of network-type coordination with respect to the extent of cooperation between organizations, ranging from simple information exchange between bodies, to platforms for concertation to negotiation, and to joint decision-making bodies and even joint organizations (see 6 2005: 50; or Alter and Hage 1993: 44–80; see Alexander 1995: 63 for a somewhat similar continuum).

As well, management systems may support the public sector in order to act as a network of mutual interdependent actors, collaborating for collective goals. Some countries experiment with financial management systems which focus on the consolidation and exchange of financial and non-financial information over organizations. These systems also provide for joint budgets, or budget sharing, in order to encourage the achievement of joint goals. Systems for strategic planning may be predominantly bottom-up or interactive, allowing for a heavy input of lower-level bodies in the construction of overall objectives.

Even the use of contracts can be an expression of network forms of coordination, more specifically when contracts have a strong 'relational' nature (Williamson 1985, 1993). In this context, contracts are intended to solidify long-term relationships among the actors, rather than simply to create a one-time relationship between a buyer and a seller. In a strictly market conception of policy each 'deal' would be struck from new, but in practice a great deal of contracting is repetitive, and the participants minimize their decision-making costs rather than maximize possible economic gains.[5] This style of decision-making demonstrates the importance of trust in the creation and maintenance of networks (Williamson 1993). In relational contracts, the emphasis is on procedures used to strengthen the relationship, on extensive interaction, and on common objectives, instead of detailed targets, extensive reporting and auditing provisions, and hard sanctions (Williamson 1985; Walsh 1995; Davis and Walker 1998; Verhoest 2005).

Coordination through networks can also take more informal forms. Chisholm (1989) has argued that although most analyses of coordination are based on hierarchy and the use of formal powers, effective coordination can be achieved by relying upon more informal mechanisms. There is a long and important literature (Gouldner 1954; Crozier 1964) on informal organization within individual organizations, and some of the same logic can be applied to the study of groups of organizations within the public sector. Just as informal patterns of interaction within an organization can enhance the performance of that organization by supplementing and bypassing the formal structure, the same may be true of the role of informal interactions as a means of coping with rigidities in the interactions among organizations in the public sector.

Within networks common values as well as common problem definitions among partners are crucial in order to achieve collective action (Kickert et al. 1997). Likewise, Mintzberg considers 'standardization of norms and values' as an important means for intra-organizational coordination. In that perspective, a common political or corporate culture that may exist among a set of actors may produce coordination with minimal formal interaction (OECD 1996; Oden 1997). One description of the logic of cartels has been that rather than formal collusion there may simply be a *corpsgeist* held by the executives that results in similar behaviour (see Alexander 1995: 74). Further, as already noted, professionals in different organizations may well respond in similar ways when confronted with a particular policy challenge, and therefore the organizations in which those professionals work may appear more coordinated than they actually are. Finally, the public sector itself may have a management culture that is sufficiently consistent to produce relatively common behaviour across a wide range of organizations.

Besides that, there are the informal contacts and linkages between individuals and organizations. The civil service itself is one of the most important informal structures in government. Although the civil service can be conceptualized as an institution in its own right, it can also be seen as a network of individuals who occupy crucial roles in the system of governance. Perhaps most importantly, the majority of civil servants experience a long career in government and may work with one another, and with politicians, over decades. The civil service is especially viable as a coordination network in civil service systems such as those of the United Kingdom in which civil servants continue to occupy positions in a number of government ministries over the course of their careers (Page and Wright 1999). Given these diverse careers, the civil servants are more likely to have some understanding of the full range of government activity than those in civil services such as that of the United States with its more specialized career patterns (Peters 2001). Even in the specialized systems, however, civil services may be a natural source of coordination for government given that they are charged with implementing policy and need to find means of working with government to make that happen. Also, informal networks can cut across the civil service by linking individuals with the same political affiliation (Rouban 2003) or the same educational training, such as the '*Corps administratifs*' in France or the Oxbridge culture in the UK (Peters 2001).

From a government perspective coordination by network and cooperation among its public organizations evolves rather 'spontaneously' in a horizontal way. Coordination results from the more or less independent interactions of those organizations each attempting to pursue its own interests in that environment. However, in the contemporary 'governance' literature it is acknowledged that government can play an important role in creating, managing and sustaining cooperative networks among its public organizations (and other bodies), using 'horizontal' and 'spontaneous' coordination to enhance its policy implementation. Nevertheless, the role and position of government is totally different from where government uses hierarchy-type mechanisms to coordinate the activities of organizations (see Kickert et al. 1997: 12, Table 2). The concept of 'network management' refers to 'the coordination of the strategies of organizations with different goals and interests around a specific problem or policy issue within a network of interorganizational relations'. A distinction is made between 'process management' and 'network constitution' (Klijn and Koppenjan 2000: 140–1; Kickert et al. 1997: 170). In several policy fields, that is, those that do not belong to the Treaties and therefore cannot be covered by the EU officially, the European Commission developed the Open Method of Co-ordination. During the past decade European governments have introduced fora for coordination of activities and views between its public organizations, private organizations, interest groups and/or citizens. Examples are to be found in fields such as regional development, employment and education, mobility and infrastructure, social housing and child care. Figure 3.3 summarizes the main elements of network coordination, in which coordination occurs mainly horizontally between public-sector organizations, with government acting as a network manager.

Network
Coordination = network management + indirect control (agency A - N)
+ self-coordination

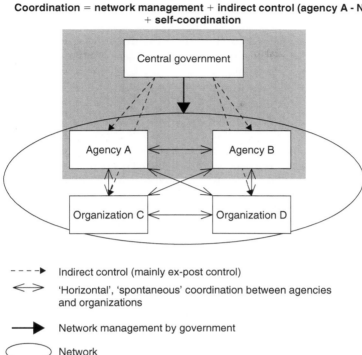

Figure legend:

- - - →   Indirect control (mainly ex-post control)

⟵⟶   'Horizontal', 'spontaneous' coordination between agencies and organizations

⟶   Network management by government

⬭   Network

▨   Public sector

Figure 3.3 Coordination by network-type mechanisms (NTM) and forms of control

To summarize, we consider coordination through three types of mechanisms.[6] First, hierarchy-type mechanisms (HTM) require, according to Peters (2003), authority (based on legitimacy) and power (use of law, budgets and coercion) as resources for coordination. HTM focus on objective-setting and rule-making, on allocation of tasks and responsibilities, and on lines of control. Second, market-type mechanisms (MTM) aim for the creation of incentives to enhance the performance of public actors. These mechanisms rest on a substantial mobilization of bargaining and information as coordination capacity resources. Third, network-type mechanisms (NTM) search for the establishment of common knowledge, common values and common strategies between partners. The fundamental resources employed by governments who coordinate by NTM are information, norms and, to a lesser extent, mutual cooptation and bargaining.

Each of the three approaches can illuminate some aspects of the politics of coordination, but each also has some important explanatory deficiencies. Although we have discussed these approaches as alternatives to one another, in reality many attempts on the part of government to enhance coordination will involve more than one of them. Under certain circumstances attempts to impose direct hierarchical control over an organization or set of organizations will work better if the coordinators can build a more cooperative network among the organizations involved or among lower-level employees in those organizations. On the other hand, attempts to coordinate more from the bottom up will work better if hierarchy casts a deep, dark shadow on the participants. As well as providing an intellectual understanding of policy coordination, these three approaches are also closely related to a set of *instruments*. In the next section we will discuss these instruments in more detail.

3.2   From mechanisms to instruments for coordination

We now turn to the *instruments* that may be used within the public sector to coordinate several organizations. The coordination instruments are specific activities or structures created to bring about coordination. The three coordination mechanisms (HTM, MTM, NTM) discussed in the previous section are of a more general and abstract level. They refer to the basic processes which may underpin coordination efforts and instruments (authority, price and competition, or trust and solidarity). As such, specific coordination instruments may refer to specific coordination mechanisms, since the instruments may function mainly by using authority (hierarchy), competition (market) or cooperation (network). But as we will argue, certain coordination instruments may be used in different ways, for example, in a hierarchical or more network-like way.

Organization and management theorists regard integration and coordination, next to task allocation and differentiation, as essential elements of organizing. The early developers of contingency theory – Lawrence and Lorsh (1967), for example – state that the more differentiation there is within organizations, the more complex coordination and integration mechanisms are needed. Several early scholars in organizational studies developed lists of coordination instruments that can be used within organizations (Thompson 1967; Galbraith 1973; March and Simon 1958; Lawrence and Lorsh 1967). Summarizing the organizational theory literature in his well-known book *The Structure of Organizations*, Mintzberg (1979) defines several means of coordination within organizations, including mutual adjustment, direct supervision, and standardization of work processes, output and skills. Later, he added standardization of norms and values as an intra-organizational coordination instrument.

In the more specific theoretical literature on inter-organizational coordination, as well as in the practitioner-oriented literature on joined-up government, several typologies of instruments are to be found (Alexander 1995; 6 2004; OECD 1996, Ling 2002), which differ to some extent in focus, level of pragmatism and completeness. The typology of 'interorganisational coordination structures' developed by Alexander (1995: 55) is probably the most elaborate and comprehensive of those mentioned, although it mainly focuses on structural tools. It is particularly interesting because of its implicit distinction between coordination structures and non-structural instruments, and for its positioning of structures on hierarchy–networks–markets continuums and on different levels of analysis (micro, meso and meta). The typology developed by Perri 6 (2004) is rather generic, setting out a continuum of increasing collaboration and integration, ranging from short-term to long-term perspectives, and ending with the most extreme form of coordination – a full merger of organizations. But the typology is rather limited; there are no market-type instruments distinguished and there is a strong emphasis on more structural forms. The two other typologies are less well-structured, less generic and more practitioner-oriented; indeed the OECD typology (1996) was developed as a toolkit for strengthening policy coherence. However, both typologies are interesting since they emphasize cultural forms of coordination such as leadership, administrative culture, exchange, joint training of staff, and the development of cross-cutting skills. In addition to the instruments related to culture and human resource management, the typologies also refer to instruments linked to the budgeting and financial management system (joint budgeting and budget sharing, for example) or the strategic management system. In that respect, they complement the typologies of Alexander and 6. Again, neither mentions market-like instruments.

Largely based on these and drawing from empirical international comparative research we developed our own typology of coordination instruments (see Table 3.2). Our typology encompasses most of the instruments in the other typologies, but frames them in very general terms. This allows the typology to be used to classify similar coordination

Table 3.2 Clusters of coordination instruments

Instrument	Underlying mechanism	Involved source of coordination capacity					
		Authority	Power	Bargaining	Information	Norms	Mutual cooptation
Management instruments							
1. Strategic management (planning and evaluation) Dependent of primary objective and process	NTM – HTM						
1.1. Bottom-up and interactive strategic management	NTM			+	+		+
1.2. Top-down and unilateral strategic management	HTM	+	+				
2. Financial management (budgeting, accounting and audit) Dependent on objective and focus	HTM – MTM – NTM						
2.1. Traditional input-oriented financial management systems	HTM	+	+	+			
2.2. Results-oriented financial management systems focused on incentives for units	MTM			+			

	Type						
2.3. Results-oriented financial management systems oriented towards information exchange and consolidation according to policy portfolios	NTM				+		
3. Inter-organizational learning: culture management (by means of training, rotation, career management, internal job market); competence and information management	Mainly NTM/ MTM				+	+	+
4. Procedural instruments concerning mandated consultation and review	Mainly HTM/NTM depending on compulsory nature	+		(+)	+		
Structural instruments							
5. Reshuffling of competencies: organizational merger or splits; centralization (decentralization)	Mainly HTM	+	+				
6. Reshuffling of lines of control	Mainly HTM	+	+				
7. Establishment of a specific coordinating function or entity; lines of control							

(Continued)

Table 3.2 Continued

Instrument	Underlying mechanism	Involved source of coordination capacity					
		Authority	Power	Bargaining	Information	Norms	Mutual cooptation
8. Regulated markets: internal markets, quasi-markets, voucher markets and external markets	Mainly MTM	(+)		+	+		
9. Systems for information exchange	Mainly NTM				+		
10. Advisory bodies and consultative/deliberative bodies	Mainly NTM			(+)	+		+
11. Entities for collective decision-making	Mainly NTM			+	+		+
12. Common organizations (partnership organization)	Mainly NTM (HTM)			+	+	+	+
13. Chain-management structures	Mainly NTM			+	+	+	+

Legend: +: primary use of this resource for coordination; (+): additional and limited use of this resource for coordination.
Sources: Verhoest and Bouckaert (2005); based on Verhoest et al. (2000); Verhoest et al. (2003); features based on Peters (2003).

efforts at very different levels of analysis (political, administrative and agency levels). Our typology differs from the others in three main ways. First, we distinguish between management and structural instruments. On the one hand, the coordination of tasks may be realized by creating new or changing existing structures and institutional forms within government (structural positioning – Alexander 1995 – or architecture – Hood 2005). A well-known strategy is the reshuffling of competencies between ministries or departments in response to changing contextual pressures. The creation of coordinating entities (for example a project minister), collective decision entities, regulated markets, and information structures or chain management structures are other examples of structural coordination mechanisms (Bouckaert et al. 2000; Verhoest et al. 2003; see also Alexander 1995). On the other hand, the abovementioned typologies also refer to non-structural instruments, based on, for example, planning, budget, evaluation and consultation procedures or on the creation of common cultural values. In our typology, most of these non-structural instruments are considered to refer to specific broad management systems used within the public sector, such as strategic management, financial management, and cultural and knowledge management.

Second, just like Alexander (1995), we assume some link between the specific coordination instruments and the three basic mechanisms of coordination (hierarchy, market and network). Table 3.2 lists the different managerial and structural coordination instruments and allocates the instruments to the institutional arrangement they predominantly refer to (HTM, NTM and MTM), using Peters' classification of resources and mechanisms (Peters 2003). Moreover, Table 3.2 indicates what kinds of resources for coordination capacity are activated when a specific coordination instrument is used. However, two cautionary notes should be made. As Alexander clearly points out (see also Verhoest et al. 2003), most instruments are not clear-cut, extreme manifestations of hierarchy, market or networks. Most instruments reflect attenuated degrees of hierarchy, market or networks. For example, according to Alexander (1995), the need for authority and power (hierarchy) lessens when one moves from coordinating units and coordinators, to interorganizational groups, to liaison or boundary spanners. In Table 3.2 we merely classify the instruments according to their basic interaction pattern and do not really elaborate on the different degrees of hierarchy, market or network they represent. Thus, characterizing several instruments as being basically forms of HTM does not mean that they exercise similar levels of authority and power. Some instruments will only need attenuated levels of hierarchy. Similarly, we discern increasing levels of cooperation (NTM) when we move from simple information exchange structures between organizations, to negotiation bodies, to common steering bodies and to joint organizations.

Characterizing 'joint organizations' as an extreme form of networks points to another issue. Most instruments are to some extent hybrid and combine aspects of different mechanisms (like the combinations of networks and hierarchies in the creation of joint organizations). Moreover, depending on the context, several coordination instruments may be used in different ways. A strategic planning process may serve predominantly as a top-down task allocation or as a two-way process of establishing common strategies. Likewise, the budgetary cycle may function as a means of task allocation or as a way of creating market-like incentives linked to performance. Where necessary, we distinguish between different ways of using the same instrument.

Thirdly, our typology has a bias towards more formal forms of coordination within the public sector. There is not much attention given to coordination between organizations via interpersonal contacts and informal channels of communication. However, by referring to instruments for cultural coordination we grasp some of these more informal channels. However, our broad focus on coordination within the public sector at the central level, as well as the research methodology chosen, do not allow for an extensive analysis of informal channels for coordinating public-sector organizations. We come back to this issue when we discuss the research methodology in Chapter 4.

Now we will define the various coordination instruments more clearly, link them with other typologies, and argue why they predominantly may be considered as manifestations of HTM, MTM or NTM. We will discuss the structural instruments first and then turn to the nonstructural instruments.

A first set of coordination instruments clearly associated with authority and power fall into the category of *organizational restructuring by shifting tasks and competencies* between organizations. Here, coordination is enhanced by bringing related activities together by merging organizations (see merger as an extreme level of coordination in 6 2004) or by separating them from other organizations with completely different activities. This reflects the basic principle of work division or departmentalization in organization theory (Thompson 1967; Galbraith 1973). An historical example in several countries is the creation of independent ministries of the environment by combining competencies from different departments such as health, natural resources, energy and others, and centralizing related or overlapping activities. A number of countries, such as Australia, Canada and the United States, have created superministries which encompass a wide range of programmes by integrating (parts of) other ministries. Such superministries internalize formerly inter-ministry/interdepartmental coordination efforts (OECD 1996). On the other hand, decentralization can enhance the coordination of related policy fields. For example, in France competencies were decentralized from the central ministries to the regional *départements* because it was believed that '*interministerialité*', or coordination between policy fields, could occur better at the *département* level than at the level of the highly segregated centralized ministries. Such organizational restructuring through the transfer of competencies may also be used to change the basic principle of specialization of the involved organizations (for example, from functionally to territorially based organizations).

Reorganizing and changing lines and levels of control involves another set of hierarchy-type coordination instruments. As made clear earlier in this book, politicians and administrative superiors may issue orders through the lines of control to subordinate organizations. Changing these lines of control may also improve coordination, like letting one minister control several ministries with common or related competencies. Similarly, establishing cross-cutting lines of control, such as in matrix management or lateral management, may increase coordination.

Strongly associated with influencing lines of control is the *creation of coordinating functions or entities* (Lawrence and Lorsch 1967). Alexander (1995) distinguishes between a coordinator, respectively an individual or unit whose only or main function is to coordinate the activities of the different organizations in an inter-organizational system, and a lead organization which has, besides its coordinating function, some line functions. For instance, the OECD (1996) distinguishes between coordinating ministers without a portfolio and lead ministers. In most Western countries, the prime minister has a coordinating function with regard to the other ministers. Special units that monitor and stimulate cross-cutting policy objectives throughout the public sector can be established within the department of the prime minister. Process managers can be appointed to enhance joined-up working between agencies (Pollitt 2003). The exact position of the coordinating entity within the public sector *vis-à-vis* the other organizations will determine to what extent hierarchical authority and power as resource is used. However, most common coordinating functions or entities within the public sector imply some hierarchical difference between the coordinator and the coordinated organizations. Moreover, their coordinating power is mostly stipulated and enforced by laws and statutes. Their task is often to streamline, monitor and control the implementation of a centrally decided specific objective, goal or policy. In that perspective, this kind of coordination instrument's 'coordinating function or entity' is to be distinguished from negotiation bodies or common steering groups which could be created by different organizations and which are more based on the principle of cooperation.

Another set of structural coordination instruments relate to the *creation of regulated markets* in order to create stimuli and sanctions that induce appropriate behaviour by public organizations. The coordination of tasks and activities by different organizations is done through mechanisms of price and competition, offer and demand. Money and incentives are crucial. Providers are mainly funded through sales to their customers and purchasers, and their demand determines the activities of the providers. Such a market can be created by government and, depending on the kind and number of purchasers and providers, the kind and level of competitition and the level of regulation, the market can be internal, a quasi-market, a voucher market or an external market.

Several coordination structures can be considered predominantly as forms which increasingly rely on solidarity and cooperation (NTM). First, the creation of *systems for information exchange and sharing* may induce organizations to take into account the actions of other organizations through processes of mutual adjustment (Galbraith 1977; Alexander 1995; Pollitt 2003 for 'joint information-gathering'; OECD 1996 for 'informed decision-making'). Through new or reoriented flows and systems of information, decision-making organizations can be better informed about the latest developments and activities of other organizations. This helps them to adjust their activities in line with those of other organizations. Through systems and arrangements for information exchange, information flows and exchange can be better organized; the development of common IT systems and joint databases is a good example of this (Pollitt 2003). Information from various organizations can also be integrated in a government-wide information system, giving a strategic overview of government activities. The focus would be on both on technical ICT systems as a basis for making information accessible as well as on the content of the information systems.

A further coordination instrument is the *creation of consultation or negotiation bodies* (Galbraith 1973; Lawrence and Lorsch 1967). Whereas 'information systems' as a coordination instrument focus on the ICT and other impersonal systems of information exchange, in these consultation and negotiation bodies, representatives of different organizations exchange information in one or both directions, and organizations can mutually adjust their activities based on the information exchanged. Besides information exchange, issues relevant to the different organizations can be discussed and negotiated, and even joint strategies can be elaborated. Decisions made by such bodies have to be ratified and implemented by the member organizations or by a higher body before the decision takes effect. Such bodies may be permanent or temporary, and their advice can be binding to differing degrees (legally, morally or politically). Alexander (1995) would call these 'negotiation bodies', together with the collective decision-making bodies as coordination instruments known as 'inter-organizational groups'. One could think of all kinds of committees which do not have formal decision-making power and which involve members of different organizations: advisory committees (Pollitt 2003); committees of senior-level civil servants which prepare the meetings of interministerial committees (OECD 1996); or inter-agency task forces.

Entities for collective decision-making represent even a higher level of cooperation between organizations. In contrast to the 'concertative' bodies discussed above, these entities can make binding decisions. For instance, in many countries the Cabinet meets as a collective decision-making body. Another example is the governing board of a one-stop delivery agency with representatives from the collaborating organizations or governmental levels. In some countries (in the Netherlands with '*Bestuursraden*' and in Flanders with the '*Beleidsraad*'), strategic decision-making boards consisting of senior officials of the different organizations belonging to a policy domain (departments and/or agencies) were created in order to collectively set out strategy and control the implementation of it. Such joint decision-making bodies enable joint planning and joint working more easily than weaker forms of cooperation. In the private sector this cooperation takes the form of strategic alliances (6 2004).

The most extreme form of cooperation is the creation of a *joint organization*. In this form of coordination two or more organizations create a common organization controlled by the different 'parent' organizations in order to perform joint tasks. 6 (2004) refers to project-linked joint ventures, satellites or unions (see also Alexander 1995). Other examples are public-private partnership organizations; organizations for shared services (in the field of HR, ICT, financial management, for example) controlled by different departments or agencies; or jointly owned cross-border organizations (such as those between Northern Ireland and the Irish Republic).

Besides these more general network-type coordination structures (that is, systems for information exchange, advisory and negotiation bodies, entities for collective decision-making and joint organizations), we define one more specific type of instrument separately in our typology. *Chain-management structures* refer to structural devices used to coordinate a network of different organizations involved in subsequent steps of the production of a good, a service or a policy (Van Dalen, in Duivenboden et al. 2000). The organizations in such a chain are interdependent, their actions are sequential, and each step adds value to the end product. Within the public sector, one could define different kinds of chains depending on the level they function on, such as policy chains versus implementation chains. Or one could distinguish chains in relation to the product they aim to create; logistic chains (in defence), information or knowledge chains (in the social security field), or chains focusing on individuals (in local social policy). In the Netherlands, for example, chain-management structures and procedures have been set up in the policy areas of food safety, agriculture, asylum policy and water management (Duivenboden et al. 2000). There are also different levels of chain management. Besides self-organization, there is 'relay'-coordination, with each individual organization gearing its actions to those of organizations before and after it in the chain. In these, coordination may be more formalized through specific structures, such as a permanent body for consultation. In this body all main public (and private) actors involved in the different phases of the policy issue are represented. The consultation body may monitor the preparation, implementation and evaluation of the policy. Most of the time, all actors are involved as 'equal' partners, although one actor may take the strategic lead as chain manager.

In addition to these structural forms, we can also discern coordination instruments which do not involve a change in structures, but which rely more on procedures, incentives and values. We will refer to these different coordination instruments on a very general level by clustering them in the category of management systems. Management systems are understood here as a set of instruments and procedures which plan, monitor and evaluate the use of resources (HRM, finances, etc) or the implementation of policies.

A first set of coordination instruments is linked to the processes of the policy cycle within a government, encompassing policy design, implementation and evaluation. More specifically, this set of coordination instruments will be labelled 'strategic management' (Bryson 1988), by which we refer to the alignment of activities of public organizations according to a system of interconnected levels of plans, objectives and targets (levels – cabinet; department; agency). Examples are the SRAs and KRAs in New Zealand. Fundamentally, coordination between organizations is fostered by giving individual organizations clear objectives within a framework of broader inter-organizational or even government-wide goals. These different levels of plans are linked to one another in order to avoid duplication, gaps and to enhance the pursuit of overarching goals. These plans are monitored and evaluated, after which plans can be adjusted and fine-tuned. Such strategic management at the government-wide level often goes hand in hand with more outcome- and effectiveness-focused modes of policy making, as well as the integration of cross-cutting issues in the planning of individual organizations (Pollitt 2003).

Intuitively, one would consider the strategic management system to be rather hierarchically oriented. The plans on lower levels are derived from the higher-level plans, objectives and targets. The process of planning relies heavily on top-down instructions and the unilateral setting of objectives and targets for lower levels. Monitoring and evaluation is a one-way process applied by higher levels over lower levels. However, this need not be the case, and strategic management processes may be designed to allow for strong bottom-up involvement. In such a more network-type variant, the process of planning on the different levels of objectives and targets has heavy input from lower levels and features a strong emphasis on negotiation. Plans at the higher level therefore consist of aggregating and integrating lower-level plans. The process of planning is bi-directional and based on consultation and involvement of lower levels. Monitoring and evaluation of progress is a joint process between the different levels by joint committees or networks.

Moving from a top-down to a bottom-up system, we may distinguish between four types of strategic management.[7] The first type is strategic management in the form of a detailed common planning instrument, integrating policy objectives in terms of effects with the specific contributions of individual agencies to these objectives in terms of inputs, activities and outputs. In 2000 Canada introduced the Result-based Management Accountability Framework as a condition for approval of programmes by the Treasury Board. In the case of horizontal initiatives it details the role and contribution of each partner. Such detailed planning instruments provide clear, explicit guidelines for organizations involved and enable a transparent accountability system. However, collective policy objectives are not always easily chopped into pieces and tasks for individual organizations. Moreover, such a system may suffer from a lack of ownership and may constrain innovation and creativity at the level of individual organizations. More common is a 'cascade' system, where general policy objectives are linked to more concrete objectives at the level of the individual organization. Mostly, the individual organizations make this link themselves, which is then reviewed by some central department. The New Zealand strategic management system in the 1990s using Strategic Result Areas (SRAs) and Key Result Areas (KRAs) is a typical example of this. This system allowed for a clear view on how policy outcomes are supported by organizational outputs as well as for a reconciliation of top-down and bottom-up input. Still, the risk of artificial linkages between higher and lower objectives remains and the cost of monitoring progress at the different levels can be very high. A third model would be to allow organizations themselves to develop strategic partnerships with other organizations in order to achieve objectives for which these organizations are collectively responsible. Such objectives are then defined at the outcome level, or represent final outputs to which organizations have to deliver as chain-partners. This model obviously stimulates ownership and creativity but also assumes substantial autonomy, a strong strategic vision, and sufficient goodwill and capacity at organizational level to make collaboration possible. Moreover, the role of central departments is more facilitating than directive. The New Zealand new-generation strategic management programme 'managing for shared outcomes' would fit in that scheme. In the UK, shared public-service agreements may set joint objectives for departments.

The fourth model of strategic management is the most loosely coupled, in that it only sets out a broad collective mission for the whole government, which acts as guidance for the day-to-day work of public-sector organizations. However, no monitoring systems are attached, which makes it dependent purely on the goodwill of individual organizations. Again in New Zealand, the State Service Commissioner developed a set of State Development Goals for periods of five years; the encompassing goals were 'being the employer of choice, excellent state servants, coordinated state agencies'. Here, strategic management was more a tool to develop a corporate culture, rather than a fully fledged planning and guidance instrument.

The budget process gives rise to another set of powerful 'tools of coherence' (OECD 1996), for three reasons. First, the budget process involves all policy sectors. Moreover, it gives a cyclic opportunity to assess the strategic orientation for the future and, third, it plays an important role in setting and monitoring the policy priorities of government. If we take it more broadly, the *financial management system,* encompassing processes and instruments of budgeting, accounting and auditing, can be used as a coordinating vehicle in different ways, depending on the dominant emphasis on authority, market or cooperation principles. The set of instruments may entail budgetary guidelines, framework letters, expenditure review committees, bilateral negotiations and conflict resolution processes, budgetary advice at the centre, formats, systems and provisions for accounting and audits (OECD 1996, 1999).

The role and capacity of the ministry (ministries) of budget and finance, as well as its relations with line ministries and other central ministries, is of course crucial to the effectiveness of this set of coordination instruments. Different dimensions in budget and financial management systems may have coordinating effects. First, the focus and content of financial management systems may help to align the tasks and efforts of different actors. This can be done by assigning objectives and means to individual organizations, or by linking individual organizations to common cross-cutting or outcome-oriented objectives. Moreover, because of its time frame, the budget cycle may have a coordinating function over time. A multi-year budget system coordinates expenses (and sometimes policies) between different moments in time. Finally, budget and financial management systems often entail consolidation techniques and formats, enabling the aggregation of information across organizations and policy domains.

The hierarchical, input-oriented budget process defines clearly what resources should be spent on, and in great detail. There is not much autonomy for organizations to spend the budget as they see fit. Making savings are expressed as unilateral demands, to which all organizations have to comply with. Through the budget, policy priorities are set and communicated downwards.

Alternatively, financial management systems can be more result-oriented, with a heavy emphasis on organizational incentives for performance. The focus of the financial management system is on providing incentives to organizational units to increase their performance. The budget is linked to the expected or past performance (price times quantity: $p*q$) of the organizations, and financial sanctions in case of underperformance are possible. Such budgeting is a precondition for creating (quasi-)markets. In such systems budgets, accounts and audits will be geared towards the performance of individual organizations and hence they will be accrued. Negotiations on the exchange of financial resources for delivered services, competition and benchmarking between public (and private) organizations are important elements in such a system.

However, financial management systems can also be used to foster joined-up working and cooperation between public organizations. In such a perspective, the focus of the financial management system is on the consolidation of financial and performance information across organizations and policy fields. The emphasis is on information consolidation and exchange, new budget formats, geared towards horizontal policies (for example, outcome- or programme-based budgets), as well as joined and exchangeable budgets in order to achieve cross-cutting objectives (OECD 1996; Pollitt 2003; 6 2004). If organizational or individual incentives for collaboration are present in financial management systems, they are heavily geared towards joined-up activities and cooperation (Pollitt 2003). Such financial management systems oriented towards collaboration will usually include great flexibilities for budget shifts between organizations and years, a limitation of input controls, as well as a longer time-span (say, three years).

Another set of coordination instruments relates more to human resources as a important resource. *Interorganizational culture and knowledge management* is a somewhat heavyweight label for all activities that enhance coordination and cooperation by fostering shared visions, values, norms and knowledge between organizations (Weick 1994). As such, this set of coordination instruments fosters the creation and growth of inter-organizational networks (Kickert et al. 1997; Klijn and Koppejan 2000) and hence is predominantly linked to the network-type coordination mechanism. An affiliated concept in private-sector management literature is 'inter-organizational learning', the creation of common rules and knowledge (explicit knowledge) and common values, norms, habits and routines (latent knowledge) (Holmqvist 1999; Hjalager 1999; Levinson and Minoru 1995). This could be done by means of the development of cross-cutting skills among staff; common education (for example, the Ecole Nationale d'Administration in France) or common training; management development; mobility of staff between organizations; collocation; and the creation of systems for inter-organizational career management and competence management (Alexander 1995; Pollitt 2003). Some countries (such as Australia, Canada, the USA, New Zealand, the UK and the Netherlands) have experimented with the creation of a 'senior executive service', which gathers, develops and rotates senior civil servants among departments as well as agencies (Halligan 2003). The introduction of behavioural and ethical codes for civil servants may be another vehicle for creating such common values and norms. Although somewhat debatable, we also may include here the more informal cultural contexts and processes that may influence politico-administrative behaviour to a large extent (OECD 1996). One could think of politicization or partisan control of (senior) civil servants (Rouban 2003). A strong affiliation of public managers to political parties may create informal networks and may have a socialization function with respect to common objectives and values. Also, more broad politico-administrative settings in a country may enhance common culture. For example, traditionally the New Zealand central government, which is based in Wellington, was known for its close relationships between politicians and senior civil servants, with high levels of mutual interaction. The consensual culture is referred to as the 'Wellington village' culture.

A last set of coordination instruments, which is somewhat of a catch-all category, refers to procedures for mandatory consultation or review for policy proposals, draft legislation or other plans (Alexander 1995). Some countries use forced points of passage during preparation of policy initiatives, with ministries having to comment on policy proposals that potentially affect their own policy. Australia has, for example, a procedure for 'co-ordination comments' for new policies (OECD 1996). Also, review procedures of draft legislation with respect to, for example, regulatory quality are quite common, and they may involve the assessment of the extent to which the draft legislation is in line with government policies or cross-cutting issues in order to avoid conflict or duplication among programmes (OECD 1996). Policy audits and evaluation, such as landscape reviews in the UK, may also have a coordination function as long as they are focused on horizontal objectives and on the policy effects of the interplay of different public organizations involved in policy implementation.

3.3 Conclusion: a typology of coordination mechanisms and coordination instruments

In this chapter we developed a typology of coordination instruments and linked them to the three dominant coordination mechanisms that we distinguished. In sum, the three fundamental modes of coordination in the public sector are elaborated in this chapter as follows (Verhoest and Bouckaert 2005):

1 Coordination by hierarchy-type mechanisms (HTM): HTM refer to a
   set of coordination mechanisms which are based on authority and

dominance. They involve the setting of objectives and rules, allocation of tasks and responsibilities and establishing lines of direct control and accountability. Both management instruments (such as procedural rules, top-down planning systems or traditional input-oriented financial management systems) and structural instruments (such as organizational mergers, coordinating function, direct lines of control and accountability) can be used.

2   Coordination by network-type mechanisms (NTM): NTM are based on mutual interdependencies and trust. NTM search for the establishment of common knowledge, common values and common strategies between partners. While most cooperative networks grow 'spontaneously' between organizations, governments may create, take over and sustain network-like structures between organizations by, for example, the creation of common information systems, concertation structures, collective decision-making structures, or even common partnership organizations. Inter-organizational learning instruments such as culture management may foster common knowledge and values.

3   Coordination by market-type mechanisms (MTM) (OECD 1993): MTM are based on competition and exchange between actors, aiming to create incentives for performance. Although markets establish 'spontaneous' coordination among the market participants, governments can 'purposefully' create and guard markets (for example, internal and quasi-markets) to foster coordination by competition among organizations.

4
How To Map Coordination: Issues of Methodology

Empirical research on coordination in general and in the public sector in particular is quite limited. But empirical coordination research based on a systematic research methodology is even more scarce. Exceptions are case studies on specific inter-organizational cooperation between organizations and within networks of organizations (James and Moseley 2006; Bardach 1998; Torfing and Sorenson 2002). These case studies have examined the manner in which decisions on particular coordination problems have been made, and the characteristics of the individual policy networks that can serve as the basis for coordination. However, even these scarce descriptive studies on coordination strategies, used by governments within policy domains or at government-wide level (6, 2004; Röber and Schröter 2006) refer in most cases to more anecdotal, illustrative evidence without much systematic data-gathering, analysis and presentation.

For this comparative research on coordination strategies in seven OECD countries, we have developed a research methodology that enables us to gather, map, analyse and compare in a systematic way, on the one hand, the level and kind of specialization within central government and, on the other hand, the coordination instruments (and coordination mechanisms) employed by those governments. In addition, this methodology was designed to look at the evolution of these two dimensions of organizations over the time period 1980 to 2005. The comparative static analysis method which we have developed allows us to compare several country cases over time.

In this chapter we will outline the methodology. First, we specify the central research questions once again, and then we proceed with discussing the comparative static method, its merits and drawbacks compared to other methods, as well as the steps for gathering, mapping, analysing and representing data. Finally, we will justify our selection of cases, that is, the countries we studied.

4.1   How to analyse central research questions on specialization and coordination

As spelled out in Chapter 1, the central research questions in this book are:

To what extent have countries indeed increased the coordination of management and policy as a reaction to excessively high levels of specialization, resulting in centrifugal fragmentation?

To what extent have countries indeed introduced new coordination mechanisms (more markets and networks rather than hierarchies) to cope with the negative consequences of increased specialization?

For the seven selected countries we will discuss the following more specific research questions. The first two sets of research questions are mainly descriptive.

• First, we analyse evolutions with respect to the level of specialization within each country for the period 1980–2005: How does the basic structure of government change over time? Does the level of specialization increase and at what levels (political, departmental and/or agency)? The individual country studies also raise a comparative question: Is an increasing level of specialization and fragmentation a common evolution, which can be discerned in each of the seven countries to the same extent?
• Second, we study the coordination strategies pursued in each country, with respect to the instruments used and the mechanisms emphasized: What kind of coordination instruments are used by governments at different levels and in different time periods? What are the changes over time in intensity and kind of coordination instruments used? On what coordination mechanisms (HTM, NTM, MTM) do the instruments mainly rely?

The three other sets of more specific research questions are more inter-pretative and comparative, and will be discussed extensively in the summary chapter.

- We will compare the trajectories of the countries. To what extent do we observe in each of the seven countries the hypothesized pattern of an increased level of specialization and organizational proliferation followed by an increase of coordination and consolidation? Are there other patterns? Moreover, we try to analyse the role of specialization as the driver for increased coordination: Does specialization increase the need for coordination or are other drivers also important? Do governments use new coordinating mechanisms, apart from hierarchy, to deal with higher levels of fragmentation and specialization?
- Moreover, we will focus on different aspects of the coordination strategy *as (a set of) reform initiative(s)* in each of the countries. Are strategies in some countries more radical than in others?; Are they more politically explicit. Are they more comprehensive? In addition, what kind of implementation (*de jure* or *de facto*) strategy is used? Who are the principal change agents and their position within government, and what is the impetus for change (top-down versus bottom-up)?
- Finally, we compare the coordination strategies in the seven countries with respect to the kind of coordination mechanisms (HTM, NTM, MTM) which were dominant and the changes over time in that respect. Do coordination strategies on instruments differ within coordination mechanisms? Is there really an overall shift towards the increased use of MTM and NTM in a fragmented institutional setting, to the detriment of the traditional HTM, as we hypothesize?

The upgraded comparative static analysis as a general approach

In our empirical research we used a comparative static methodology by taking several cross-sections of the government apparatus over time. Comparative static analysis combines the advantages of static analysis (in-depth snapshots at one moment in time to enable comparison between countries) and their juxtaposition in time (longitudinal analysis of evolutions to track changes within a country over time). This comparative static methodology thus makes it possible to compare between periods and between countries (Bouckaert et al. 2000: 35–6).

The comparative static analysis used here is upgraded since we are attempting not just to describe the differences but also to account for the dynamics of change. Thus, what we are doing is in essence a qualitative version of pooled time-series analysis almost as if we were able to do quantitative research on coordination. Understanding the dynamics and logic of change therefore becomes the final and perhaps most important part of the analysis. It would be very nice to have annual or even continuous pictures of change. We take the (roughly) five-year snapshots which tend to leave out changes occurring and disappearing between the observations. This is the problem of 'censorship' as described in events-history analysis (Tuma 1991). However, we believe we still have sufficient information to provide a meaningful understanding of changes in the public sector in these countries.

4.2   Analysing coordination: a five-step approach

For the seven countries under study, we analysed two dimensions in the period 1980–2005: the organizational specialization and fragmentation within government and the coordination strategies (Bouckaert et al. 2000; Verhoest et al. 2003). Using figures and symbols, we drew for each country a 'picture' of the organizational specialization and the coordination instruments used, reflecting several moments in the period 1980–2005. These moments are mostly related to changes in cabinets or administrations (mostly about five-year terms). Each picture was created in two steps. First, we mapped the basic government structure and its components on the political level, the level of the ministries and the level of the agencies and other semi-autonomous bodies. In a second step symbols representing difference were inserted in the basic schemes, enabling us to study the coordination strategies used by the country under study.

It is useful to discuss each step in more detail and to provide information on how the schemes were made and how they should be read.

First step: mapping the 'initial' government structure and its components (specialization)

Firstly, we distinguish three levels of analysis within the public sector at central level:

1 The political level (indicated as L1) which refers to the Cabinet, the prime minister and the other ministers (including junior ministers and state secretaries). All countries have a parliament. Parliament was not taken into account, except in those countries where parliament has a direct control relationship with ministries and agencies (for example, the USA). In the countries with a presidential regime, the president was mapped too.

2 The level of ministries/departments (indicated as L2). This is the level of the core-administration directly under the Cabinet and with a ministerial representation within the Cabinet. In some countries

these organizations are called ministries, in others departments. This level includes both line ministries and the central ministries, which have competencies mainly directed towards the other ministries or the rest of the public sector, for example, finance, budget and civil service matters, as well as the services supporting the prime minister in his/her role as head of the government.

3 The level of the quasi-autonomous public and hybrid agencies and other bodies, performing tasks for government (indicated as L3). At this level we have included different kinds of agencies (ranging from departmental agencies to public law agencies to private law agencies) and other quasi-autonomous bodies (OECD 2002). The bodies include non-commercial agencies as well as public corporations and state-owned enterprises.

For each level we frame its basic structure and its composing elements in a *standardized and simplified* way. Over time, the comparison of such subsequent basic schemes allows us to analyse (the evolution in) the degree of specialization and organizational fragmentation.

Figure 4.1 shows a simple example of such a basic initial scheme. This example is purely hypothetical and refers to the central government structure in country X. The scheme in Figure 4.1 shows in a simplified way the main actors at the different levels. Actors are represented by squares/rectangles. Besides the prime minister and the other ministers, the Cabinet is also depicted, although the Cabinet is, if we take it strictly, considered as a coordination instrument, that is, more precisely, an entity for collective decision-making (represented by a triangle). At the level of ministries and departments the difference between line ministries and central ministries is visible. At the third level of analysis, we see different types of quasi-autonomous bodies with a different legal structural distance with regard to the core administration. Departmental agencies are legally closer to government, compared to public law bodies, public companies or private law bodies (OECD 2002). Again, this representation is simplified, and certainly does not represent all actors, nor their exact numbers (that is, the total number of agencies). The schemes are supported by an extensive text, outlining the relevant details.

In order to make this basic scheme for each period for each country, we tried to deal systematically with a standard list of questions in order to collect relevant data.

Comparing schemes over time may reveal an increase or decrease in numbers, types and a change of position of actors in such a way that we

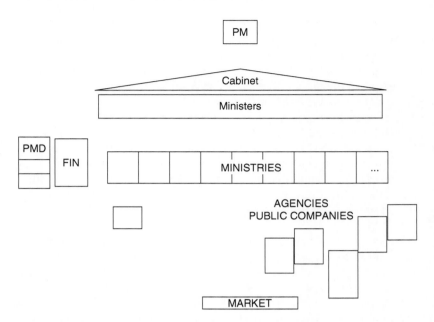

Legend PM: Prime Minister; PMD: Prime Minister's Department; FIN: Department of Finance

Figure 4.1   An example of a basic scheme of specialization within the central government of country X at moment T(0)

are able to depict very schematically vertical and horizontal specialization within the central public sector and changes over time.

Second step: mapping coordination instruments

In a second step, we map the different coordination instruments used within central government. Therefore, symbols representing different coordination mechanisms are added to the basic schemes for each period. Mapping all the coordination instruments and linking them with the three coordination mechanisms (HTM, MTM, NTM) enables us in subsequent steps to study the coordination strategies used by the country under study.

In Chapter 3 we developed our typology of (sets of) coordination instruments. Each of these instruments will be represented on the schemes with a specific symbol. Table 4.1 lists the different coordination instruments with the related symbols. The relevant symbol is

Table 4.1 Symbols representing the coordination mechanisms

Instrument	Predominant underlying mechanism	Symbol
1. *Strategic management (planning and evaluation) Dependent of primary objective and process*	NTM–HTM	
1.1 *Bottom-up and interactive strategic management*	NTM	
1.2 *Top-down and unilateral strategic management*	HTM	
2. *Financial management (budgeting, accounting and audit). Dependent of objective and focus*	HTM–MTM–NTM	∿∿∿
2.1 *Traditional input-oriented financial management systems*	HTM	
2.2 *Results-oriented financial management systems focused on incentives for units*	MTM	
2.3 *Results-oriented financial management systems based on information exchange and consolidation according to policy portfolios*	NTM	
3. *Inter-organizational culture and knowledge management*	Predominantly NTM	
4. *Mandated consultation or review system*		
5. *Reshuffling of competencies: organizational merger or splits; centralization (decentralization)*	Predominantly HTM	
6. *Reshuffling of lines of control*	Predominantly HTM	→
7. *Creating coordinating functions: establishment of a specific coordinating function or entity*	Predominantly HTM	*
8. *Regulated markets: internal markets, quasi-markets, voucher markets and external markets, competitive tendering*	Predominantly MTM	$$$
9. *Systems for information exchange*	Predominantly NTM	

(Continued)

Table 4.1   Continued

Instrument	Predominant underlying mechanism	Symbol
10. *Negotiation bodies and advisory bodies*	Predominantly NTM	⬯
11. *Entities for collective decision-making*	Predominantly NTM	△
11. *Common organizations (partnership organizations)*	Predominantly NTM (HTM)	⬭
12. *Chain-management structures*	Predominantly NTM	∞∞
	Entities of a temporary nature are represented by the same shape but with dotted line/borders	▢

inserted on the scheme close to the squares, representing the actors or institutions involved in these instruments.

Moreover, the newly introduced coordination instruments are numbered on the scheme. Below each scheme, a full list of the numbered coordination instruments is given. When we describe in the accompanying text the coordination instrument involved and its main features, we refer between brackets and in bold font to the relevant number, which is displayed in the list and the scheme (for example, **(8)**). In that way, this representation of coordination instruments with the symbols and numbers within the schemes is supported by a list of the coordination instruments and a clear reference in the extensive accompanying text.

Let us illustrate this with the example of country X in the period T(0) to T(4). Figure 4.2 shows what kind of coordination instruments are used within this country. The coordination instruments are made visible by inserting visible symbols on to the basic structure of the government.

The scheme in Figure 4.2, together with the list of the numbered coordination instruments, gives us insight on how the government of country X coordinates its public sector within the period T(0) to T(4). First, the scheme shows that the prime minister and his ministry have a strong coordinating function (denoted with an *asterix*) in relation to the other actors in the public sector in order to get the agreed policies implemented **(2) (3)**. Also the ministry of finance and civil service is a main coordinating actor, since it controls resource use within the line

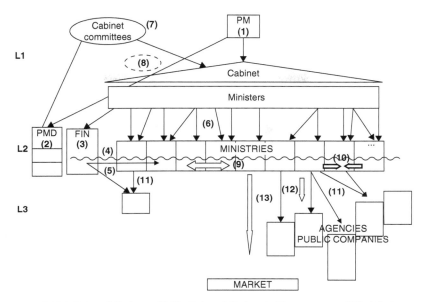

Legend PM: Prime Minister; PMD: Prime Minister's Department; FIN: Ministry of Finance

Number Relevant events

	Cabinet as entity for collegial decision-making
(1)	Coordinating power of the Prime Minister
(2)	Coordination role of the Department of the Prime Minister
(3)	Coordination capacity of the Treasury
(4)	Input-oriented budget cycle
(5)	Strong control by the Ministry of Finance and civil service on financial management transactions and civil service matters within line ministries by ex-ante approved procedures and strict regulations
(6)	Direct control by ministers on ministries with some departments controlled by several ministers and with some ministers solely controlling several departments
(7)	Existence of an elaborated system of cabinet committees
(8)	Introduction of ad hoc task forces at the level of cabinet
(9)	Split of the Ministry of Health and Social Security into two separate ministries
(10)	Merger of the former Ministry of Education and the Ministry of Employment to a new Ministry of Education and Employment
(11)	Detailed process-oriented control by ministries of the departmental agency, public companies, public law bodies and private law agencies
(12)	The creation of a new public company for postal services by the shift of tasks and competencies from the Ministry of Trade and Industry
(13)	Limited privatization of telecommunication and banking services by the shift of competencies from the Ministry of Trade and Industry to the private market

Figure 4.2 Coordination instruments within the central government of country X from Year. T(0) to T(4)

ministries and even quasi-autonomous bodies very strictly through an input-oriented budget cycle (4) (represented by a *wave*) and strict ex-ante control procedures (5). Departments and agencies are quite strictly controlled by their superiors, with, in some cases, several ministers being responsible for one ministry (6) (respectively several ministries being responsible for one agency) (11). Control lines are depicted as simple thin black lines.

Several structural changes happen in this period, such as both the split (9) and the merger (10) of two departments. These shifts of competencies are represented by large arrows. While the merger aims at enhancing coordination between education and employment policy and services by bringing them structurally together, the split is actually an example of horizontal specialization. Other shifts of competencies are the creation of another public company (12), out of the Ministry of Trade and Industry, as well as a privatization of the telecommunications services (13). The latter will be subject to market competition instead of political control.

Coordination at the level of the Cabinet is enhanced by a system of permanent committees (cabinet committees), composed of ministers and senior officials (7). These committees prepare Cabinet decisions, but have no decision-making powers in themselves. For policy domains which are not dealt with in the cabinet committee structure, as well as for urgent ad hoc problems, temporary task forces are created in order to prepare well-balanced policy proposals (8). The cabinet committees as well as the task forces are symbolized by an oval form, representing advisory and negotiation bodies. Temporary coordination instruments, such as the temporary task forces, are displayed as interrupted black frames.

Third step: presenting changes over time

Such schemes are generated about every five to seven years in the period 1980–2005. The periods dealt with are largely determined by the term of successive cabinets, in particular when clear shifts in power occurred. The succession of different schemes allows for inter-time comparison and for analysing evolutions and changes. Figure 4.3 shows the changes in specialization and coordination in country X in a new cabinet period, from year T(5) to T(9).

First, if we just consider in Figure 4.3 the underlying structure of rectangles and squares and compare it to the previous period (Figure 4.1), we learn how the specialization at the different levels (political, departmental and agency) changes in this new period.

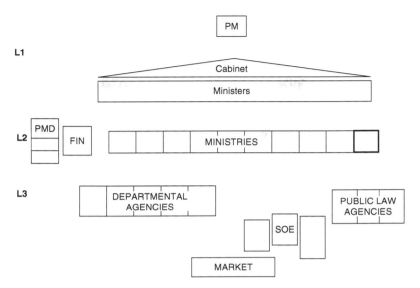

Legend PM: Prime Minister; PMD: Prime Minister's Department; FIN: Ministry of Finance; SOE: State-owned enterprises

Figure 4.3 The basic scheme of specialization within the central government of country X from year T(5) to T(9)

At the level of the departments one additional ministry was created, seen in the extra square. Moreover, the size of the line departments is considerably smaller compared to the previous period, referring to a considerable devolution of competencies, tasks and staff towards new and existing agencies. The same holds for the size of the Ministry of Finance and civil service, which lost competencies and tasks in relation to the line ministries and agencies. At the agency level, the representation by squares and rectangles shows that numerous new departmental agencies were created. This group is located nearer to the departments than the formerly existing groups of agencies, the public law bodies and public companies, referring to their relative legal distance. As to these initial groups of agencies, the squares representing the group of public law agencies are depicted all at the same distance in relation to the departments, which is clearly different from the previous period where there was a huge variety in distance. This means that in the period under review, the autonomy and governance structures of these public law bodies was harmonized and made more homogenous.

As for the formerly existing group of public companies, no such bodies are shown on Figure 4.3. However, some new rectangles, further away from the departments, refer to the creation of state-owned enterprises. In effect, the former public companies were corporatized and reorganized as state-owned enterprises.

In our country analyses, the entire evolution with respect to specialization is not shown. However, we show for each period the completed scheme, with the coordination instruments. In Figure 4.4 the completed scheme for the period T(5) to T(9) is presented, showing both the evolution with respect to specialization and to coordination in this period. Again, the changes are marked explicitly. The coordination instruments, which were initiated before this period, and which are still in operation, remain in the scheme.

Figure 4.4 shows that in this period many new coordination instruments were introduced, or more generally, that much change with respect to coordination took place. The temporary task forces are crossed as a signal of their abolition **(14)**. Two structural changes at the level of ministries occur: the split of two formerly merged ministries **(15)**, represented as a shift of competencies, and the creation of a new Ministry for Equal Opportunities with a coordinating function **(16)** (denoted by an asterix). This new ministry performs new tasks, as there has been no shift of competencies from other bodies (that is, no thick arrow).

Several structural and other changes are interrelated and refer to a major process of devolution. First, shown by large arrows, there is a shift of competencies from the Ministry of Finance and civil service to line ministries and agencies **(19)**. This points at an enlargement of the managerial autonomy of line ministries.

Detailed input control of agencies by the central Ministry of Finance and civil service is abolished. The coordinating capacity of this ministry is reduced, as shown by the smaller asterix **(18)**, but not totally lost. The budget cycle is reoriented more towards outputs, with strong incentives for individual organizations to meet performance targets – shown by the wave **(20)**. There is a shift of input control to output control, also at the political–administrative interface. Each individual ministry is now controlled by one minister, in order to clarify the accountability lines, compared to the more messy situation in the period T(0) to T(4). Moreover, this control by the ministers of ministries is now based on output-oriented contracts, with the ministers as purchasers and the ministries as providers (17, see the thin arrows). So, the secretaries-general have more managerial autonomy, but are held accountable for output-related objectives.

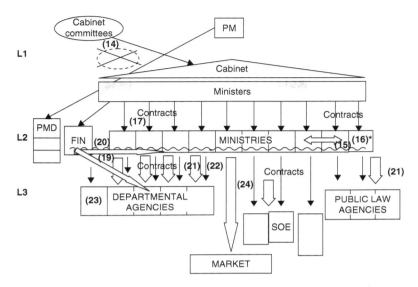

Legend PM: Prime Minister; PMD: Prime Minister's Department; FIN: Ministry of Finance; SOE: State-owned enterprises

Number   Relevant events

(14)   Abolition of ad hoc task forces
(15)   Split of Ministry of Education and Employment back into two separate ministries
(16)   Creation of a new coordinating Ministry of Equal Opportunities
(17)   Restructuring of control lines between ministers to ministries: shift to one-to-one control relationships with one ministry controlled by one minister, and with the control relationship based on output-oriented contracts
(18)   Coordination capacity of Ministry of Finance and civil service is reduced
(19)   Shift of competences concerning financial and HR management from Ministry of Finance and civil service to line departments, and to a even greater extent to agencies and other quasi-autonomous bodies
(20)   Reorientation of the budget cycle towards more output-orientedness, with strong incentives for individual organizations to meet performance targets
(21)   Devolution of competences from line ministries to newly created agencies, with a large number of departmental agencies created, as well as some public law bodies. Public companies are restructured as state-owned enterprises in anticipation of partial and full privatization
(22)   Reorientation of control of ministries on agencies towards output-oriented contracts, with one agency controlled by one ministry
(23)   Introduction of regulated markets as well as liberalization of existing markets in which some agencies and some State-owned enterprises have to compete for customers and resources
(24)   Major privatization of several public bodies in the field of transport, energy and water

Figure 4.4 Coordination instruments within the central government of country X from year T(5) to T(9)

Second, a major agencification, through shifting competencies from ministries to the lower agency level, leads to the creation of many more departmental agencies and to the relative reduction of the size of ministries (21 as shown by the large arrows). This increase in specialization is accompanied by other changes at the agency level, such as corporatization. Again the control of the now more autonomous agencies is contractualized with an emphasis on objectives to achieve and with clearer lines of control and accountability (one-to-one) (22). This is shown by the changed thin arrows. Moreover, market incentives are introduced to make several of these autonomized agencies perform optimally, through the introduction of quasi-markets in some policy fields, as well as by liberalization processes. Agencies in these markets are subject to coordination by price, supply and demand – denoted by a dollar sign (23). In the same perspective, several public bodies are privatized, and becoming subject to pressures stemming from competitive markets and private ownership (24). Privatization is shown as a shift of competencies from the public sector towards the private market.

In T(10) a new Cabinet is elected and the new prime minister stresses the need for a more whole-of-government approach and more inter-organizational collaboration within the public sector in order to meet pressing problems and cross-cutting policy issues such as poverty and national security. Figure 4.5 shows the changes under this new Cabinet.

A government-wide strategic management system was introduced, with planning, monitoring and evaluation of whole-of-government objectives aligned with the objectives of ministries and agencies through negotiation and bottom-up input (shown with turning arrows). A strategic management committee for monitoring each of the overarching objectives was created. This committee cannot take decisions but aims to coordinate between the different actors involved in the achievement of the objective concerned (shown as an oval form, 25). This is supported by a government-wide information system for information exchange, managed by the Department of the Prime Minister (28). A common culture and set of values between ministries and departments was pursued by creating a senior executive service providing common training for senior civil servants, as well as mobility programmes between ministries and departments (26). The senior executive service is depicted as a cultural coordination instrument in the form of a star. Specific negotiation committees (shown by an oval form) are set up in social policy fields in order to enhance joint working.

Notice that in this period no new ministries or agencies are created and no changes in specialization are to be observed: the basic structure of this

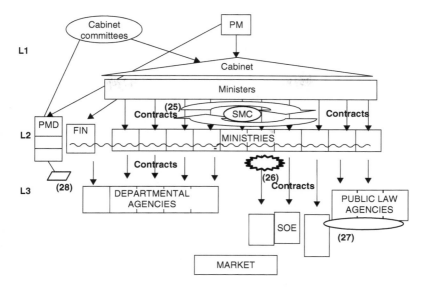

Legend PM: Prime Minister; PMD: Prime Minister´s Department; FIN: Ministry of Finance; SOE: State-owned enterprises

Number	Relevant events
(25)	Introduction of government-wide strategic management with linkages to plans at the level of departments and with extensive input from the departmental level, as well as negotiation. Outcome-oriented and horizontal objectives are negotiated among actors and monitored/evaluated through negotiation bodies ('strategic management committees') with the responsible ministers and departmental senior civil servants
(26)	Creation of a senior executive service encompassing senior civil servants from all departments, agencies and other quasi-autonomous bodies, providing common training and extensive mobility programmes
(27)	In social policy fields, several cross-cutting networks of agencies are created in order to enhance one-stop shops and integrated service delivery
(28)	The introduction of an information system for monitoring cross-cutting issues and government-wide objectives, encompassing modes for information exchange and sharing between individual organizations through common ICT platforms. The Department of the Prime Minister supervises this information system.

Figure 4.5 Coordination instruments within the central government of country X from year T(10) to T(14)

scheme remains the same as in the previous period T(5) to T(9). Moreover, all coordination instruments introduced in the previous period remain active, as they are reproduced in the scheme for the period T(10) to T(14).

Fourth step: analysing changes in coordination mechanisms over time

This simple example of three cabinet periods in country X shows that we can learn a lot simply by comparing the subsequent figures. However, apart from these specific observations at the level of individual coordination instruments, we may bring the analysis one step further, by linking specific coordination instruments to the three broad coordination mechanisms we identified: HTM, MTM and NTM. In Chapter 3 we described the conceptual and theoretical link between the three mechanisms and the individual coordination instruments. In this section we will outline how we make this link in our empirical analyses and what kind of information on this link for each country we will produce further in this book.

A crucial research question in the comparison of the different countries in this book is in relation to the kind of coordination mechanisms (HTM, MTM, NTM) that were dominant and the changes that occurred in them over time. Our zero hypothesis is that all countries will change in similar ways, but in reality that hypothesis is very likely to be rejected. We make a judgement on which coordination mechanism(s) prevail in a certain period, based on the link between coordination instruments used and the coordination mechanisms referred to or the *predominantly emphasized* coordination mechanism or mechanisms in a specific period (such as T(0) to T(4)), in order to detect *changes* in coordination strategies. The example of country X is quite simple and clear-cut. The three periods we have presented here show clear changes in the emphasis on specific coordination mechanisms (see Table 4.2).

In the first period T(0) to T(4) (see Figure 4.2), coordination is mainly about *hierarchy-type coordination mechanisms*, with a strict input-oriented and detailed control of ministries by their ministers and by central ministries, which have substantial coordination power and capacity. The few existing agencies have little autonomy and are also controlled in a detailed way by their parent ministries. Structural shifts of competencies are important instruments in order to enhance coordination. The use of an elaborate system of negotiation bodies at the political level (cabinet committees and task forces) also point to a network-type mechanism. However, the use of market-type mechanisms is largely absent, except for the privatizing function.

Table 4.2 Chronological overview of coordination tendencies in Country X

	Country X
Start position and period T(0)–T(4)	**HTM rather strongly emphasized** **Some traditional NTM** (such as cabinet committee system and task forces) MTM largely absent
Period T(5) –T(9)	HTM attenuated and reoriented towards outputs NTM attenuated to some extent (abolition of temporary task forces) **MTM strongly emphasized**
Period T(10)–T(14)	HTM equal as previous period **NTM heavily emphasized** **MTM remains in place**

In the second period T(5) to T(9), a considerable increase in specialization through devolution of competencies from central ministries to other bodies on the one hand and from line ministries to newly created agencies on the other is combined with specific shifts in coordination strategies. Compared to the previous period, coordination through hierarchy-type mechanisms is to some extent attenuated (despite the frequent shifts of competencies), since the control shifts from a detailed input to a more strategic output orientation, based on negotiated contracts. Moreover, the coordinating capacity of a central ministry is reduced. In the new setting of more bodies with more managerial autonomy, a strong emphasis is put on the introduction of *market-like* incentives and competition, through a change in the budget cycle, through output-oriented contracts, and through the emphasis on quasi- and liberalized markets, as well as major privatizations.

The third period T(10) to T(14) again witnesses a certain shift of emphasis. Most coordination instruments in place during the previous period remain, but several new coordination instruments are added which refer more to *network-type coordination* mechanisms: a bottom-up strategic management system with monitoring committees and supported by information-sharing systems, cultural coordination through a senior executive service, as well as specific networks and negotiation bodies to enhance collaborative efforts between agencies.

These judgements are mainly based on our assessments and supported by the observations of other scholars. Not all country analyses show clear-cut and straightforward shifts in emphasis over time. In many cases, we will observe hybrid combinations in which instruments related to HTM, MTM and NTM are all present. Again, in these situations we mainly look for broad changes, distilled from our detailed analysis of coordination instruments.

In the concluding chapter of this book we will also compare the overall approach of governments in the seven countries, and discuss for each of the coordination mechanisms the extent to which they have been used, through which vehicles (instruments), in which periods, as well as what kind of corrective measures have been applied. Moreover we will analyse the main features of the coordination strategy within countries' reform programs.

Fifth step: summarizing trajectories of specialization and coordination

A final kind of analysis is to summarize the trajectory that the central public sector follows in terms of specialization and organizational proliferation on the one hand and consolidation and coordination on the other. Essentially, we will indicatively present the trajectory of each country on the two-axis scheme developed earlier, which displayed the basic argument of the book (see Figure 1.1). Figure 4.6 shows the indicative trajectory for country X during the period T(0) to T(14).

This graphical presentation is qualitative and indicative. The first quadrant refers to a relative starting position with a relative number and variety of organizations in the initial situation and a relative level of consolidation within and between policies. The fourth quadrant refers to quite the opposite. There is a proliferation of organizations, a broad range of which are barely consolidated, even decoupled. The second quadrant refers to a corrected position where it is not so much a matter of the number and variety of organizations being reduced but of the way they are coupled, consolidated or coordinated being modified. The level of coordination has increased and makes a qualitative difference, that is, it is visible and slightly significant.

There are three qualifications to be made in using this synthetic way of presenting a country trajectory. First, the axes in this scheme cover complex phenomena.

Horizontal specialization and organizational proliferation relate to the raw number of public sector bodies on the one hand, and to the range of types of organizations as well as the heterogeneity within these types with regard to autonomy and governance structures on the other. The vertical axis of consolidation, coordination and (de)coupling refers both to the level of intra-policy cycle consolidation or coordination (that is, of policy design, implementation and evaluation), as well as inter-policy

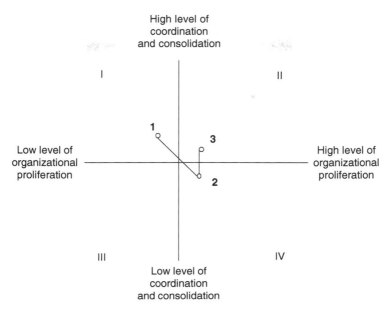

Figure 4.6 Trajectory of specialization and coordination in country X, indicatively displayed on a two-axis scheme

coordination or consolidation between policy fields. It means that a position in relation to the axes of organizational proliferation refers to some aggregated judgement as to changes in the number of organizations, as well as to their variety. It is clear that in some cases these changes may go hand in hand. However, this is not always the case.

Second, the position on the respective axes is not measured quantitatively, but rather qualitatively. We neither have simple measurement scales, nor data of sufficient quality to measure quantitatively. To our knowledge no quantitative measurement scales and ratios exist for these dimensions, particularly not for the dimension of coordination and consolidation. Instead of using quantitative measures, relative positions may be estimated qualitatively by taking several sub-dimensions into account and by making informed expert judgements. These judgements may then be validated by checking with country experts, through focus groups or with Delphi techniques. We have carried out some validation of these summary schemes by presenting them to country experts (academics and civil servants), and at several conferences and scientific meetings.

Third, because of these measurement and scaling difficulties, the most important element in these schemes, which display the overall trajectory of a country, is mainly the relative shape of the trajectory that the country follows rather than the exact positions on the respective axes. The schemes demonstrate to us to what extent countries do follow the assumed two-step trajectory; that is, first, more organizational proliferation and, second, a corrective strengthening of coordination. Figure 4.6 points to a two-step trajectory for country X, as it moved from an initial position that combined strong hierarchical coordination with some organizational proliferation, to a second position in which the organizational proliferation increased (at least in terms of numbers of organizations) combined with an attenuation of existing coordination and an emphasis on MTM. In the third position, in a context of equal organizational proliferation, additional NTM are introduced to enhance inter-organizational coordination. However, countries could follow, for example, a trajectory which is mainly horizontal, in which increasing organizational proliferation is combined with simultaneously enhanced coordination mechanisms. So, it is mainly the relative shape that is of interest in these schemes, as well as the extent that countries move upwards to the second upper quadrant or not.

Consequently, when we display the different schemes for the seven countries in the summary chapter, it is only the relative shapes of the trajectories that should be compared, rather than the exact positions of the countries in the axes. These diagrams allow us to compare conditions within one country over time rather than between countries, and therefore we do not display the trajectories of the seven countries on one two-axis scheme.

4.3   Additional research issues

Selection and delineation of cases

In this book we study the evolution of specialization and coordination strategies within the public sector. More specifically, we focus on central government within the following seven OECD countries: New Zealand, the United Kingdom, the United States, Sweden, the Netherlands, France and Belgium.

This selection is to some extent based on practical and pragmatic grounds – hence including the home countries of the authors and making use of data in languages known to the researchers. However, the selection of the cases in this book is justifiable on more theoretical grounds, including differences in the extent of the implementation of

NPM-like reforms and of agencification, as well as fundamental differences in politico–administrative cultures and management traditions (Painter and Peters 2010; Beuselinck and Verhoest 2005).

The basic assumption of this book is that an increase in specialization and organizational proliferation within the public sector, as a consequence of NPM-like administrative reforms, will be followed, quasi-automatically, with an increase in coordination efforts and the introduction of new coordination mechanisms. But, not all OECD countries have radically followed NPM doctrines in their administrative reforms; some have even been quite reluctant to embark on administrative reforms at all (Pollitt and Bouckaert 2004; Wollman 2003). In our sample of countries, clearly the Anglo countries implemented the most radical and comprehensive New Public Management (NPM)-based reforms, whereas Sweden and the Netherlands adopted only selected NPM elements in their reform strategy and that in a consensus-oriented, moderate way. France and Belgium, two Latin countries, were more reluctant to adopt NPM elements. The USA was the exception among Anglo countries, introducing only modest NPM reforms (Pollitt and Bouckaert 2004).

The disaggregation of government bureaucracy is considered a central feature of NPM reform packages (Hood 1991). Likewise, this strategy of disaggregation by agencification, outsourcing and privatization was not pursued equally enthusiastically in all OECD countries (OECD 2002; Pollitt and Bouckaert 2004). The extent of NPM-based agencification from 1980 onwards was much greater in countries such as New Zealand and the UK than in Nordic, Continental or Latin European countries (in order of decreasing extent) (OECD 2002).

That is not to say that in the latter countries organizational proliferation was absent or that agency-like bodies did not exist. On the contrary, Sweden has a long tradition of numerous large agencies, with their autonomy enshrined in the constitution. Similarly, the USA, France, the Netherlands and Belgium have had many legally independent public bodies for some time, created on many different grounds (such as corporatism, expertise, independent decision-making or as institutions of countervailing power). In countries with a tradition of numerous organizational types and forms, such as the UK, coordination is a long-lived problem facing government, rather than a recent one.

Moreover, and somewhat related to the previous point (Pollitt and Bouckaert 2004; Christensen and Laegreid 2001), the countries considered in this book can be considered as belonging to different administrative–cultural 'families of nations' (Lalenis et al. 2002), following

Anglo-American, Scandinavian (Nordic European), continental European or Latin European traditions. For example, these families differ in their legal tradition (Lalenis et al. 2002). France and Belgium have a strongly legalistic '*Rechtsstaat*' tradition, whereas the common law tradition and the public interest model is central to Anglo-American administrative cultures. Sweden's and the Netherlands' legal traditions and governance models shift between *Rechtsstaat* and the public interest model (Kickert and Hakvoort 2000). The families also differ in their broader cultural values (Hofstede 2001; House and Hanges 2004, Lalenis et al. 2002) with Latin cultures relatively more predisposed to hierarchical relations and avoidance of uncertainty and Nordic countries (including the Netherlands) less focused on these 'masculine' values. Finally, the country families differ in their type of democracy, with the Anglo countries having more clear majoritarian political systems, with the others having more consensus-oriented structures (Lijphart considers France to be an exception; see Lijphart 1999: 248). This variation is also apparent in the nature of executive government in these countries (Pollitt and Bouckaert 2004), as well as in the distinction that can be made between the countries with a presidential or semi-presidential system (the USA and France) and the others.

For each country we researched the period between 1980 and 2005. The motivation for the time span for the analysis mainly had to do with the rise (and subsequent fall?) of NPM as a reform ideology in the OECD. NPM found its way in politico-administrative mindsets during the 1980s or even later, with the UK and New Zealand being early adopters. The year 1980 is therefore appropriate for the start of the analysis, because in that year the more traditional forms of government organization and coordination were still prevalent. NPM only came later. Making 2005 the end year of the analysis is of course somewhat arbitrary, and has mainly to do with the deadline for this book. But next to that, it is clear that since the late 1990s a new wind has blown through the public management literature, putting public governance or similar ideas at the core of the next reform paradigm (Moore 1995). This emphasis on governance broadly indicates a shift from a focus on internal administrative reforms to an externally oriented emphasis on relations between the state and other sections of society in order to form and implement policies.

Methods of data gathering and analysis validation

The analysis of seven countries was carried out to a large extent in the period 1998 to 2003, resulting in two research reports commissioned by the Flemish and Belgian governments (Bouckaert et al. 2000; Verhoest et al. 2003[1]), with a major update from 2005 to 2006. The USA was added as a country case in the same period.

Until now, we have mainly discussed the analytical tools used. But how did we gather the data for the analysis of specialization and coordination? Our data mainly comes from an extensive document analysis, covering government publications as well as academic sources. Relevant government publications were gathered from existing databases (mainly the Public Management Institute database of government publications in OECD countries), web searching and targeted requests for documents to governments, public bodies or country experts. Moreover, we screened the public management literature on relevant scientific accounts and evaluations of public administration systems and reforms in the seven countries under review. For some countries, this scholarly literature is vast, but for others quite limited (for instance, Belgium). By no means is our use of scholarly literature exhaustive, but we tried to use several authoritative sources per country. All of the authors of this book have been involved themselves in major international comparative works on administrative reforms and public management (Pollitt and Bouckaert 2004; Peters 2003, 2004; Verhoest et al. 2003, 2007, 2010) which included some or all of the countries studied in this book. This experience helped us in finding relevant sources and detecting relevant reform initiatives. Also some information was gathered through networks in which the researchers participate, such as the COBRA network which studies international processes of agencification and organizational proliferation.

In addition, during the first phase of research (1998–2003) for several countries site visits and interviews were conducted with government representatives or country experts. Many of these interviews focused on individual coordination instruments, instead of broad coordination strategies (Verhoest et al. 2003).

An important additional step was performed. For each country, we asked at least one or two scholars or practitioners, considered to be experts with regards to the public sector in their country, to check the lists of initiatives that we had selected as having an effect on the level of specialization and coordination in their country. They were provided with the analytical schemes as well as the full text of the country chapters. This provided both a check for the comprehensiveness of our selection, as well as a check as to the relevance of the decisions taken regarding that initiative to the evolution of specialization and coordination in the country involved. Additionally, several country studies have been presented on different academic platforms of which some have been published in reviewed journals or books (Verhoest and Bouckaert 2005; Legrain and Verhoest 2004).

Strengths and weaknesses of the methodology used

It is clear that the analyses in this book build on a highly innovative analytical methodology. However, the outline of the methodology in the paragraphs above points to some inherent deficiencies or weaknesses. In this section we will elaborate on these weaknesses, try to estimate their effect on the overall findings of the research, but also indicate what we see as the strengths of this methodology. In this way, we can respond proactively to any criticism that this methodology and way of presenting our results may invoke.

A first obvious weakness of the methodology used here is in *what we do not include in our analysis*. The analysis is focused on coordination within the public sector at the central level in these countries. Principally, *coordination with the private sector or with other governmental levels* is not included, except in those cases where this is needed in order to understand coordination at the central level (such as in France). When studying specialization and coordination within the public sector of a specific country, one could choose a holistic approach, dealing with evolutions on all governmental levels at the same time. Or one could use a rather modular approach, in which the analysis focuses on one governmental level and its interfaces with other governmental levels at the time, with the objective being to integrate the analyses of different governmental levels at a later stage. This approach is followed in this book.

A related limitation is in the empirical focus on specialization and coordination at a generic level and focusing on general initiatives, rather than on initiatives *within specific policy sectors*. It may be assumed that sectoral analyses of specialization and coordination may show somewhat different patterns. On the other hand, general initiatives may originate from or be stimulated through sectoral dynamics. Sectors may be important analytically, since policy sectors differ in crucial features which may influence the extent of specialization and coordination. For instance, policy sectors differ in terms of their political salience (see Pollitt et al. 2004 for the influence of political salience on the autonomy and control of agencies). This deficiency is acknowledged as our analysis is generic, and does not exclude adjusted or more pronounced changes in specific sectors (such as privatization and marketization in economic sectors versus socially oriented policy fields). In the perspective of the abovementioned modular approach, subsequent work has set out to link our generic analyses with sector-specific analyses in different countries (Beuselinck 2006).

Similarly, our methodology is not able to detect all kinds of coordination. As the emphasis is more on formal coordination instruments, including some obvious initiatives to stimulate cultural coordination, we miss to a large extent the informal means of coordination within the public sector. The government-wide influence of administrative corps and of politicization is normally obvious and acknowledged in scholarly publications. But the extent to which interpersonal contacts, informal discussions and platforms, and bilateral and multilateral discussions affect coordination within a public sector is much harder to grasp. Moreover, our taxonomy does not really provide labels and symbols for these elements. In some cases, the accompanying text for a country refers to elements of informal coordination. But it is hard to know if we have been able to detect the most important elements in that respect, because of missing data.

Other weaknesses of our methodology relate to *what we select to include in the analysis*. This plays at several levels. First, there is the question of to what extent the initiatives we list with respect to specialization and coordination refer to models or strategies of governments (talk and decisions) or effectively implemented realities (action). Are the initiatives shown *announced reforms or reforms in effect?* The history of the public sector is filled with examples of attempted reforms that were never implemented, or if implemented had no real effect. Because we extensively used government documents as data sources, many of the framed initiatives are announced reforms (talk and decisions) and not necessarily reforms in effect. We tried to overcome this by looking for evaluative studies or scholarly publications which assess the implementation of reforms, but in several instances we failed to find such sources. Moreover, the academic and non-academic experts who checked the country chapters helped us to some extent to distinguish rhetoric from reality. However, there remains a bias towards announced reforms. This bias is not too problematic, because talk and decisions tell us a lot about changes in thinking about coordination, and therefore about changes in coordination strategies.

Second, there is the *criteria for selection of relevant events*. What initiatives endanger or strengthen coordination and how do we know this? And how do we avoid a bias in our selection, given the difficulties of data-gathering? We attempted to overcome this difficulty by having a consistent checklist of topics. Further, we cast our net sufficiently widely so that all types of reform – policy design, policy implementation and management – were included in the analysis.

A third element of potential criticism is the *degree of subjectivity in linking instruments to HTM, MTM or NTM mechanisms*. Some sets of instruments and reforms are clearly hybrids and mixtures. Indeed, NTM instruments are particularly ambiguous, implicitly containing some elements of hierarchy. We have, both through careful review of the theoretical literature and the operation of the instruments, attempted to ensure that the coordination instruments are classified in a defendable way.

Part 2
Specialization and Coordination in Seven Countries (1980–2005)

5
Coordination in New Zealand (1980–2005)

This chapter discusses the changes in New Zealand in five stages: 1980–4 as an 'initial stage' under the National Party cabinet of Prime Minister Muldoon; 1984–90, under PM Lange's Labour cabinet; 1990–6, under PM Bolger's National Party cabinet; 1996–9 (for the Bolger and Shipley stage); and finally from 2000 to 2005 under PM Clark's Labour cabinet. Over all these stages we have registered 45 observations of changes in the degree of specialization and coordination.

5.1 The early 1980s: the National Party cabinet under PM Muldoon, 1975–84

At the beginning of the 1980s the New Zealand public sector had two main characteristics. First, the ministerial departments were the dominant actors in government. The functions of policy advice, preparation, execution and regulation were performed all within a department, and the sectoral model was prevalent **(1)** (See Figure 5.1). Second, the governmental apparatus was already fragmented for a country with no more than 3.5 million inhabitants (Boston et al. 1996: 77–8). Until 1984, the public sector comprised: three central departments; about 36 departments in the core Public Service with 88,000 staff; a number of offices of Parliament (Audit Office and Ombudsman's Office); a number of non-core departments including the Post Office and the police; various public corporations and Crown-owned companies including broadcasting and railways, the education and health services; and numerous other public bodies (such as boards, tribunals and agencies) most of which were later called 'Crown Entities'. More than 400 government-funded public bodies existed at that time **(2)**.

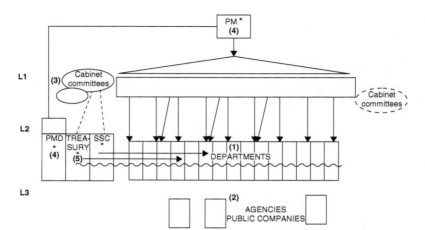

Legend PM: Prime Minister; PMD: Prime Minister's Department; SSC: State Service Commission

(1) Strong departments (36 core)
(2) About 400 smaller agencies, and non-departmental public bodies
(3) System of cabinet committees
(4) Position of the Prime Minister
(5) State Service Commission (SSC) and Treasury: interdepartmental coordination

Figure 5.1 Specialization and coordination in New Zealand in the early 1980s, before the public management reforms

Figure 5.1 shows the situation in 1984, reflecting the fragmentation. The coordination of activities at that time was primarily done through a committee structure, composed of a large number of permanent and temporary cabinet committees (3). The 'system of cabinet committees' was supplemented and serviced by a system of interdepartmental committees, either permanent or ad hoc. The position of the Prime Minister and his department was formally rather weak in comparative terms. However, in reality the New Zealand Prime Minister was perceived as being *primus inter pares* among ministers and the focal point of executive power. Although the PM's department was relatively small by overseas standards, officials within this department exercised significant influence and played a key role in policy formulation and decision-making across a wide range of policy areas (4). The State Service Commission (SSC) and the Treasury, the two other central agencies, were responsible for interdepartmental coordination and had an important role in the committee structure. Moreover, these central agencies coordinated and controlled financial and human resources management in the line departments using, among other things, the budget procedure (5).

Up to this time changes in the government apparatus occurred in a rather ad hoc way, being the consequence of new policy initiatives, changing societal needs and political decisions. There was no master plan involved.

5.2 From 1984 to late 1990: reforms under the Labour cabinets of PMs Lange and Palmer

From 1984, New Zealand embarked upon a number of drastic reform initiatives in order to reverse the major economic decline of the country, its budgetary problems and threats of inflation (Schick 1996: 13). These reforms were facilitated by, among other factors, an accommodating political system, with a unitary government, unicameral parliament and a single-party cabinet with a parliamentary majority (Schick 1996: 14, see Pollitt and Bouckaert 2004). The new Labour government under Prime Minister Lange changed its control model of society and its own apparatus from an interventionist to a more market-like stance. Figure 5.2 reflects these changes, which had four central principles (Mulgan 1997).

First, the state should restrict itself to its core business, shedding tasks that can be performed more efficiently and effectively by the private sector. Therefore, commercial activities were separated from administrative and regulatory activities by the establishment of state-owned enterprises (State-owned Enterprise Act 1986) (6), some which were privatized in a second stage. By 1992 14 state-owned enterprises were active under the Act and 15 former state assets were sold, including Air New Zealand (7) (OECD 1993: 216).

A second principle was that departments should have non-conflicting objectives, just like private businesses. This principle led to the division of policy functions and operational executive functions through the creation of a large number of quasi-autonomous executive bodies, called Crown Entities (8). In some policy domains such as environment administration competencies were reallocated to several ministries (Environment, Agriculture and Forestry, Fisheries, Conservation). The remaining, rather small, ministries were limited to policy advice, management and monitoring of the budget and corporate services. However, this agencification did not decrease the number of ministries.

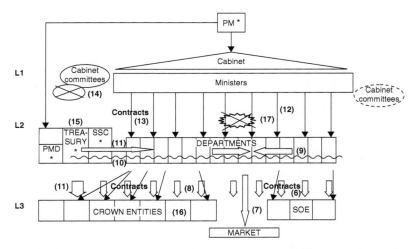

Legend PM: Prime Minister; PMD: Prime Minister's Department; SSC: State Service Commission; SOE: State-owned enterprises

(6) State-owned Enterprise Act 1986
(7) Privatize some state-owned enterprises
(8) Quasi-autonomous executive bodies (Crown Entities)
(9) Reshuffle (policy advice) competencies between small but numerous ministries (−15 +20; several agencies)
(10) Public Finance Act 1989 (internal markets)
(11) State Sector Act 1988 (reduce input control, increase autonomy)
(12) One-to-one relation between minister and administration
(13) Puchaser–provider relationship
(14) Weakened system of cabinet committees
(15) Relation between minister and chief executive is crucial; central agencies; weakened horizontal capacity; functions of Prime Minister's Department split; SSC lost regulatory powers
(16) Market-type mechanisms
(17) Senior Executive Service fails

Figure 5.2   Specialization and coordination in New Zealand in the period 1984–9

New ministries were created to respond more adequately to the needs of certain groups, such as the Maori, Pacific Islanders, women and the elderly. Some of these ministries had a horizontal coordinating role (9). Overall, this structural disaggregation resulted in highly diverse organizational structures within the ministries and at the level of the agencies, since there was no generic blueprint or law in place to encourage uniformity.

A third principle was the creation of internal markets through allocating purchaser and provider roles to different actors in this field (minister, department and autonomous entities). According to this principle, the cost of public activities should be set by market forces, reflecting the demand of the purchaser (Public Finance Act 1989; see Pallot 1991) **(10)**.

A fourth principle was reduction of central input control and the decentralization of substantial management autonomy to departmental managers (State Sector Act 1988) **(11)**. The responsibility of chief executives towards ministers was redefined, making them accountable for the outputs of their department. A system emerged that was a combination of one-to-one lines of control, with ministers purchasing services from departments and contracting relationships among the various actors. Departments were generally controlled by one minister **(12)**,[1] who had in general two roles: one as a purchaser of its output, the other as the 'owner' of the organizations. As purchaser a minister may opt to obtain output from the department or from alternative suppliers such as Crown Entities or non-governmental actors **(13)** (Schick 1996: 29). This was at least theoretically the case, but in reality this model was very difficult to implement.

These changes in micro-control increased the level of specialization in the New Zealand state apparatus, which already suffered from problems of coordination (departmentalism, poor inter-actor communication and information exchange) (Boston 1992). Between 1984 and 1990 several elements aggravated this coordination deficit. Political problems and power struggles within government, the exclusion of senior civil servants from cabinet committees and the abolition of preparatory administrative committees further eroded communication between the political and the administrative levels and the possibilities for overall coordination (Boston, 1992) **(14)**. Interdepartmental coordination became more difficult because of drastic organizational changes, including the abolition of 15 departments, the creation of 20 new departments and of several agencies (see **(9)**). Important policy changes had to be implemented by the departments while they were in turmoil and while existing networks were destroyed, leaving little time or opportunity for interdepartmental coordination. Furthermore, because of the narrow objectives assigned to the different departments, more competitive attitudes arose within the public sector (Steering Group 1991: 46–8). In addition, the State Sector Act emphasized minister–chief executive relationships to the detriment of cabinet–chief executive relationships and the horizontal relationships among chief executives.

The central agencies were then unable to take the leading role in setting up new coordination systems, as they were adjusting to their own loss of competencies **(15)**. The functions of the Prime Minister's Department were split and allocated to two separate offices (the Prime Minister's Office, which was essentially a political office, and the Department of Prime Minister and Cabinet), which suffered both to some extent from a lack of resources and policy capacity. Although the State Sector Act gave the SSC a role in coordination and advice on structural and management matters, the SSC lost its regulatory powers in relation to the other ministries.[2] Coordination among autonomous organizations was mainly done by the introduction of market-type mechanisms **(16)**. The Treasury was by far the most dominant central department during this time. Its bureaucratic power was almost uncontested, despite it being concerned to see that every other agency's policy advice was made 'contestable'. However, the Treasury did not introduce new coordination mechanisms at that time.

Although some limited corrective actions were taken at the end of the 1980s, they had only limited success in enhancing policy capacity because of the lack of political consensus. For senior civil servants, the attempt by the SSC to create a senior executive service **(17)**, which could create more horizontal mobility and a more common culture, failed because of resistance by the senior managers themselves (Schick 1996: 50). In 1989 and 1990 two subsequent cabinets resigned and the 1990 election brought a conservative government to power.

5.3   From late 1990 to late 1996: reforms under the National Party cabinet of PM Bolger

From the 1990s onwards the New Zealand government tried to strengthen its coordination system with a variety of structural and procedural changes (see Figure 5.3). First, the coordination role of the central agencies was strengthened. Prime Minister Bolger, who came to power in 1990, preserved the structures of the recently created Department of Prime Minister and Cabinet (DPMC), combining the analytical group (long-term, strategic policy advice) and the advisory group (short-term advice) into one group **(18)**. In this way, the DPMC was better equipped to play a stronger coordinating role. The coordination of financial management and the budget process by the Treasury was also further enhanced **(19)**. The SSC got the task of coordinating the different Result Areas in the new strategic planning system and harmonizing the performance agreements between ministers and chief executives **(20)**.

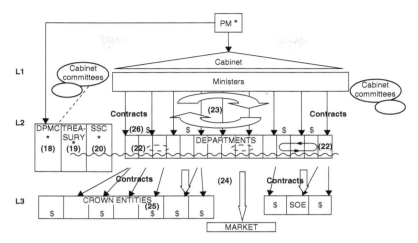

Legend PM: Prime Minister: DPMC: Department of Prime Minister and Cabinet (New Zealand); SSC: State Service Commission; SOE: State-owned enterprises; SRA: Strategic Result Area; KRA: Key Result Area

(18) Department of Prime Minister and Cabinet (DPMC)
(19) Enhanced coordination by Treasury of budget process
(20) SSC: coordinate Result Areas, harmonize performance agreements (minister–chief executives)
(21) Re-establish cabinet committees
(22) Ad hoc interdepartmental working committees and the system for mandated interdepartmental consultation
(23) Strategic Management System: Strategic Result Areas (SRAs)/Key Result Areas (KRAs)
(24) (S) Further hiving-off and privatization
(25) Further purchaser–provider split; increased competition
(26) Competition for policy advice, but only to a limited extent

Figure 5.3 Specialization and coordination in New Zealand in the period 1990–5

In addition, the three central agencies aimed for better coordination between the coordination mechanisms at their disposal: the budgeting process; decision-making in cabinet; performance agreements; performance evaluation; and the selection of chief executives. The standard performance agreements of the chief executives incorporated an appendix issued by the SSC which set forth government-wide requirements for internal control, human resources management, financial management and other practices. Aimed at coordinating management, these requirements were, however, quite general and not targeted sufficiently to allow for assessing progress and remedying deficiencies (see Schick 1996: 45).

Second, the system of cabinet committees was restructured, with revamped high-level officials' committees to assist them **(21)**. Highly ranked civil servants were again admitted to the cabinet committees, in order to increase the information exchange between the political and administrative levels. Efforts also were made to increase interdepartmental consultation before cabinet decision-making. Departments were asked to consult one another and the Department of the Prime Minister and Cabinet concerning important policy proposals **(22)**. For specific policy themes, some ministries were designated as 'forced points of passage' (for example, the Environment Ministry for policy proposals with environmental repercussions) (OECD 1996: 21). A review by the SSC in 1999 with a broader focus on policy advice revealed some remaining problems in this coordination structure (SSC 1999b).[3] However, despite the weaknesses the SSC recommended no fundamental changes to this set of coordination mechanisms, but stressed the importance of leadership, clear expectations from ministers and the selection of high-quality members (SSC 1999b: 47–52).

Third, in order to remedy some shortcomings identified by the Logan Report (Steering Group 1991), the government enhanced its capacity for strategic management. The report identified major problems in how governments set strategic priorities and how the public service helped them meet those goals. Furthermore, it noted that clearer specification and better achievement of outputs was effective only if there was certainty 'that the production of the outputs led to the achievement of the outcomes, and only if the outcomes could be broken down into measurable parts and distributed among the various departments as outputs' (Steering Group 1991).

In order to link departmental actions and budgets to the policy priorities of government and to enhance a long-term strategic perspective, three initiatives were taken. A planning capacity was developed at the centre of government. The Fiscal Responsibility Act of 1994 introduced a medium-term fiscal strategy. Moreover, following the publication of the government's vision statement *Path to 2010* in 1993 (National Party 1993), the government introduced a strategic management system, by formulating cross-portfolio Strategic Result Areas (SRAs) which reflected the long-term policy objectives of government and by inducing departments to develop Key Result Areas (KRAs) **(23)**. These KRAs and their measurable milestones had to be linked to the SRAs and formed the basis of performance agreements. The alignment of the SRAs and the KRAs was mainly done by a more or less continuously informal strategic conversation between ministers, chief executives and central agencies

(SSC 1998a: 15). By embedding individual performance and purchase agreements (that is, micro-level control) in a framework of government-wide objectives (macro-level control) the government tried to reorient departments towards the policy priorities of the cabinet.

Figure 5.3 shows how the hiving-off and privatization of government activities proceeded in the period 1990–5 (24). By 1995 the structure of the state sector had changed dramatically, compared to the situation before reform. The core public service comprised 39 departments, but employed only 39,000 staff compared to 88,000 staff in 1984. Departments were therefore generally much smaller than their counterparts in 1984 (except for the Department of Social Welfare and the Inland Revenue Department). Twelve departments had fewer than 100 staff. The large number of departments and their small size generated diseconomies of scale. Moreover, in some departments there were insufficient skills and capacities to strategically control the proliferation of Crown Entities (Schick 1996).

A new tier of Crown Companies and Crown Research Institutes and other Crown Entities was established. They performed many of the functions previously carried out by the core departments. This tier of Crown Entities comprised more than 2700 bodies, including 2600 school boards of trustees, 23 Crown health enterprises, four regional health authorities, 21 business development boards and various other bodies. Unlike the departmental 'Next Steps' agencies which were the main type of autonomous bodies set up during the 1980s and the 1990s in the UK, all Crown Entities were separate legal entities. Moreover, most were governed by a board of directors, appointed by government and who themselves appointed the senior management of the entities. This group of organizations spent approximately two-thirds of the budgeted resources for the operation of government and one-third of total Crown expenses (Schick 1996). However, despite considerable accountability requirements, the operations and finances of these bodies remained rather opaque, according to the 1996 report by Schick (Schick 1996).

This fragmentation was, however, to some extent counterbalanced by the three corrective actions already described. Besides these actions, coordination by markets was strengthened for quasi-autonomous bodies. In sectors such as health and education major restructuring had taken place and market-type mechanisms were introduced via purchaser–provider splits and by increasing competition (25). In this period competition for policy advice by departments themselves was introduced (26).

5.4   From late 1996 to 1999: reforms under the National Party coalition cabinets of PMs Bolger and Shipley

Proportional representation, introduced in 1996, had a major impact on the parliamentary–executive relationship and the policy process. Issued in the same year, the highly influential Schick Report was largely positive about the coordination capacity of the New Zealand state sector. Important factors included the positive influence of informal networks, the small size and population of New Zealand and the capital city Wellington's village atmosphere, as well as the value attached to inter-departmental work (Schick 1996: 46). Formal mechanisms, in particularly the SRA–KRA system, were considered to be performing well. The system had 'a marked, and generally favourable, influence on budget decisions and managerial accountability', with KRAs and milestones cast in actionable terms (Schick 1996: 55). Schick stated:

> [w]ith so many departments contributing to the same SRA, the process gives the government a much clearer picture than before of how the various activities relate to one another. The process may also become a tool for examining duplication or inconsistencies in public policies. (Schick 1996: 56)

However, he pointed to some possible improvements: the strategic planning in the departments themselves needed to be enhanced; the strategic planning should be more clearly linked with multi-year budgets; and the priorities as framed by the SRAs and KRAs should direct more clearly resource allocation (1996: 60). These observations of improved strategic alignment and coordination and cooperation across departments on the one hand as well as a lack of impact on budget allocations on the other hand were largely supported by subsequent reports by the SSC (SSC 1997a; SSC 1998b).

Other reports were more critical about central coordination capacity and pointed to the lack of a 'whole-of-government' perspective in policy advice. They linked this to the substantial disaggregation of the New Zealand state sector at departmental level. At the same time, the level of disaggregation did not appear to enhance contestability of policy advice to a great extent (27) (SSC 1998c; Washington 1998).

At that time there were increasing concerns in the New Zealand cabinet about the responsiveness of the Public Service to government strategic goals and the coordination of policy and service delivery. A subsequent report of the SSC, *A Better Focus on Outcomes through SRA*

Networks (1998d), listed a number of weaknesses in the existing strategic management system, some of which mirrored the mild criticisms of the Schick Report. But some reported deficiencies were rather new, like a lack of clarity about government strategic objectives and a lack of real integration of SRAs into departmental strategy and operations, and a lack of outcome-based evaluation. There was also a lack of leadership for individual SRAs. Both within and across portfolios there was a lack of review and coordination resources and inadequate efforts directed toward strategic goals. The SSC noted that although there were a few instances of cross-portfolio consideration of new initiatives (environment, transport, justice), 'the Cabinet, Budget and purchase systems focus almost exclusively on individual portfolios' (SSC 1998d: 4). Incentives for coordination, such as sharing joint Key Result Areas between departments, were not widely adopted because of a lack of incentives (SSC 1999b: 52).

The SSC proposed a SRA-network plan in order to improve the coordination of activities and their objectives (SSC 1998d). Each SRA was to be championed by one minister, who was responsible to cabinet for the achievement of the SRA and responsible for coordination related to that SRA. The SRA minister would chair an SRA committee consisting of the network ministers likely to purchase substantial strategic outputs from their departments or Crown Entity in support of an SRA. The SRA committee would both direct the purchase decisions of each individual network minister and monitor progress of the SRA. Steps were also suggested to improve the ex-ante specification of the SRAs, and the evaluation and the integration of the budget process into strategic management.

Just before 2000 the cabinet changed the labelling of the strategic management system, referring to 'overarching goals and strategic priorities', but in general the functions remained the same. Ministerial teams functioning somewhat alike the SRA networks were announced, as was the creation of super-portfolios. These SRA teams of ministers did not function for long since in 2000 the new cabinet did not retain the programme (28). Sectors were asked to develop supporting indicators in order to measure progress towards Strategic Priorities and departments were to develop an intervention logic that linked their KRAs to the Strategic Priorities. Performance agreements asked for additional emphasis by chief executives for 'inter-agency cooperation, coordination and regard for the collective interest' (SSC 1999b).

In the second half of the 1990s it became increasingly clear that the overemphasis on the purchaser–provider roles of, respectively, ministers and departments needed some modification. The basic conditions for the internal market as initially envisioned in the reforms, such as competitive supply, efficient price and symmetrical information, had proven to be very hard to achieve in the New Zealand Public Service. As the SSC noted,

> the concept of an efficient market fundamentally misrepresents the nature of NZPS production and exchange. Few Ministers have chosen to be energetic purchasers, preferring to concentrate their attention on adjustments at the margin. Few have taken advantage of the provision for Ministers to employ purchase advisors. There is little evidence of the scope for reprioritisation within Votes being utilised, or of Ministers seeking alternative suppliers. (SSC 1998b: 10) (see **(27)**

Moreover, the ownership role of ministers became overshadowed by the purchaser role. 'Purchase promotes a narrow contractual, vertically integrated and short-term view on performance; ownership connotes a broad, permissive, horizontally integrated and longer-term view' (ibid.). The responsible ministers for departments were encouraged to enhance their ownership role.

Related to the above was the introduction in 1999 of the Integrated Performance System (IPS) that sought to coordinate both the multiple accountability requirements and the different ministerial roles **(29)**, as well as seeking to introduce mandatory strategic planning at the departmental level, aligning departments more clearly with government priorities **(30)**. Besides a longer term 'Statement of Intent', one ex-ante (the 'performance forecast') and one ex-post accountability document ('the ex-post performance report') were introduced to replace the numerous individual ex-ante and ex-post accountability requirements. In the 'integrated performance planning' process a department had to balance purchase intentions with ownership investments by outlining internal management priorities and relevant government strategic priorities, the core ongoing business, and its current and future capability. Moreover, departments had to integrate financial and performance information in their documents. The accountability concept that had been 'narrowed by contractualism' to a checklist mentality was thus expanded (Schick 1996; Putseys and Hondeghem 2003; SSC 1999c). The IPS was also envisaged as a platform to facilitate developing cross-portfolio information. The planning process was thought to 'increase cooperation, shared objectives and strategies'. At a minimum, departments would need to consider the 'activities and capabilities of other organizations whose business is related or can impact the success of their own' (SSC 1999c: 15). In 2000 pilots were set up to try out this system and it was used government-wide from 2001 onwards (OECD 2000).

From the mid-1990s onwards the government also started to develop a more coherent e-government and ICT strategy. Until then the online presence of governmental units was driven by their own initiatives, without central coordination. The first coordination initiative was the launch of an online government directory by the Ministry of Commerce, which was later merged with the directory of the Department of Internal Affairs to become the New Zealand Government Online website. An IT Policy Taskforce was established by the SSC in 1997 **(31)**, which worked with the Chief Executives' Group on Information Management and Technology to advise government on a government-wide e-government strategy, issued in 2000 (Millar 2004: 1).

In this period several initiatives were undertaken to improve management development for senior and other managers. Several reports pointed out that since the failure of the SES very little senior management development was taking place in the New Zealand Public Service (SSC 1997a; SSC 1998b). The Management Development Centre (MDC) was created, with responsibility for the career management of public managers **(32)**. This collective approach to development of managerial talent at senior levels had the objective of increasing the quality of chief executives, but also potentially enhanced the cultural coordination of values and norms within government. Figure 5.4 maps the various initiatives for further coordination undertaken in the period 1996–9.

Structural changes such as merging departments were increasingly considered costly and ineffective. Non-structural measures such as the strategic management system or virtual organizations through ICT were being propagated as better options (SSC 1998c; Washington 1998; OECD 2000). However the increasing use of non-structural coordination measures did not imply that structural reorganizations were absent. Several new ministries and departments were created through mergers and splits. A major departmental restructuring occurred in 1998 with the establishment of the Department of Work and Income (branded as Work and Income New Zealand or WINZ), merging three organizations **(33)**. The aim was to provide integrated service delivery and joint provision of employment and income maintenance services, as was increasingly promoted by government (SSC 1999d).

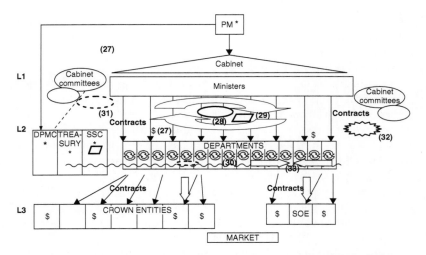

Legend SRA: Strategic Result Area; KRA: Key Result Area; IPS: Integrated Performance System; PM: Prime Minister; DPMC: Department of Prime Minister and Cabinet; SSC: State Service Commission; SOE: State-owned enterprises

(27) Problems of limited contestability with respect to policy advice
(28) SRA/KRA: Strategic Priorities plus SRA committee (chaired by minister)
(29) Integrated Performance System (1999)
(30) Integrated performance planning
(31) IT Policy Taskforce
(32) Management Development Centre (MDC)
(33) Merger of three departments (Work and Income New Zealand: WINZ)

Figure 5.4   Specialization and coordination in New Zealand in the period 1996–9

5.5   From 2000 to 2005: reforms under the Labour cabinet of PM Clark

At the end of 1999 a new cabinet came into power under Prime Minister Clark, and attempts to strengthen coordination and 'whole-of-government' capacity initiated during the later 1990s were intensified after 2000 by several initiatives. On 15 July 1999 the Minister of State Services announced the Crown Entities Initiative in order to respond to some flaws identified in some SSC studies on different aspects of the governance of Crown Entities; these included:

• inappropriate behaviours and payments (such as severance payments to board members);

- an apparent lack of public service ethos in some entities (including extravagant expenditure on travel);
- uneven monitoring of Crown Entities by departments on behalf of responsible ministers;
- variable processes for appointment to Crown Entity boards – transparency issues arose with some of the processes, and there was unresponsiveness to government requirements in some cases
- lack of clarity about the roles and responsibilities of ministers and boards, and monitoring departments and central agencies in relation to Crown Entities;
- inconsistent and incomplete legislation including inadequate governance arrangements and patchy accountability requirements;
- no single minister with overall responsibility and no clear central agency mandate (for example, the State Services Commission had a very limited legal mandate in relation to the wider state sector); and
- ad hoc establishment processes with no agreed criteria for setting up organizations as Crown Entities rather than as departments or state-owned enterprises (SSC 2000a).

From 2000 onwards, a first set of decisions was made to enhance the 'vertical accountability' of the Crown Entities, including allocation of responsibility for general oversight of the governance and accountability regime of the Crown Entities to the Minister of State Services (34), the issuing of several guidelines and standards of behaviour, and the assignment of the Crown Entities to different classes with distinct governance and accountability frameworks (35). Greater consistency of reporting and financial arrangements was introduced.

The governance of the Crown Entities was also a major topic in the Review of the Centre initiative, launched in 2001 (Minister of State Services 2002). With this initiative the New Zealand government aimed at 'strengthening the "whole of government" strategic capacity by overcoming problems of excessive structural "fragmentation" and "siloization", the weakening of longer-term executive and managerial capability, and the attenuation of a coherent state sector ethos' (Gregory 2006, see also Cabinet Committee on Government Expenditure and Administration 2002a).

To ensure that the work of Crown Entities was well aligned with whole-of-government interests and that better 'horizontal connections' with related organizations were made, the government was now given the power to direct an entire class of Crown Entities toward specific cross-government policies, standards and generic provisions, such as equal employment-opportunity requirements and e-government (36).

Moreover, the extent to which ministers responsible for individual Crown Entities could direct these Crown Entities to follow certain policy was clarified (37). All these measures were integrated in the 2004 Crown Entities Act.

Two other legislative changes followed from the Review of the Centre initiative. The State Sector Amendment Act (No. 2) 2004 strengthened the role of the SSC in reviewing the machinery of government (38), created a strategy for common senior management development, and set minimum standards for integrity across the public service and the Crown Entities (39). This Act, according to Gregory (2006), expanded the power of the SSC over the wider public sector and made it the central actor in public-sector reform. The Treasury, which was the principal architect of the earlier reforms, nevertheless remained strong.

The Public Finance Amendment Act 2004 changed the budget structure in order to facilitate transferring appropriations between organizations and creating resources for joint objectives (40). Parliamentary appropriations were no longer confined to one output class only, enabling public managers to switch resources. However the Ministry of Finance was required to approve multi-class appropriations (Gregory 2006). This fitted into the 'managing for outcome' moves that had been taken since 2001. Other measures included the increased emphasis on consultation and sharing of information and plans by departments with other actors (Cabinet Committee on Government Expenditure and Administration 2002b).

The Review of the Centre also included measures for integrated service delivery such as 'cross-agency circuit breaker teams' and efforts to increase regional coordination with local government and non-governmental organizations and networks of agencies to integrate policy, delivery and capacity-building (Cabinet Committee on Government Expenditure and Administration 2002c) (41). Although several steps had been taken, mainly in the social sector, and guidebooks written (Minister of State Services 2004a), the actual results of these efforts to create networks were considered to be rather limited. According to Gregory (2006: 151), this was probably due to the persisting main emphasis on individual accountability for single organization outputs, despite changes to the original Public Finance Act.

Other important evolutions after 2000 were that the quasi-markets in health were 'largely rolled back' (Gauld 2001, quoted in Gregory 2006) (42). Moreover, the reintegration of some operational departments into policy ministries, first observed at the end of the 1990s, was implemented to varying extents in policy fields such as education, housing, justice and transport (43). For example, in the social policy domain, the Ministry of Social Development integrated three former public service organizations. Another example was the reintegration of the Building Industry Authority (BIA), a Crown Entity, into a newly created Department of Building and Housing, under full ministerial control, after a political scandal due to regulatory fragmentation (Minister of State Services 2004b). One observer considered these measures as a break from the doctrine of splitting policy and implementation:

> In making these moves the government has implicitly deemed that any problems stemming from 'provider capture', as posited by the public choice theoretical tenets that underpinned the original reforms, have been less important than the need to reconnect, for their mutual benefit, policy ivory towers with street-level experience. Now, in the move to so-called 'evidence-informed' policymaking, it is being recognised that those working at the 'coal-face' have important experiential knowledge to offer. (Gregory 2006)

A final important evolution in relation to policy coordination was the enhanced role given to the Ministry of Maori Development (**44**). After 2000, this ministry took on a central agency role towards the other governmental organizations to ensure that Maori issues were adequately addressed over government (OECD 2000). The crucial position of the SSC was further strengthened by creation of an e-government unit with a coordinating and monitoring role in the implementation of the e-government policy (OECD 2000) (**45**). The New Zealand government further emphasized the 'planned, systematic implementation' of e-government in a Vision Statement, issued in 2000. But even in the early stages of planning, the involvement of the various ministries and agencies was reflected in their participation in the E-government Unit Advisory Board, steering groups and project groups (Millar 2004: 2). An evaluation in 2004 was largely positive about the progress made (E-government Unit 2004).

Despite all the coordination initiatives, structural changes and reclassification after 2000, the New Zealand government remained highly articulated. In mid-2005 the state sector still comprised 36 Public Service Departments and four Non-Public Service Departments, 2567 Crown Entities, with 2472 School Boards of Trustees, 49 Crown Agents (including 21 District Health Boards), 21 Autonomous Crown Entities, 15 Independent Crown Entities, 9 Crown Research Institutes and three other Crown Entity Companies. Also within the State Services, but not considered as Crown Entities, are 50 organizations listed under the 4th Schedule of the Public Finance Act, while 18 state-owned enterprises exist outside the State Services (SSC 2005). This proliferation and coordination during the period 2000–5 is shown in Figure 5.5.

5.6   Conclusion

The public sector in New Zealand went on a rollercoaster ride during the time period that we investigated. Beginning as a traditional Westminster

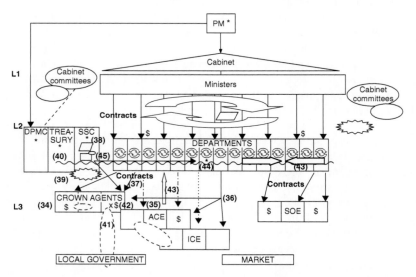

Legend IPS: Integrated Performance System; ACE: Autonomous Crown Entities; ICE: Independent Crown Entities; PM: Prime Minister; DPMC: Department of Prime Minister and Cabinet; SSC; State Service Commission; SOE: State-owned enterprises

(34)   Crown Entities Initiatives (1999)
(35)   Vertical accountability of Crown Entities to Minister of State Services
(36)   Review of the Centre (2001): strengthening whole-of-government capacity
(37)   Crown Entities accountable to minister; Crown Entities Act (2004)
(38)   State Sector Amendment Act (No. 2) (2004)
(39)   Common senior management development; standards for integrity
(40)   Public Finance Amendment Act (2004)
(41)   Cross-agency circuit-breaker teams (including local government)
(42)   Rolled back quasi-markets in health
(43)   Reintegration of policy ministers and operational departments
(44)   Ministry of Maori Development
(45)   SSC: e-government unit

Figure 5.5   Specialization and coordination in New Zealand in the period 2000–5

system, New Zealand became a leader in New Public Management. It implemented one of the most radical sets of reforms in the world, moving most of its functions into Crown Entities and using market-based forms of governing whenever possible. However, this is not to say that reforms were uniformly applied in all sectors. On the contrary, while there were various organizational solutions adopted in different policy sectors (such as health, education and social services), some sectors were never subject to 'organizational decoupling'; subsequently some large organizations which were decoupled have been recombined, others partially recombined, while others have remained decoupled. Despite some successes among the reforms, many were seen to have gone too far and subsequent governments returned to more traditional forms of governing.

Although the state structure changed dramatically, the problem of coordination continued and to some extent these problems were exacerbated by the reforms of the state. Many efforts were made to enhance coordination throughout this period. These efforts to some extent mirrored the particular ideology of the government at the time, but also represented reactions to those ideologies. The use of performance management as a strategic and coordination tool represents one of the most important policy interventions of this period. This method too has had some successes but the process of learning how to make these coordination mechanisms as effective as they promise to be continues.

6
Coordination in the United Kingdom (1980–2005)

Eva Beuselinck[1]

The British administration is characterized by a considerable number of reforms that have taken place during the 25 years up to 2005, under both the Conservative governments of Margaret Thatcher and John Major, and under the rule of the Labour government of Tony Blair. Although a certain degree of continuity in the styles of reform is discernable throughout this era, each period of government encompasses specific approaches with regard to the search for a more coordinated and coherent public sector. Therefore, the analytic task is to distinguish common patterns of change from the particular approach of each government.

6.1   The situation before 1979

For a clear understanding of the British central government, the concept of the 'core executive' is crucial. This concept primarily includes three components (Moran 2005: 115–25): the Prime Ministerial machine, the Cabinet machine (Cabinet, Cabinet Committees and Cabinet Office), and the machinery of government departments. Within this setting, the Prime Minister and his or her entourage play an important coordination function within the government (1). Both the Cabinet Office (2) and the Treasury (3) play a major role as well in the coordination of the public service. In addition to their specific role at certain moments – for example, founding the Efficiency Unit and the Financial Management Initiative – they are, generally speaking, of crucial importance within the coordination process. The Treasury – as a virtually permanent member of the core executive – fulfils this role by coordinating the allocation of public spending, and the Cabinet Office has a role in tracking interdepartmental issues in case they need closer examination by

Cabinet Committees (of permanent and temporary nature). This system of Cabinet Committees[2] **(4)** is also a crucial element that should be taken into consideration when attempting to understand coordination. Whereas the Cabinet – chaired by the Prime Minister and composed of all cabinet ministers[3] – meets weekly, and therefore has some importance as a setting for information exchange, the Cabinet Committees (with a varying composition of members, depending on the subject to be discussed) are vital for coordinating governmental policy and inter-departmental harmonization. Ministers without portfolio, such as the Chancellor of the Duchy of Lancaster, are another element that can play a role in promoting coordination among different policy areas **(5)**, next to the existence of super-ministries such as the Department of Health and Social Security at that time, covering a wide policy area **(6)**.

As compared to the different components of the 'core executive', the departments constitute solid organizations with activities related to both policy development and implementation. A number of externally autonomous agencies such as Non-departmental Public Bodies and Quasi-non-governmental Organizations complete the picture of the British administration in this initial, pre-reform period (Hogwood 1997).

A final characteristic of British public administration that should be taken into account, and that was still omnipresent in the early 1980s, is the Oxbridge domination in senior ranks of the civil service **(7)**. The common social and educational backgrounds of these Oxbridge graduates generated a particular culture within the public administration, fostering a certain degree of common elitist identity (Kavanagh and Richards 2003) among civil servants, politicians and between civil servants and political elites.

Taking a closer look at the general structure of the British public administration at the end of the seventies, Figure 6.1 presents a general overview, portraying the different actors in a schematic manner and also indicating the different centres of coordination capacity and power. Figure 6.1 also provides a list of the main coordination instruments at that time.

6.2   Transformations under Thatcher (1979–90)

In the early 1980s, British public administration was marked by a clear shift towards managerialism, under the influence of the Conservative, and neoconservative, government elected in 1979. When Margaret Thatcher took office, she introduced a series of reforms focusing on

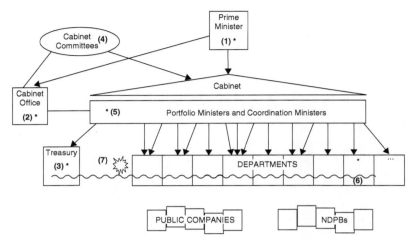

Legend NDPB: Non-departmental Public Body

Number	Coordination instrument
(1)	Strength of the Prime Minister
(2)	Coordination capacity of the Cabinet Office
(3)	Coordination capacity of the Treasury
(4)	Application of an elaborated system of Cabinet Committees
(5)	Coordination capacity of ministers without portfolio
(6)	Coordination capacity of super-ministries
(7)	'Oxbridge' culture among senior ranks of the civil service

Figure 6.1   Specialization and coordination in the UK: the situation before 1979

implementing the principles of this managerialism. This approach was inspired by a firm belief in the ideas stemming from private-sector management, and their applicability to the setting of public administration (Pollitt and Bouckaert 2004: 292). On the one hand, these precepts resulted in a focus on the intra-organizational level, pleading for efficiency and performance indicators. On the other hand, there was a general concern about downsizing the public sector, which was considered to be too big, and too intrusive (Pollitt and Bouckaert 2004: 294). Mrs Thatcher in particular railed against the excesses of the 'Nanny State'. Moreover, the striving for change was reinforced by the particularly difficult and tense relationship between the Prime Minister and the `traditional` civil service, which was illustrated by the 21-week strike of the civil service in 1981 and the fact that Sir Ian Bancroft, Head of the Home Civil Service, was given early retirement in the same year (Fry 1988).

The drive for eliminating redundancy is illustrated by two major initiatives that were launched in the early days of the neoconservative rule, and that were oriented towards the improvement of both general and financial management within the public sector. First, in 1979, the Efficiency Unit (8) was founded within the Cabinet Office. This Efficiency Unit then carried out the Rayner Scrutinies under the guidance of Lord Derek Rayner, consisting of efficiency reviews that investigated individual areas of government activities, with the aim of limiting the expenses of departments and streamlining procedures. By 1983, this process had resulted in more than 150 scrutinies, as indicated by Fry (1988: 7) (see Figure 6.2).

In the first half of the 1980s, the coordination capacity of a number of institutional actors was weakened because they were either split up or abolished. The Civil Service Department, for instance, was abolished in November 1981, because it was considered by Prime Minister Thatcher and by Rayner to be losing touch with its actual duties of running departments (Seldon 1990: 106). Its functions were divided between the Treasury and the Cabinet Office (9). On the one hand, the Treasury was granted responsibility for pay and staff numbers. On the other hand, the Cabinet Office – through the creation of the Management and Personnel Office – took over responsibilities for recruitment, training and personnel. This Management and Personnel Office was itself abolished in 1987, when its competencies were transferred to the Treasury (10).

Also in the early 1980s, the Central Policy Review Staff (CPRS) was abolished (11). This think tank (part of the Cabinet Office, and founded in 1971 by then Prime Minister Edward Heath), aimed at providing capacity development for planning and coordination of governmental policy in order to take better policy decisions. At the time of its foundation, the idea behind it was putting an end to departmentalism and to introducing a managerial approach focused on the achievement of governmental goals instead of departmental goals (Blackstone and Lowden 1988). However, in the 1980s the CPRS became involved with a number of politically controversial exercises. Consequently, Margaret Thatcher closed it down after the 1983 election. This action mainly strengthened the coordination function of the Prime Minister (12): Mrs Thatcher took this opportunity to strengthen the Downing Street Policy Unit (Peele 1995: 120) and informal committees played an important role in coordination processes.

While some organizations were terminated, new initiatives were launched in the early 1980s, including the Financial Management

Initiative (FMI), initially jointly run by the Treasury and the Management and Personnel Office (Seldon 1998: 106). The aim of this initiative was to improve financial management in departments, and to introduce a 'value for money' approach by scrutinizing the allocation, management and control of resources throughout central government.

At the departmental level, in 1988 the Department of Health and Social Security was broken up into component parts **(13)**. Consecutive Conservative governments carried out a broad series of privatizations, and by 1991 half of the public sector had been transferred to the private sector (March 1991: 462) or transferred to more independently functioning bodies **(14)**. This privatization process continued until the end of Conservative rule in 1997. However, this does not imply a decreasing role for the governmental apparatus. Government remained in control of the privatized monopolies (for the importance of the regulatory agencies, see Hogwood 1997: 706) and the level of public expenditure hardly changed (Richardson 1993). Furthermore, a separation of policy from implementation stimulated the foundation of the Next Steps Agencies (executive agencies) **(15)**, that were either newly created or hived off from civil service departments (Moran 2005: 140). One reason this programme was launched appeared to be the excessively slow evolution of the FMI and other management reforms, according to the new head of the Efficiency Unit, Sir Robin Ibbs. The Efficiency Unit published a report – *Improving Management in Government: The Next Steps* (1988) – that set out the future challenges for administrative reform of the British public sector.

The Next Steps report – also called the Ibbs Report – was based upon an examination of reforms already implemented within the civil service. The report indicates five problem areas in total, related to the organization of public administration:

1 Too little responsibility at the management level and lack of (self)confidence;
2 The necessity to make expectations *vis-à-vis* organizations and people more explicit;
3 The necessity to give more attention to outputs and not only to inputs;
4 The search for a uniform organizational system within the civil service in order to facilitate coordination;
5 The necessity to strive for continuous improvement.

These concerns were translated into four important priorities for the future: a separation between strategic policy advice and decisions on the one hand and service delivery on the other hand; a clear definition of the relationship between the agency and the department; management guided by performance indicators; and a more flexible position *vis-à-vis* traditional civil service organization (Moran 2005: 144–7). This flexible position was – among others – advocated in the Ibbs report as part of its proposals for breaking up the career civil service; standardized terms and conditions of service normally accorded to career civil servants were considered to be an obstacle to effective management (Fry et al. 1988: 435).

The executive agencies became widely implemented on a broad scale within the government apparatus, presenting great diversity with respect to size, responsibilities and political salience. Within ten years, more than 140 executive agencies were created, employing more than 70 per cent of non-industrial civil servants. These agencies are units contracted by the departments and, as such, remain part of them. The chief executives of the agencies are responsible for their organization and are monitored by framework documents which are drawn up by the agencies, and which include a system of corporate plans and annual targets. At the departmental level, duties shifted towards pure policy preparation, whereas implementation became located in the executive agencies. It should be noted that among the agencies, considerable variation occurred with respect to their status, degree of autonomy and their overall relationship with their parent departments (Pollitt et al. 2001: 280).

As a result of the agencification process, the structure of government moved from a pattern of monolithic, 'inward-looking' departments encompassing both policy and executive functions, to one of small policy departments with executive activities carried out by 'single-purpose' agencies, focusing on better service delivery (Ling 2002: 618).

6.3 Transformations under John Major (1990–7)

The period between 1990 and 1997 was characterized by the continuation and completion of the previous reform initiatives begun under the Conservative government during the 1980s, focusing on customer service and oriented towards continued processes of contracting-out and marketization, both at the departmental and the agency levels. The previous period was characterized by a significant increase in the number of privatizations, which involved the indirect introduction of market principles. These principles were now translated into quasi-markets (such as

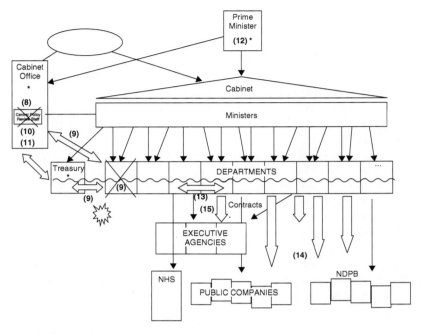

Legend NHS: National Health Service; NDPB: Non-departmental Public Body

- **(8)**   Creation of the Efficiency Unit within the Cabinet Office
- **(9)**   Disbandment of the Civil Service Department
- **(10)** Disbandment of the Management and Personnel Office
- **(11)** Disbandment of the Central Policy Review Staff
- **(12)** Strengthening of the coordination function of the PM (through informal committees)
- **(13)** Reshuffling of competencies between Ministry of Health and Social Security
- **(14)** Transfer of considerable parts of the public sector towards private sector/more independently functioning bodies
- **(15)** Autonomization through the foundation of Next Steps Agencies (1988)

Figure 6.2   Specialization and coordination in the UK under Thatcher (1979–90)

in the National Health Service) or growing competition between public and private-sector organizations. In 1991, two important papers were published following this line of thought: the *Competing for Quality* White Paper and the *Citizen's Charter Programme*. The *Competing for Quality* paper referred to a programme designed to concentrate government activity on the essentials (OECD 1999), these being benchmarking, restructuring and the implementation of efficiency techniques. As such, this initiative strived to introduce market-oriented procedures at the agency level, operating through a system of mutual competition (market forces) **(16)**. This approach was completed in the early 1990s by a market-testing programme **(17)**, involving compulsory competitive tendering that focused on giving customers the option of having services provided internally or externally, depending on which department or organization offered the best value for money. The *Citizen's Charter Programme* was launched by the Prime Minister as a ten-year programme (over the years, there have been four further White Papers setting out progress and future plans). This programme aimed to improve the quality of public services and make them more answerable to the wishes of their users **(18)**. The introduction of this Charter was in line with the Next Steps Initiative and was part of the agenda of agencies and framework agreements. In 1992, a new cabinet minister was appointed and put in charge of the execution of this programme. The civil service White Papers *Continuity and Change* (1994) and *Taking Forward Continuity and Change* (1995) continued on the same path while also reaffirming a number of key principles of the Civil Service: integrity, honesty and objectivity; non-politicization; recruitment by fair and open competition; selection and promotion on merit; and accountability through ministers to Parliament. The revised *Civil Service Management Code*, issued in 1993, is another illustration of a central framework for the management of the Civil Service developed throughout these years **(19)**.

An important reshuffle took place in the management of the civil service between 1992 and 1995. In 1992, these competencies were transferred to the Office of Public Service and Science **(20)** – located within the Cabinet Office – merging the Office of the Minister of Civil Service, the Next Steps Team, the Citizen's Charter, the Efficiency Unit and the Market-Testing Unit. This concentration of competencies at the level of the Cabinet Office also implied the strengthening of the coordination function of the Prime Minister **(21)**.

In 1995, the Office of Public Service and Science became the Office of Public Service and the remaining responsibilities for Civil Service management were transferred from the Treasury to the Office of Public Service **(22)**. A few other competency reshuffles took place at the departmental level. Examples of these reshuffles were the abolition of the Department of Energy in 1992 and the reallocation of its functions relating to energy efficiency in housing to the Department of the Environment, and for international trade to Trade and Industry, and the merging of the Department of Employment with the Department of Education into a new Department for Education and Employment in 1996 (23). Moreover, a number of central ministries were significantly downsized, following a programme of management reviews in 1993.

Information policy was the final element that gained importance during the first half of the 1990s. The *Code of Practice on Access to Government Information* (1994) (24) was an important element here. The Code was not simply concerned with answering requests for information, but also with providing facts and analysis connected with major policy decisions. The aims of the Code were – among others – to:

- improve policy-making and the democratic process by extending access to the facts and analyses which provide the basis for the consideration of proposed policy;
- support and extend the principles of public service established under the Citizen's Charter.

The Code committed departments and public bodies under the jurisdiction of the Parliamentary Commissioner for Administration (the Ombudsman) and aimed to:

- publish the facts and analysis of the facts which the government considers relevant and important in framing major policy proposals and decisions;
- give reasons for administrative decisions to those affected;
- publish in accordance with the Citizen's Charter:
  - full information about how public services are run, how much they cost, who is in charge, and what complaints and redress procedures are available;
  - full and, where possible, comparable information about what services are being provided, what targets are set, what standards of service are expected and the results achieved.

On a more practical level, the 1996 Green Paper *Government.direct* set the direction for the development and implementation of an integrated information system: it proposed a new system for information management in the public sector by using a common electronic system for the entry and retrieval of basic personal information and a common customer interface for public services (6 et al. 1999: 42). This Green Paper was elaborated by the installation in 1995 of the Central IT Unit (a unit within the Cabinet Office) (25) and would be adapted and further developed after 1997 by the Labour government.

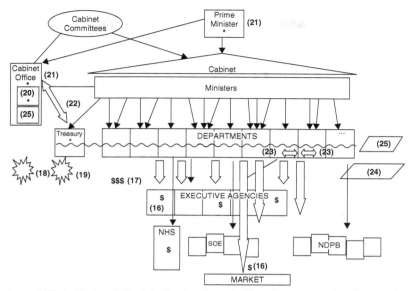

Legend NHS: National Health Service; NDPB: Non-departmental Public Body; SOE: State-owned enterprises

(16) Introduction of market-oriented procedures at the agency level and continued privatization
(17) Launching of the Market-Testing Programme
(18) Introduction of the Citizen's Charter Programme
(19) Revised Civil Service Management Code (ethical values and management practices)
(20) Office of Public Service and Science: merging of the Office of the Minister of Civil Service, the Next Steps Team, the Citizen's Charter, the Efficiency Unit and the Market-testing Unit
(21) Strengthening of the coordination capacity of the Prime Minister through strengthening of the Cabinet Office
(22) Office of Public Service and Science transformed into the Office of Public Service and transfer of the remaining responsibilities for civil service management from the Treasury to the Office of Public Service
(23) Departmental reshuffles and mergers
(24) Launching of Code of Practice on Access to Government Information
(25) Installation of Central IT Unit within the Cabinet Office and publication of Green Paper *Government.direct* (further developed after 1997)

Figure 6.3 Specialization and coordination in the UK under Major (1990–7)

6.4   Transformations under Blair (1997–2000)

When Tony Blair's Labour government took office, there was no radical break with the previously launched public-sector reforms. The Prime Minister, the Cabinet Committees and the Cabinet Office remained crucial for coordination, albeit with a few adjustments. The system of Cabinet Committees was maintained, but it was complemented with task forces **(26)** with very specific assignments and political advisers became increasingly important as actors (Blick 2004), both playing a significant role in the coordination machinery (see Figure 6.4). The main focus for coordination remained the Prime Minister and the partially restructured Cabinet Office. Separate coordination units were created within the Cabinet Office for handling cross-organizational policy fields, including the Performance and Innovation Unit (PIU), the Social Exclusion Unit (SEU), the Women's Unit and the UK Anti-drugs Innovation Unit **(27)**.

In the first years of the Labour government, important new principles and procedures for public expenditure planning and control were also introduced, such as the Comprehensive Spending Reviews **(28)**. Replacing the normal public spending survey, the Comprehensive Spending Reviews were launched in 1997. These consisted of both a large number of separate departmental reviews and a wider overall review conducted by a Cabinet Committee of senior ministers looking across government as a whole (OECD 1999). It allowed the government to bring public spending programmes into line with its own priorities and with a coherent set of objectives. The White Paper *Modern Public Services* (14 July 1998) set out the results of the Comprehensive Spending Reviews and the new public spending plans for 1999–2002.

The aforementioned initiatives are all illustrations of the first experiments with holistic budgeting and a search for greater policy coordination that appeared in late 1997 and early 1998 (6 et al. 1999: 21). In 1999, the White Paper *Modernising Government* **(29)** was published: it set out interventions related to the coordination problem that emerged following the creation of executing agencies and the further development of coordination instruments, as well as the introduction of ICT, functions based on performance agreements and the striving for cultural coordination through HR policy. The paper elaborated on five areas that it was thought led to a high-standard and responsive public service delivery:

1 Policy-making: more emphasis on outcomes, and improved risk management; horizontal policy should be tackled in a better way; departments and other organizations with overlapping competencies

should be urged to collaborate (joined-up government); regulation to be better coordinated and the impact of public programmes to be evaluated.

2 Responsive Public Services: tackling public-service delivery in a more coordinated way in the future by encouraging partnerships at all levels of the public administration – called 'joined-up government'.

3 Improving the Quality of Public Services: through Public Service Agreements, the emphasis to shift from inputs to outcomes; best practices to be circulated and followed by others through the process of benchmarking; and systems of performance management and inspection to be further developed and refined.

4 Information-age Government: encourage the further spread of e-government or electronic service delivery.

5 Public Service: with respect to HR policy, initiatives to be announced related to training, offering extra incentives, with more emphasis on innovation based on skills found in the private sector.

The White Paper led to further restructuring, including the development of joined-up government (JUG) structures (**30**), whereby several organizations at different levels collaborate in areas where competencies overlap or are vaguely distributed. This approach was designed to allow cross-governmental solutions to tackle underlying causes and not only symptoms of 'wicked problems'. The coordination of policy fields has to be optimized in this way. Moreover, for each of the five main commitments towards modernizing government, workstreams were established within the Cabinet Office. In practice, these JUG initiatives were on the one hand enforced through different units within Cabinet Office (see 27) – strengthening the position of the Prime Minister – and on the other hand administered through the strategic alliance by a range of actors, such as sponsor ministries established for specific joined-up policy initiatives (Kavanagh and Richards 2001). As such, both permanent and ad hoc institutions were created for promoting a holistic approach to government.

The entities playing a key role in the *Modernising Government* approach were (Cabinet Office, 1999: 6):

- The Social Exclusion Unit: a cross-departmental team based in the Cabinet Office to tackle in a joined-up way issues arising from social inequalities.
- The Performance and Innovation Unit: set up to report directly to the Prime Minister on selected cross-departmental issues. Reviews

policy to improve coordination and practical delivery of services involving more than one public body.

- Service First: the new Charter programme focusing on the service to the citizen.
- Civil Service Management: a body developing a more corporate approach to achieve cross-cutting goals and providing the leadership needed to drive cultural change in the civil service. One of its tasks was to ensure that the principles of better policy-making are translated into staff selection, appraisal, promotion, posting, and the pay system
- Public Services and Public Expenditure: charged with monitoring progress on Public Service Agreements with relevant Secretaries of State, including tracking the performance of departments in delivering better-quality services
- Public Sector Benchmarking Project: set up to spread use of the Business Excellence Model across the public sector.

The broad range of existing quangos and other *non-departmental public bodies* (NDPBs) were reviewed and the number of NDPBs declined moderately over the late 1990s, mainly provoked by reclassifications and the devolution of tasks and responsibilities towards the Scottish and Welsh Assemblies (Flinders 2004: 887) **(31)**. This devolution of responsibilities towards the Scottish and Welsh levels was one aspect of the broad decentralization of power that gained full force by the end of the 1990s **(32)**.

6.5   Continued transformations under Blair (2001–5)

From 2000, reforms focused on promoting leadership and service delivery on the one hand, and continued the reaggregation of public services in accordance with the initiatives launched by the end of the 1990s on the other. The *Wiring It Up* report (Cabinet Office 2000) **(33)** examined how existing accountability arrangements and incentive systems could be reformed to facilitate joined-up working and promote the extension of non-departmental coordinating mechanisms at the centre, along with enabling the centrifugal coordination of activities of public bodies and agencies. However, the same report stressed the efficiency of the traditional vertical management structures in departments (Judge 2005: 127). Taking into account the existence of a large number of ministerial departments, non-ministerial departments, executive agencies and non-departmental bodies, the Cabinet Office (cited by Judge 2005: 123)

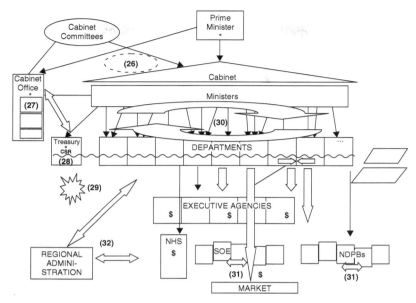

Legend NHS: National Health Service; NDPB: Non-departmental Public Body;
SOE: State-owned enterprises

(26)   Installation of task forces to complete the system of cabinet committees
(27)   Creation of cross-cutting units with the Cabinet Office (PIU, SEU)
(28)   Comprehensive Spending Reviews
(29)   White Paper *Modernising Government* (five cross-cutting policy fields)
(30)   Introduction of the joined-up government (JUG) approach
(31)   Review of NPDBs
(32)   Devolution towards the Scottish and Welsh level

Figure 6.4   Specialization and coordination in the UK under Blair (1997–2000)

underlined the important role that departments play in this complex
setting: departments of state are identified as 'the lead element in a
linked set of public, private and voluntary sector bodies responsible
for delivering services' **(34)**. The Office of Public Services Reform
(OPSR – established in 2001 and broken up in 2006) **(35)** was important in strengthening public-service delivery. It was responsible for
pushing forward the reform of public services in accordance with the
Prime Minister's four principles of reform – 'standards', 'devolution
and delegation', 'flexibility' and 'expanding choice'. An important
initiative developed by the OPSR was the 'Departmental Change
Programme', consisting of a number of tools such as Landscape

Reviews, End-to-End Reviews, Improving Management and Project Delivery. This programme was oriented towards organizational capacity development, increased accountability, customer focus and appropriate delegation of responsibility.

Among the coordinating institutions, a distinction should be made between the 'old' institutions such as the Cabinet Office, Treasury, Prime Minister's Office, and a broad range of task forces and specific coordinating units within these institutions. Moreover, the intertwined role of the different actors at 'the centre' (Cabinet Office, Prime Minister's Office, Deputy Prime Minister's Office – hived off in 2002 from the Cabinet Office and a key actor in the coordination of the JUG initiatives **(36)** – and the Treasury) is highly relevant: in line with the basic principles of JUG, coordination was identified as being an inter-institutional issue involving complex interaction. The coordination of coordination was an important concern, as illustrated by the establishment (2002) of the Delivery and Reform Team (based in the Cabinet Office) **(37)** responsible for coordination of a variety of units and groups such as the Reform Strategy Group, the Efficiency Review Team and the Office of Public Services Reform; it was also involved in departmental strategic planning. This strategic planning was – among other things – fostered by the use of Performance Partnership Agreements. Another example underlining the importance and challenges of coordinating the coordinators can be found in the area of regulation inside government (Hood et al. 2000).

Next to the Cabinet Office, the Treasury continued to play a significant role in the JUG approach, oriented towards value for money and accountability for results (including cross-organizational results). The emphasis on cross-organizational performance is important: a setting had to be created in which sufficient attention was given to these inter-organizational aims and goals. Initially this emphasis was stimulated through initiatives such as the Single Regeneration Budget in the 1990s, or the Invest to Save Budget. More recently, Public Service Agreements were used to address cross-cutting concerns **(38)**. However, it has been argued (James, 2004: 416) that these Public Service Agreements might lose their initial incentive system when the emphasis shifted from organizational performance towards 'cross-cutting' accountability.

Technology continued to play an important role in the JUG approach as a medium for service delivery: it is a critical factor in successful holistic government. The importance of technology was underlined by the continued concern within the Cabinet Office about this specific domain, as illustrated, for instance, by the report *Transformational Government Enabled by Technology* (Cabinet Office 2005) **(39)**.

Finally, there were strong calls for a bottom-up approach to make JUG a successful story (6 et al. 1999: 14, 31). Although the importance of the role of centrally located entities such as the Cabinet Office and the Treasury in stimulating cross-departmental working can not be denied, it was also stressed that genuine JUG and effective integration

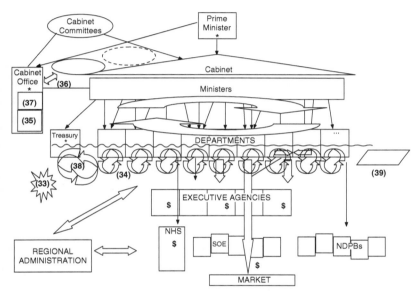

Legend NHS: National Health Service; NDPB: Non-departmental Public Body; SOE: State-owned enterprises

(33) Collaborative culture promoted by *Wiring It Up* report and joined-up government
(34) Coordination capacity of departments is underlined with the introduction of PSA
(35) Establishment of the Office of Public Services Reform
(36) Coordination capacity of the Deputy Prime Minister's Office (hived off from the Cabinet Office)
(37) Establishment of the Delivery and Reform Team
(38) Public Service Agreements focusing on cross-cutting issues
(39) *Transformational Government Enabled by Technology* report

Figure 6.5 Continued specialization and coordination in the UK under Blair (2001–5)

are essentially bottom-up processes and that such an approach has to be mainstreamed instead of being limited to special initiatives.

6.6　Conclusion

Coordination in the UK has to be situated within the context of the country's historical tendencies towards specialization and proliferation of public organizations. Specialization became particularly evident after the creation of the Next Steps Agencies in 1988. The specialization process was followed by an increased emphasis on coordination. In general, the positions of the Prime Minister, the Cabinet Office and – to a certain extent – the Treasury appeared to be particularly important for the UK's coordination policy: throughout the period under study (1980–2005), these actors (or their sub-units) played a major role in ensuring coordination among the different levels of the central government and their associated actors. In addition, informal or ad hoc consultative bodies and task forces were an important tool for further supporting different coordination initiatives. Although numerous, these coordination efforts were not particularly coherent, especially before the mid-1990s. Afterwards, more broad-based initiatives were fostered and, more recently, actions aimed towards the 'coordination of coordination' became part of coordination policy.

The underlying motives for reforms have changed considerably over time. Under Margaret Thatcher, the dominant motivation for increased coordination was the quest for transparency and sound financial management. In the 1990s, a search for high-quality service delivery became the overwhelming stimulus, while during the second half of that decade the growing interest in ICT-related issues (such as e-government) appeared to be an important driver for new coordination initiatives. Finally, around the turn of the century, the awareness of policy-makers of the challenge of dealing with complex, intractable problems created a new boost for launching coordination initiatives. Overall, the interest in coordination and its associated challenges appears to have been much more prevalent from the mid-1990s, compared to the 1980s.

For several particular types of coordination mechanisms, several tendencies are traceable to the period 1980–2005. First, hierarchical coordination seems to be evident for the whole period: the Prime Minister and the Cabinet Office played a key role in coordinating the different actors within the government. After the initial decentralization, by the end of the 1990s the hierarchical position of the ministry *vis-à-vis* the broad range of existing agencies had strengthened. The core function of departments in assuring high standards of service delivery by coordinating all involved actors was reconfirmed. Second, the UK's trajectory shows that using market-based coordination instruments was important over the whole period, reaching a peak during the second half of the 1980s and the first half of the 1990s, when a broad range of instruments such as privatization, quasi-markets and incentives was established. Finally, some network-based instruments (Oxbridge culture, ad hoc committees) were relatively important in the early 1980s while others (task forces, joined-up government initiatives, political advisers) received a boost during the late 1990s.

In conclusion, the coordination trajectory of the UK over time displays a number of relatively clear tendencies. Its starting point is characterized by the different layers of the central government functioning in a relatively consolidated and only mildly dispersed manner. The Prime Minister, the Cabinet Office and the Treasury were the main actors at that time for coordinating all other actors, in a predominantly hierarchical way, supplemented by some network-based initiatives. During the 1980s and the first half of the 1990s, a strong movement towards a more dispersed administration – combined with a decoupling of the various policy stages – was brought about by the creation of a large number of independently functioning bodies; this supplemented privatization. At that time, coordination was largely achieved through market-based instruments, although the hierarchical position of entities such as the Cabinet Office remained extremely important. In the second half of the 1990s the emphasis shifted to harmonization of all the actors involved in central government. Initiatives oriented towards the creation of an integrated information system or an overall spending review underlined the renewed attention being paid to a more consolidated, holistic approach. Although a broad range of actors remained, the re-aggregation of public services became a high priority and cross-organizational performance was put on the agenda. Network-based coordination instruments, and to a certain extent hierarchy-based coordination instruments, (re)-appeared at this stage.

7
Coordination in Sweden (1980–2005)

The Swedish public sector has particular features which distinguish it from other European or Western models. In Sweden the Constitution requires collective decision-making, producing a system 'which is collective in the extreme and individual ministers may decide themselves only in exceptional circumstances' (Larsson 1995). The government – not individual ministers – issues directives to administration, although the individual minister can take some decisions concerning the internal organization and staffing of his department (Hustedt and Tiessen 2006). Moreover, Sweden has a dual administrative structure, with rather small government offices – mainly focusing on policy design, planning and coordination – and a large number of independent executive agencies. Moreover, there is a high level of decentralization with substantial responsibility located at the level of local authorities. The Swedish administrative culture has been described as 'cooperative, consensus seeking, problem oriented and pragmatic and is characterized by a high degree of informality, bridging organizational borders and hierarchical levels' (Hustedt and Tiessen 2006: 38).

The Swedish administrative system is composed of three levels (Statskontoret 1999) – central, regional and local. The central level, the main focus of this chapter, consists of the parliament, government offices, agencies and public utility companies. The agencies implement the decisions taken by the government and the parliament within the area of the central government's duties. There are about 300 agencies, and they differ in size (ranging from a few employees to 28,000, as in the case of the recently established agency for the army). About 70 agencies are considered 'central agencies', performing tasks of major social importance, operating on a nationwide basis and in many cases split into sub-units. The agencies at regional and local level execute central government duties at their level. Moreover, at the beginning of the 1980s, a limited number of 'public enterprises' such as Swedish Post, Swedish Telecom and the Swedish State Railways existed.

7.1 Around 1980

Figure 7.1 shows the mechanisms for coordination within Swedish central government in 1980. On the one hand there was the limited number

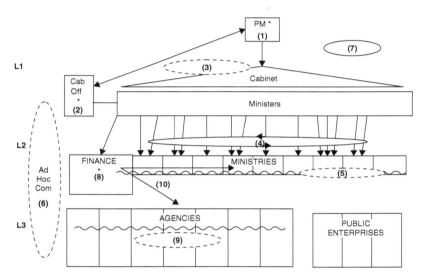

Legend PM: Prime Minister; Cab Off: Cabinet Office; Ad Hoc Com: Ad hoc Commissions

(1)   Coordinating function of Prime Minister
(2)   Prime Ministers' Office
(3)   No formal cabinet committee structure, but informal cabinet and interministerial discussions
(4)   Mandated interdepartmental coordination by *delning*
(5)   Ad hoc interdepartmental coordination (facilitated by small ministries)
(6)   Commissions of inquiry
(7)   Advisory committees
(8)   Coordination role of Ministry of Finance
(9)   Multiple objectives agencies, laymen boards and ad hoc coordination between agencies
(10) Input control of departments and agencies by central agencies
(NR) Informal network between civil servants (and politicians) through political affiliation and by careers

Figure 7.1   Specialization and coordination in Sweden in the early 1980s

of government offices (about 10) which were in some cases controlled by several ministers (about 19 in 1982) (Mackie and Hogwood 1985). The small size of the departments was maintained deliberately by simplifying laws and decentralizing responsibilities to public agencies. The small size provides 'great flexibility and facilitates coordination between departments' (Dahlberg 1993: 12).

On the other hand about 300 agencies were involved in policy implementation, but they also acted as centres of expertise. They carried out analyses, which were made public, as a basis for government decisions on important issues. In contrast to the 'executive agencies' created in many countries, Swedish central government agencies' autonomy was protected by the Constitution: the agencies themselves could decide on specific issues where the exercise of authority and application of law were concerned. Autonomous agencies did not preclude some government control, but the control had to be general and based on the following instruments: legislative provisions and appropriations approved by Parliament; the government's interpretations of the law in its instructions, and specifications in its official appropriation documents; appointments of senior management and board members; and discussions with agency representatives concerning matters not relating to application of law or the exercise of authority (OECD 2000a).

In this dual setting there were several mechanisms to facilitate coordination and planning at the different levels. Most mechanisms were used throughout the whole period under review. Two instruments were of particular importance in this context of highly independent agencies and small ministries: collective decision-making at cabinet level and policy preparation by commissions of inquiry (OECD 1992). At the political level, the cabinet had collective responsibility for the decisions taken (Statskontoret 1998). The Prime Minister had a coordinating function (1). The practical support for this function is assured by the Prime Ministers' Office (*Statsrådsberedningen*; see Larsson 1986) in which a group of political advisers keep themselves informed about what is going on within the other ministries (OECD 2002: 196) (2). In contrast to most other countries discussed in this book, a formal cabinet committee structure is lacking. Many negotiations within the government take place outside the formal cabinet meetings during 'informal' sessions of the cabinet (*allmän beredning*), issued by the Prime Minister's Office, or during the daily luncheon meetings (*lunch beredning*) (OECD 2002: 196; Mackie and Hogwood: 17) (3). Bilateral negotiations or joint preparation between ministers and ministries is obligatory when more than one ministry is involved, and usually includes the Ministry of Finance (OECD 2002: 196). According to two scholars (Mackie and Hogwood 1985: 17), this absence of formal committee structures and the popularity of informal meetings in Sweden came about because of the stability of party control in Sweden as well as the stability of the individuals holding office.

Another way of coordinating policy at the political and interdepartmental level was to circulate draft decisions to all government offices before they were addressed at cabinet meetings (*delning*) (OECD 2002: 197). In this way, each involved minister and office had the opportunity to express their opinion (4). At departmental level officials of different ministries often met ad hoc in order to prepare decisions (5). In addition to the formal and informal cabinet decision-making processes, there is a second mechanism typical of the coordination between actors at the policy development stage: commissions of inquiry (6). These commissions are appointed by government in order to prepare specific policy issues based on specific terms of reference. As organizationally independent units they are created ad hoc (for periods of one to two years). Committees normally include experts familiar with the area or the matter to be examined, including civil servants from ministries and agencies and, in some cases, politicians. The committee process is one way of accessing knowledge about a particular issue found in society. Furthermore, the parliamentary opposition and different advocacy groups have an opportunity to follow reforms from an early stage. Approximately 250–300 such committees are active at a given time involving about 600 people (OECD 2002: 184; Hinnfors, 1999). After being sent to the relevant minister the reports of the committees are referred for written comments to relevant authorities, municipalities, advocacy groups and the public, which would be affected by the policy. This referral process is time-consuming but considered valuable (OECD 1992). In addition, there are advisory committees comprising leading personalities in management, labour, industry and trade for specific policies such as employment policy (7) (OECD 1992).

At the beginning of the 1980s the Ministry of Finance also performed a coordinating role for public finance, personnel matters and economy, and was occasionally represented on the boards of agencies and in commissions of inquiry (8). Its coordinating role would increase substantially in the next decade as the state of public finances deteriorated. The problem of coordination and an excessively narrow focus of agencies was tackled during the 1960s and 1970s by giving agencies broad fields of competence, and by including representatives of other agencies, political parties and societal groups ('laymen boards') (OECD

2002: 189). Moreover in many regulations governing the work of the agencies, government included the requirement that they coordinate their activities in specific areas with other agencies (9) (OECD 2002: 189). They were obliged to cooperate with each other, although without the interference of the ministries (Pierre 1993). Because of the large policy autonomy of the agencies, control focused strongly on resource use through line-item budgeting and restricted freedom in human resources management (10).

According to Larsson (1993), the relationship between the ministries and the agencies may be depicted as interdependent. Since the ministries had only limited expert knowledge, because of their small size, government had to rely on the active participation of agencies in the preparation and formulation of policies. Moreover, there was substantial mobility between departments and agencies, which contributed to the 'development of shared epistemic and normative communities that span the ministry/agency divide'. Besides, there was a substantial informal network of politicians and civil servants in departments and agencies. This network originated from, and was reinforced by, political party lines, that is, the Social Democratic Party (SAP), which traditionally dominated Swedish politics.

7.2   From 1982 to 1985: Social Democratic cabinets under PM Palme

In the first half of the 1980s the idea emerged that the problems in the public sector were due to inefficient resource use and high costs of regulation. Sweden had the largest public sector in the Western world in terms of share of GNP, tax ratio and share of labour force (Dahlberg 1993: 4). Together with an increasingly large national budget deficit and other emerging societal problems, the high cost of the public services required action. In addition, the Social Democrats, who regained power in 1982, wanted to make the state machine more responsive and accessible to citizens. A Ministry of Public Administration (11) was created in order to suggest and coordinate reforms in the public sector. The Independent Expert Group on Public Finance (ESO), which stimulated information-sharing between government organizations and placed government productivity on the political agenda, was also established (12). ESO became an ad hoc committee with a semi-permanent status, and published reports on the finance, the productivity and efficiency of the public sector, distributional effects of public programmes and wage-related data for the public sector. In subsequent years this think-tank withered away (see Figure 7.2)

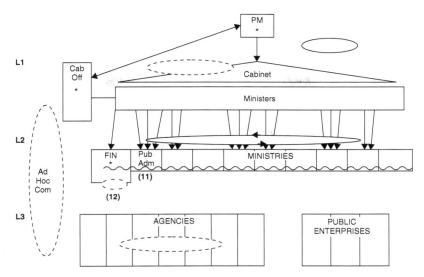

Legend PM: Prime Minister; Cab Off: Cabinet Office; Ad Hoc Com: Ad hoc Commissions; FIN: Department of Finance; Pub Adm: Department of Public Administration

(11) Creation of Ministry of Public Administration
(12) ESO Group

Figure 7.2 Specialization and coordination in Sweden: Social Democratic cabinets under PM Palme (1982–5)

7.3 From 1986 to 1990: a Social Democratic cabinet under PM Carlsson

In 1985 a government modernization programme was announced, designed to reduce the size of central government and its costs through several initiatives. A major decentralization of central competencies to the county – and above all, the local – level was prepared, which would have a profound impact on the tasks and structures of the central agencies **(13)**. Moreover deregulation efforts increased **(14)**. However, the initiative affecting the functioning of the agencies directly involved a substantial delegation of management responsibilities for financial and human resource issues to agency heads in 1988 **(15)** as well as the introduction of 'results-based management' **(16)**. Agencies could now hire their own staff and set their own salary ranges. This change was part of a larger programme to increase efficiency by reforming the budget process, expanding its time-frame to three years and stressing ex-post

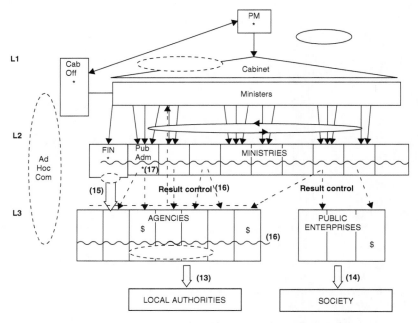

Legend PM: Prime Minister; Cab Off: Cabinet Office; Ad Hoc Com: Ad hoc Commissions; FIN: Department of Finance; Pub Adm: Department of Public Administration

(13)   Decentralization
(14)   Deregulation
(15)   Devolution of management
(16)   First steps in management by results of agencies through '*reglingbrefs*' and informal consultation
(17)   Stronger role for Ministry of Public Administration

Figure 7.3   Specialization and coordination in Sweden: the Social Democratic cabinet under PM Carlsson (1986–90)

analysis of efficiency and performance (Dahlberg 1993; Blöndal 2001). At that time the Ministry of Public Administration was strengthened as the leader in, and coordinator of, the reform process (**17**).

The pace of change increased at the beginning of the 1990s, and decreased afterwards. The reason for the increase was primarily the deteriorating public finances. At that moment, the complete Swedish economy found itself in a crisis, marked by declining productivity and high unemployment. In 1993, the budgetary deficit amounted to 16 per cent of GNP. Improved efficiency within the public sector became a spearhead of the austerity measures taken. A programme to slim down the central government by 10 per cent through decentralization, deregulation, structural reorganization and internationalization was approved by Parliament in 1990.

7.4   From 1991 to 1994: a conservative coalition cabinet under PM Bildt

The first – important – steps of administrative reform in Sweden were thus launched by the Social Democratic government. The conservative government that was in power from 1991 to 1994 – a minority government of Moderates, Liberals, and Centre and Christian Democratic parties – did not implement major changes to the reform progamme, except for a greater stress on marketization and privatization as well as a change of the main coordinating actors. In 1991 the Parliament approved a programme to reorganize and restrain the public sector (Budget and Finance Bill, Bill on Growth-oriented Industrial Policy). For the first time the use of market-based principles and the introduction of competition was announced by the government. As for general policy coordination, groups of political appointees within the Cabinet Office secured a major role in coordinating the political parties and ministers within the coalition government **(18)**. The political parties each had their own coordination groups, with the Prime Minister's Office largely responsible for coordinating the coordinators. In the administrative reform process, the Ministry of Finance became the central coordinating actor **(19)** (as well for administrative reforms, regulation and ICT), since the Ministry of Public Administration's remit was now reduced to regional and local government, with its competencies transferred to the Ministry of Finance and its Agency for Administrative Development (*Statskontoret*). The Ministry of Justice had some coordination role in the regulatory reform policies, with the Ministry of Finance. A division within the Ministry of Industry and Commerce was responsible for the control and coordination of the major state-owned enterprises (OECD 1992) **(20)**.

In this period both the decentralization and deregulation programme **(21, 22)** were accelerated. At the agency level saving and reform programmes began to show a major impact in several ways. The government aimed at distinguishing more clearly among the different public functions and their organizational forms (Statskontoret 1998). First, after 1990 a range of changes took place, both structurally and with respect to competencies at the sub-departmental level. Agencies were merged or abolished, new agencies were founded and some received new competencies, changed their activities or were internally reorganized (23). Agencies with control tasks over lower governmental levels saw their tasks redefined to those of support and evaluation (OECD 2002: 183). Approximately 160 agencies were shut down, and about 100 new ones were created. The number of central-government agencies eventually fell by more than half; from 1360 in 1990 to 590 in 1998. But these figures also include agencies that were part of groups of agencies. The remaining agencies were, however, larger on average than their predecessors. Most reform took place through consolidation of agencies at the regional level (mainly in the fields of public order and safety, defence and business and industrial services) as well as by corporatization.

The government also developed criteria to choose the right organizational form for state activities, including privatization and corporatization (24). Between 1990 and 1996 about 13 public enterprises with activities in competitive environments became limited companies (including Sweden Telecom and Sweden Post) with about 100,000 state employees involved (OECD 1999: 5; Statskontoret 1999: 18). New independent regulatory agencies were created to guarantee competitive neutrality in liberalized markets.

Third, the management autonomy of agencies was further increased with respect to shifting budgets over years (25). Since the National Institute for Civil Service Training and Development was abolished in 1992 each agency became responsible for its own training and development. Moreover, negotiations for wage agreements with labour unions were decentralized to the agencies because the new Swedish Agency for Government Employers responsible for negotiations was now controlled and financed by them (26). This agency is governed by the Employers' Council, composed of 80 members elected by the agencies and in which the agencies with the biggest staff hold the most seats. The agencies' staff are seconded by the member agencies. The financial management of the agencies as well as of the government offices was modernized by introducing accrual accounting systems, partly in order to facilitate the implementation of results management (Scheers and Bouckaert 2003) (27). Moreover, the control of expenditure was significantly strengthened by issuing expenditure ceilings, a reform implemented in 1996, and agencies had to publish an annual financial and performance report, based on uniform templates. This report was audited by the National Audit Office, because uniform and sound financial and performance information was lacking (OECD 1999). The National Audit Office also developed a rating and benchmarking system, evaluating the

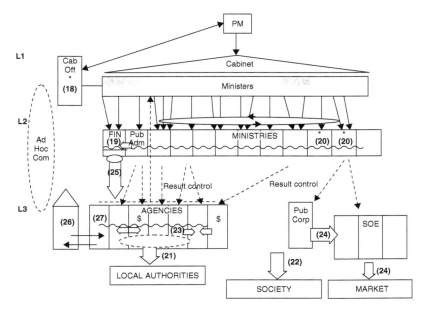

Legend PM: Prime Minister; Cab Off: Cabinet Office; Ad Hoc Com: Ad hoc Commissions; FIN: Department of Finances; Pub Adm: Department of Public Administration; SOE: State-owned enterprises; Pub Corp: Public Corporations

(18) Coalition control unit within Cabinet Office
(19) Ministry of Finance and Statskontoret central coordinating actors for administrative reforms, regulation and ICT
(20) Other ministries with some coordination role in reform programmes: Ministry of Justice regarding regulation, and the Ministry of Industry and Commerce regarding the control of major state-owned enterprises
(21) Further decentralization
(22) Further deregulation
(23) Major restructuring at agency level as effect of decentralization and deregulation
(24) Corporatization and privatization of public enterprises
(25) Further devolution of financial management autonomy to agencies (mainly regarding shifting budgets over years)
(26) Joint agency for wage negotiations (Swedish Agency for Government Employers), which is controlled by the other agencies
(27) Introduction of accrual accounting system and uniform templates for annual financial and performance reports for agencies; stronger central control by expenditure ceilings

Figure 7.4 Specialization and coordination in Sweden: the conservative coalition cabinet under PM Bildt (1991–4)

financial management of government agencies (Dahlberg and Isakson 1996).

So, forced by the poor state of public finances, a number of institutional changes were implemented during the 'budget process', which became much more top-down (Molander et al. 2002: 8). A saving programme – expense reductions and tax increases – was implemented by government to restore the budget balance. Furthermore, HR management underwent a number of changes. Approximately 26,000 civil servants disappeared from central administration between 1990 and 1998 (12 per cent of state employees), and the job specifications of a range of functions were revised. Despite the reforms, the number of ministries and agencies (not taking into account regional sub-units) remained relatively stable (Riksrevisionsverket 1997), as did the general organizational design. The dual structure remained.

7.5   From 1995 to 1999: Social Democratic cabinets under PMs Carlsson and Persson

The 1994 and 1996 elections brought the Social Democrats back into government. In 1995–6 an evaluation of the reforms took place. When assessing the reform initiatives, the Commission on Administrative Policy stressed, among other things, the fragmentation of Swedish central government. The Commission pointed to the general problems of governance and the inadequate control of large resource flows (Molander et al. 2002). A government bill 'Central Government Administration in the Citizen's Service' of 1997 and subsequent action plans set out the main priorities for future action: concentration on core activities; development of the quality and skills of state employers; focus on performance; and effective provision of information and services. The issues stated in the bill were aimed at fine-tuning the past reforms, rather than setting new strategic directions. Crucial challenges, such as Sweden's membership in the European Union (EU), internationalization, the rapid development of information technology, and cooperation and functional division between central and local government, called for new and increased coordination among governmental actors.

Before discussing these challenges and the response of the Swedish government, two other changes in the context of a new leadership policy issued in 1995 should be noted. The government initiated a regular dialogue about the goals and results of agencies between agency heads and ministers in order to intensify contacts and management by results **(28)**. This regular dialogue was considered a very important instrument for the government's control of the agencies (OECD 1999). The leadership policy was, however, broader and involved formulating a strategy for the induction, training and mobility of senior management in agencies (OECD 1999) **(29)**.

The government also prioritized developing e-government, the use of IT within the agencies and an open electronic infrastructure as a joint basis for information exchange between agencies and levels of government. A 1996 IT Bill aimed at increasing usage of IT in Swedish society and made the supply of public information and technical infrastructure a priority (Regeringskansliet 2000: 17). Therefore, 'improved coordination between agencies is therefore necessary, and more paths for voluntary cooperation should be sought' (Statskontoret 1998: 21). The government adopted a 'light-touch' approach based on a 'joint-initiative' of networking for the exchange of experiences and training programmes (OECD 1998). The Statskontoret became responsible for 'reshap[ing] public administration using IT', by issuing studies, networks, quality assurance and support such as joint procurement initiatives. The necessary coordination was achieved through consultations, cooperative forums and consensual agreements.

The Top Leaders Forum was a crucial innovation, created as early as 1994 and chaired by the Minster of Finance **(30)**. As an informal cross-cutting management group with senior managers from 10 major central agencies and representatives of the associations of regional and local authorities, it addressed concerns about the compartmentalization of efforts to apply technology. The Forum advanced rather successful projects and policy discussions but because of 'traditions of independence of Swedish agencies, and the lack of legal authority to enforce action' it was constrained in its ability to achieve change (OECD 1998). It dissolved in 1998 when the Minister of Finance stepped down as chair. But the need for joint and enforced policy work was keenly felt by the agencies. So, in June 2000, a bottom-up approach resulted in the formation of the State Agency E-Forum, in which agency managers identified and discussed strategic issues (OECD–PUMA 2000: 26–7; **(35)** on Figure 7.5). The Central Government E-forum was an informal forum for consultations and cooperation, headed by the Director-General of Statskontoret and comprising the Deputy Directors-General of eight central government agencies (Statskontoret 2002). Actual strategies were elaborated by a high-level IT Commission.

The light-touch approach was abandoned in one case, however. The government established firm and coherent Y2K process control at the

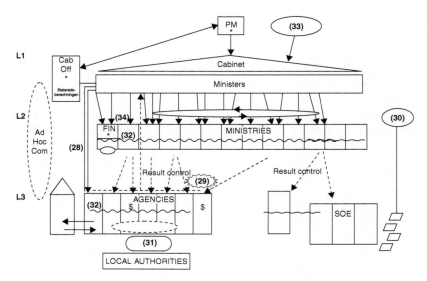

Legend PM: Prime Minister; Cab Off: Cabinet Office; Ad Hoc Com: Ad hoc Commissions; FIN: Department of Finance; SOE: State-owned enterprises; Pub Corp: Public Corporations

(28)   Regular dialogue between ministers and agency heads
(29)   More coordinated leadership policy
(30)   Networking and training for ICT and e-government. Top Leader Forum. Enforced quality insurance for Y2K
(31)   Joint agencies with local government and regional development networks
(32)   VESTA consolidated system of accrual activity-based financial management
(33)   National council for quality and development
(34)   Integration of ministries in the chancellery in 1997 (and creation of superministry for industry in 1998)

Figure 7.5   Specialization and coordination in Sweden: Social Democratic cabinets under PMs Carlsson and Persson (1995–9)

agency level, because making all the central government agencies' IT systems Y2K-compliant was considered a matter of urgency. The outcomes of enforced quality assurance, that is, the second-opinion reviews of major IT projects that were commissioned by wary or apprehensive ministries, were assessed by government (but less so by the 'health-checked' agencies) (OECD–PUMA 2000: 26–7). As well, the introduction of EMU – although Sweden decided not to participate – became a catalyst for studying and enhancing the interconnectedness of the Swedish administration (see Statskontoret 2000).

During the late 1990s new forms of cooperation between central government and other levels of government emerged in often complex and divergent forms, partly because of EU policies **(31)**. In the fields of labour-market policy and EU Structural Funds administration, new central government structures were created in which municipal representatives were in the majority. Moreover, since 1998 regional development networks have been in operation, involving public and private actors and involving the regions. The central agencies play a central role in these rather 'loose' networks. For Sweden such close cooperation of public and private actors (such as labour unions and business organizations – the new 'corporatism') below the national scale and close to individual companies is rather new (Statskontoret 1998; Niklasson 2004).

In this period the government shifted its financial strategies from across-the-board savings to the integrated improvement of financial and performance systems in the core administration, through the introduction of the VESTA project **(32)**. This project envisaged a consolidated system for central government forecasting, budgeting, accounting, performance monitoring and payment information (Pollitt and Bouckaert 2004). After changing the accounting system to one on an accrual basis (in 1993), the budgeting system was also to become based on accrual. Moreover, an activity-based structure for budgeting and accounting was envisaged in order to reduce the cost of central government activities (OECD 1998). This project was reinforced by White Book Performance Budgeting, established in 2000. In 1998, the Swedish Financial Management Authority (ESV) was created, which supported the development of sound financial management in the Swedish government. A new agency – the National Council for Quality and Development **(33)** – was established in 1999 to influence and develop public administration in strategically important areas, such as total quality management and other development issues. The Council was an arena for building up skills and competence, seminars and development programmes and close cooperation with researchers at universities and colleges (OECD 2001).

In 1997 all Swedish ministries and the Prime Minister's Office – that were previously composed of 15 independent entities – were integrated into one so-called Government Office (*Regeringskansliet*) responsible for policy preparation, planning and coordination. The Government Office was still divided into several ministries, but was nevertheless supposed to function as a collective unit **(34)**. The goals of this reform were, among others, to de-emphasise sector thinking and to promote coordination, as well as to enhance administrative efficiency. However, this merger did not meet its expectations: 'neither at unit level, nor at the political level, could changes of coordination procedures be observed' (Hustedt and Tiessen 2006: 39).

In 1998 Göran Persson announced the second large organizational reshuffle of the 1990s, the creation of a 'superministry' for industry (*näringsdepartement*). Four ministries were merged into a new Ministry of Industry, considered to be a new 'superministry for growth'. The goals of the reform were to improve coordination between the relevant ministries, to break interministerial rivalries and to foster a new, integrated organizational culture (Hustedt and Tiessen 2006: 39). The portfolio included labour market, energy, information technology and small business policy as well as infrastructure. The idea was to create the organizational preconditions for a coordinated policy to produce sustainable economic growth. However, the reforms were also symbolic, as Persson, after a major electoral defeat, needed to strengthen his position (Hustedt and Tiessen 2006: 39).

As stated by Hustedt and Tiessen (2006: 39), 'the creation of the super-department has not been subject to any systematic evaluation so far, but it appears that the effects of the reorganisations have been marginal at best, as described by Persson (2003)'. Some kind of project organization (Statskonsult 2001) was established, but with little organizational change at the unit level and resulting in far less innovativeness than claimed by the reform (Hustedt and Tiessen 2006: 39, Regeringskansliet 2003).

7.6   From 2000 to 2005: the Social Democratic cabinet under PM Persson

From 2000 onward, the e-government strategy of the government was reinforced and expanded in its bill on 'An Information Society for All' (Regeringskansliet 2000), which provided for an IT strategy for many sectors of Swedish policy. A crucial element in this strategy was the concept of the '24/7 agency' in which the highest level of IT development was 'website and network functions for joined-up services involving several agencies and institutions' (Statskontoret 2000: 3).

The interconnected government that is envisaged may be described as one in which citizens perceive public-service activities as a coherent whole; applications and database systems use standardised interfaces that enable various public systems to work together, and efficient information management eliminates the need for requests

for information that the public administration already possesses.
(Statskontoret 2002: 3)

It became obvious that a purely decentralized and voluntary development of IT in the agencies had suboptimal outcomes since it resulted in
uneven progress towards integrated e- government services, with insufficient investment, diverging norms and incompatibility of systems
(Statskontoret 2002) as well as poor development of intergovernmental
projects: 'At present, every agency is fully responsible for developing
its own business systems. There is thus a clear risk of sub-optimisation,
since each agency's decisions will necessarily be based solely on an
assessment of benefits and costs for its own activities' (Statskontoret
2004a). From 2000 onwards horizontal collaboration, coordination and
joined-up government became buzzwords in Swedish policy with regard
to IT in public administration (35).

But in promoting more IT-oriented collaboration between agencies and supporting integrated web portals the government shifted
its coordination approach to a more 'hands-on' one by including
requirements for agencies in government ordinances, the annual
dialogue between ministers and agencies, performance reporting by
agencies (Statskontoret 2000), and creation of new coordinating actors
responsible for setting norms and standards for compatibility and
quality (besides providing support in the form of user-independent
basic e-functions). The ICT Strategic Advisory Board was created in
2003 in order to advise government about strategies for an information society (36). The board was, along with others, responsible for
advocating the inclusion of ICT and e-government objectives in other
policy fields. The Government Interoperability Board was a new joint
agency, consisting of senior management of the government offices
and agencies, with mandatory powers to set common standards for
electronic information exchange for central agencies (37). Moreover, a
high-level Commission for the 24/7 Agency under the authority of the
Ministry of Finance was set up in order to promote cooperation and
innovation, while focusing on concrete actions (38). The Commission
comprised representatives of the central government, municipalities,
county councils, R&D and the business sector (Statskontoret 2004a).
Other initiatives for greater IT activities were the Municipal Platform
and the Infra-Services Procurement.

With new actors emerging and three ministries involved (the Ministry
of Finance, the Ministry of Industry, Employment and Communications,
and the Ministry of Justice, which now had the overall responsibility

over coordination of public management reforms), another coordination problem arose with respect to the central control of e-government policy. From 2006 the Swedish Agency for Public Management, the Government Interoperability Board, the Delegation for Development of Public e-services and the National Council for Quality and Development would merge into a new agency, working under the authority of the Ministry of Finance (rather than being a joint agency) (39). The aim of this new organization was to create one public body focusing on issues regarding the development of public administration, including e-government and public procurement of ICT. A new government bill on IT was issued in 2005, *From IT-policy for Society to Policy for IT-society*, which stressed the importance of increased coordination. A new Minister for Local Government and Financial Markets (40), which includes public management and e-government, was appointed in 2004 and set the following three coherent strategy targets: a joined-up administration by 2010; an efficient and just administration; and an innovative and learning administration (Statskontoret 2004a). At the end of 2004 the Statskontoret, which was now located under the Ministry of Justice, further elaborated a vision of 'network administration' and called the agencies to go beyond the Swedish model of 'contractual' cooperation in which each agency still decides whether external services and functions are sufficiently attractive for the unit to pay for their use. A rational and purposeful joint structure was needed for the public sector's information management through an interoperability framework (Statskontoret 2004a).

The gradual centralization of coordination and the strengthening of the centre with respect to IT-based reforms were obvious. However, the government emphasized fostering ownership and participation by the agencies by including them in commissions and governing boards of joint agencies and by providing sufficient central support for them. Another field where there were calls for more centralization and more coordinating power for specific central agencies was the *emergency management system* at national level in Sweden. Following the tsunami disaster in Southeast Asia the Swedish Government prepared in 2004–5 a government bill in relation to emergency management and national security. In response the Swedish Emergency Management Agency demanded more coordinating powers vis-à-vis regional and local authorities and other involved central agencies (SEMA 2004) (41).

On the other hand Swedish EU membership since 1995 has seemed to challenge traditional ways of top-down coordination in Sweden: 'In

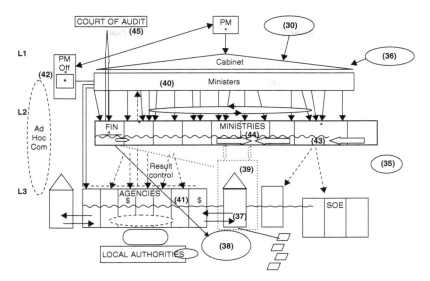

Legend PM: Prime Minister; PM Off: Prime Minister's Office; Ad Hoc Com: Ad hoc Commissions; FIN: Department of Finance; SOE: State-owned enterprises

More hands-on strategy and centralization for e-government, based on consultation and involvement of agencies

(35) Bottom-up creation of the State Agency E-Forum, which replaced the dissolved Top Leaders Forum

(36) Creation of the ICT Strategic Advisory Board

(37) Creation of the Government Interoperability Board as a joint agency

(38) Creation of a high-level Commission for the 24/7 Agency

(39) Future establishment (in 2006) of a new agency under the aegis of the Ministry of Finance, to integrate all agencies with functions related to the development of the public sector

(40) Establishment of a Minister for Local Government and Financial Markets, responsible for public management and e-government

(41) Emergency management system

(42) Centralization of coordination of EU affairs under the Prime Minister, complemented by an increased role for medium-rank civil servants in sectors

(43) Super-ministry for Growth, again headed by three ministers

(44) Reduction of ministries to ten

(45) Creation of an independent Court of Audit under the Parliament, merging the *Riksrevisionsverket* under the Minister of Finance and the Parliamentary Auditors

Figure 7.6 Specialization and coordination in Sweden: Social Democratic cabinets under PM Persson (2000–5)

particular, the coordinating role of the Swedish Foreign Office is increasingly supplemented by coordination responsibilities of the Prime Minister's Office and by coordinating activities of medium-rank civil servants within sector ministries and agencies' (Molander et al. 2002: 13). Time pressure makes collective decision-making and mutual exchange of important documents difficult. In 2004 a special secretariat for the coordination of everyday EU affairs (especially those related to the Council) moved from the Foreign Office to the Prime Minister's Office (**42**). This reform indicated that the Swedish Prime Minister had an ambition to tighten the coordination of EU affairs in the Swedish central administration (Larsson and Trondal 2005). However, civil servants from the agencies remained very active in EU forums.

After the 2002 election, the Super-ministry for Growth was headed by three ministers instead of one, with a minister for industry and trade, a minister for communications and regional policy and a minister for employment, resembling the organization before the merger (Hustedt and Tiessen 2006: 39) (**43**).

Despite the abovementioned evolutions, the relationship between the ministries and agencies, and their respective duties, did not change substantially. However, the original idea of the reforms in the late 1980s and early 1990s that operating discretion granted to the agencies would be counterbalanced by three-yearly evaluations and reports of the results achieved by the agencies was, according to these reports, not fully achieved. A major study of 2002 showed that the introduction of results management stagnated at a disappointingly low level, because of the lack of strategic control capacity within the small ministries (Molander et al. 2002). In the same report, an unclear delineation of responsibilities, tasks and ex-post accountability was reported, as well as a decline in trust between ministries and agencies. Recent debates on central agencies in Sweden discuss the feasibility of a complete decentralization to the local level on the one hand or recentralization on the other.

7.7   Conclusions

Swedish administration has retained many features that were present in the early 1980s. Indeed, some changes identified above have reinforced the pre-existing characteristics. In particular, there has been some continuing decentralization and deconcentration of administration, so that the ministerial structure that is meant to provide some coordination among the agencies and other more or less autonomous actors faces even greater challenges. The persistence of the basic administrative structure has presented significant challenges to political and administrative leaders who would want to create coherence among public programmes in Sweden.

Despite this overall stability, however, there have been some important changes in public administration and in the coordination system. For example, several experiments with reorganization of ministries have attempted to move similar activities into a single ministry, albeit with those policies continuing to be delivered by more or less autonomous agencies. There were also important political changes, particularly as the bourgeois parties attempted to coordinate not only their policies but also their political positions.

8
Coordination in the Netherlands (1980–2005)

In the Dutch case five stages of developments in coordination may be distinguished between 1980 and 2005. The initial or 'zero' stage in this study is just before the turning point of 1981 with the cabinets of Van Agt I and II, and Lubbers I. A second stage was between 1987 and 1994 with Lubbers II and III. The subsequent stage was between 1995 and 2002 with Kok I and II. The last stage in this study covers 2002–5 with Balkenende I and II.

8.1   Specialization and coordination before 1981

The individual responsibility of each minister for the organization and structure of his apparatus (the ministry and the hived-off bodies) has been central in the Dutch central government system since the enactment of the Constitution of 1848 (Kickert and in 't Veld 1995). This basic feature of ministerial responsibility significantly affects the functioning of the Dutch government and was the basis for the fragmentation and compartmentalization which is a particular feature of it. Related to that, and linked to the nature of coalition cabinets,, the coordinating power of the Prime Minister is weak (1) (Nomden 1999; Kickert 2005: 21). The function of Prime Minister is not embedded in the constitution. He is *primus inter pares* and must maintain the unity of government policy. He lacks the power to nominate and dismiss ministers. Moreover, he cannot reshuffle his cabinet by assigning ministers to other portfolios, nor can he issue any directives to an individual minister (Nomden 1999: 4; Andeweg and Bakema 1994). Unlike prime ministers in other countries, he has only limited policy support within the Ministry of General Affairs, and is mainly concerned with informative services. By the end of the 1970s the competency of the Prime Minister was extended to grant powers to ministers in the absence of clarity. Overall the influence of the Prime Minister in practice is mainly dependent upon party politics and his own personality (Kottman 1978: 422).

The doctrine of individual ministerial responsibility also restricts the scope of other coordinating instruments, like the Council of Ministers and coordinating ministers, for coordination which is more procedural and indirect. Another consequence is that the Ministry of General Affairs (which had competencies for civil service matters) and the Ministry of Internal Affairs only have very limited powers to control or coordinate other ministries, and they should not be considered real 'horizontal' ministries (Bouckaert et al. 2000). Only the Ministry of Finance has considerable coordination capacity, as it controls the budget process and financial management regulations **(1) (2)**. The quality of public service is a shared competency of the ministries of General Affairs, Internal Affairs and Finance, which complicates coordinated reforms.

Each ministry is responsible for sound organization and for exercising its duties effectively. In this context ministers and ministries function quite autonomously. As early as 1971, the Commission van Veen pointed at 'departmentalism and compartmentalism' as a most pressing problem within central government, an observation stressed by a subsequent commission (Commissie Interdepartementale taakverdeling en coördinatie 1971; MiTaCo 1977; Commission Vonhoff 1979). Individual ministerial responsibility and the resultant 'departmentalism' determined the evolutions of coordination strategies in the period from 1980 to 2005 and even beyond.

Somewhat similarly, the role of the secretary-general as the highest civil servant of a ministry in coordinating the directorates was quite unclear. Although partly depending on the way the secretary-general defines its role, most ministries were rather loosely coupled agglomerates of powerful directorates. The informal board of secretaries-general with an advisory role was largely inactive till the end of the 1980s (Kickert 2005).

Figure 8.1 shows the specialization and coordination of the central government around 1980. The one-to-one relationship between ministers and ministries **(3)** is remarkable and points to a high level of individual ministerial responsibility. There was a huge number of junior ministers ('state secretaries') but these operated within the competencies of the full ministers. In order to cope with deficient interministerial coordination and following the advice of the Van Veen Commission, the Netherlands installed an extended system of consultation bodies around the central Council of Ministers *('ministerraad')* **(4)**, consisting of ministerial sub-councils **(5)** and ministerial committees *('onderraden'* and *'ministeriële commitées')* **(6)**.

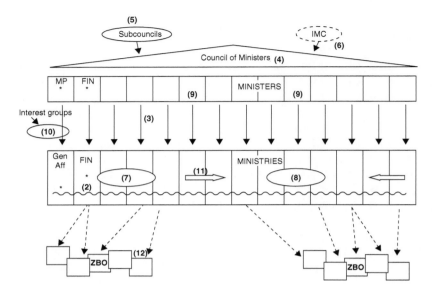

Legend IMC: Interministerial Committees; ZBO: 'Zelfstandig Bestuursorgaan' – externally decentralized body; MP: Minister-President (Prime Minister); FIN: Department of Finance; Gen Aff: General Affairs

(1)   Prime Minister as *'primus inter pares'* with weak coordination powers
(2)   Quite powerful Minister/Ministry of Finance uses the budget process as coordination mechanism
(3)   One-to-one relationship between ministers and ministries
(4)   Council of Ministers
(5)   Sub-councils (permanent)
(6)   Ministerial committees (temporary)
(7)   Preparatory interministerial coordination committees
(8)   Other interministerial committees
(9)   Coordinating ministers
(10) Large number of external advisory bodies, encompassing independent expertise as well as sectoral interest groups
(11) Reshuffling of competences between ministries
(12) An unstructured multitude of external decentralized bodies

Figure 8.1 Specialization and coordination in the Netherlands before 1981

These cabinet committees consisted of ministers, secretaries of state, highly ranked civil servants and representatives of crucial semi-autonomous bodies, like the central bank. They were each served by preparatory interministerial coordination committees, consisting of highly ranked civil servants from different ministries *('ambtelijke voorportalen')* **(7)**.

Additionally, other interministerial committees were active (8). For each cabinet committee a coordinating minister had responsibility for elaborating a coordinated policy (9). However, such a coordinating minister did not have formal powers over other ministers and his coordination efforts were merely procedural, and not substantive (Nomden 1999). This structure of committees and coordinating ministers enhanced the communication between the political and administrative levels and between ministries. Moreover, the Prime Minister was somewhat strengthened because he was chairing both the Council of Ministers and the sub-councils (Kottman 1978). However, the structure itself proliferated and fragmentated. In the beginning of the 1980s about 69 coordinating ministers and 245 interministerial committees and external advisory bodies (10) existed.

Besides interdepartmental committees, coordination efforts at the administrative level were mostly handled by reshuffling competencies between ministries and by mergers or splits to improve communication between interdependent policy domains (11). In the case of these shifts the Dutch government followed an inductive and incremental strategy with pragmatic small reshufflings of competencies, as a response to changing organizational needs or as part of compromise-building during coalition formation. In 1980 a considerable number of policy implementation tasks were handled by external decentralized bodies, the so-called *'zelfstandige bestuursorganen'* (ZBOs), partially as a way to involve societal actors in policy implementation (12). In 1983, an analysis pointed at more than 400 such bodies with a huge variety of legal and organizational forms (WRR 1983). These ZBOs were at best loosely coupled to the parent ministries with heterogeneous and incoherent governance arrangements.

8.2 Specialization and coordination from 1981 to 1986: Cabinets Van Agt I and II, Cabinet Lubbers I

In 1981 the Commission Vonhoff once again drew the attention of politicians to the considerable level of departmentalism (*'verkokering'*) resulting from individual ministerial responsibility. Policy development was a matter of highly specialized entities, which were in close contact with sectoral actors, in competition with other ministries and under weak and informal political control. The coordination system that was installed in the 1970s as a response to that departmentalism created new problems of uncontrolled growth of bodies, delays in decision-making and bottlenecks in procedures. As a consequence there were suggestions for rationalization of coordination (Commissie Hoofdstructuur Rijksdienst 1979–1981). Although the government did not follow the Vonhoff Commission's

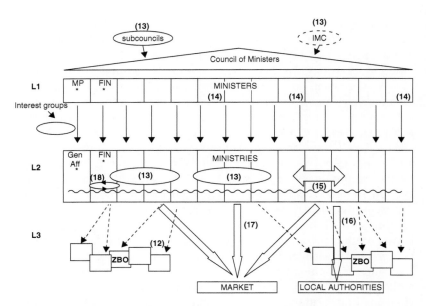

Legend IMC: Interministerial Committees; MP: Minister-President (Prime Minister); FIN: Department of Finance; Gen Aff: Department of General Affairs; ZBO: 'Zelfstandig Bestuursorgaan' – externally decentralized body

(13)   Reduction of the number of coordinating ministers and of interministerial committees
(14)   Creation of project ministers
(15)   Major reshuffling of competencies between ministries took place with the abolition of the Ministry of Public Health and Environmental Protection (*'volksgezondheid en milieuhygiëne'*) and division of the competencies among two ministries with adjacent competencies
(16)   Decentralization of competencies to local authorities
(17)   Privatization of state activities
(18)   A policy review procedure coordinated by the Ministry of Finance, which was mainly focused on savings

Figure 8.2   Specialization and coordination in the Netherlands in the period 1980–6

suggestion to increase interdepartmental coordination by identifying five main policy areas, with each having one integrating minister and one sub-council, the number of coordinating ministers was reduced to 25 and the number of interministerial commissions was limited to about 70 (**13**). A system of project ministers in charge of the implementation of the policy priorities of the cabinet was introduced but these ministers lacked the budget and personnel for these tasks **(14)** (Nomden 1999). The suggestion to create a senior civil service corps, in order to enhance inter-organizational coordination, was not followed. In 1982 a last major reshuffling of competencies between ministries took place with the abolition of the Ministry of Public Health and Environmental Protection and the division of the competencies between two ministries with adjacent competencies **(15)**. After that the strategy of organizational mergers and splits was explicitly abandoned – except for a small shift in 1994 – because of the costs, delays and discontinuity resulting from it and because of its inability to cope with constant changing societal contexts (cf. Commissie Wiegel 1993; Nomden 1999).

Six 'Major Operations' were launched in 1982, concerning among other things decentralization, privatization and deregulation. Partly as a response to the deteriorating budgetary situation of the Dutch public sector, competencies were devolved to local authorities **(16)** and privatizations of state activities were begun **(17)**. Overall, the scale of privatizations remained rather limited, since only a small number of public enterprises existed at the national level. From 1985 onwards a formal privatization policy framework and procedure was established (Zalm 2001). The decentralization of competencies to local authorities was overall quite limited in scale (Kickert 2005: 12). The Ministry of Finance coordinated from 1981 onwards a policy review procedure, which was mainly focused on savings **(18)**.

8.3 Specialization and coordination from 1987 to 1994: Cabinets Lubbers II and III

In the second half of the 1980s a new coordination strategy emerged. In this the reduction of the size of the central administration and hence of the coordination needs within it, through shifting tasks to the private market and hived-off bodies, would be made more explicit. Stated differently, specialization was considered as a way of minimizing the need for coordination in the central administration. Ongoing devolution and decentralization made the core ministries smaller in the next two decades, as will be shown in Figures 8.3 to 8.5.

In addition to the privatization wave at the end of the 1980s **(19)**, the size of the central administration was reduced further by the hiving off of state activities to newly created ZBOs **(20)** (Kickert 2005). This was primarily done because autonomy in external decentralized ZBOs allowed ministries to make savings in their own budgets (Kickert 2005: 15). Moreover, autonomization allowed public managers to avoid strict input controls within the central administration. Within the central administration some competencies concerning personnel (such as staff configuration) were devolved from the Ministry of General Affairs to the line ministries **(21)**. In order to enhance result-oriented control through a so-called integrated budget, further competencies for financial management were devolved from the Ministry of Finance in the early 1990s **(22)**. There were also rather unsuccessful experiments with limited forms of self-management, combining extended managerial autonomy for parts of ministries with a limited form of contractual output-related control (*'zelfbeheer'*) (Kickert 2005).

At the level of the ministries, the role and competencies of the secretary-general for intra-ministerial coordination was re-emphasized and partly strengthened in 1988 (Nomden 1999) **(23)**. Moreover, the secretaries-general revamped their informal consultation in the context of budgetary savings and the Great Efficiency Operations. This informal consultation allowed for a common position of the secretaries-general in major reform decisions, and strengthened the interministerial coordination with regard to management issues to some extent (Kickert 2005: 30) **(24)**.

The Great Efficiency Operations in the first half of the 1990s increased pressures for savings, and also changes in governmental structure. The autonomy of tasks was intensified, a further decentralization of competencies to local authorities occurred **(25)**, and a reflection on the core business of government begun. In 1993 a report by the secretaries-general and another by the Wiegel Commission (Commissie Wiegel 1993) pointed once again to the continuing relevance of departmentalism (see also Commission *Staatkundige en bestuurlijke vernieuwing* 1991): As the policy cycle of policy development, steering, implementation and overview fell under individual ministerial responsibility, there was considerable vertical 'compartmentalization' and the creation of administrative 'islands' with their own scientific institutions, advisory platforms, and implementation and inspection bodies. Several recommendations were made to improve coordination. One was for a generalized organizational split between 'policy' and 'administration' (that is, between policy design and implementation). The reforms were oriented toward creating small and flexible core ministries, which would focus on policy development. Policy implementation tasks were further decentralized to semi-autonomous bodies and the private market. It was intended that the reduction of the size of the central administration and the autonomization of policy implementation would improve intra- and interdepartmental policy coordination. Figure 8.3 clearly shows the shift of implementation competencies to the third level of

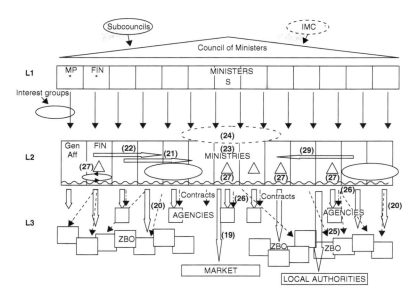

Legend Interministerial Committees; MP: Minister-President (Prime Minister); FIN: Department of Finance; Gen Aff: Department of General Affairs; ZBO: 'Zelfstandig Bestuursorgaan' – externally decentralized body; Ag: Agency.

(19) Further privatization at the end of the 1980s
(20) Hiving off of state activities to a large number of newly created ZBOs
(21) Devolution of competencies concerning personnel (such as staff configuration) by the Ministry of General Affairs to line ministries
(22) Devolution of competencies with regards to financial management by the Ministry of Finance in the early 1990s
(23) Strengthening of the role and competencies of the secretary-general for intra-ministerial coordination in 1988
(24) Informal consultation between secretaries-general revamped in context of budgetary savings and Great Efficiency Operations
(25) Further decentralization of competencies to local authorities occurred in the early 1990s
(26) Devolution of tasks from departments to internally decentralized bodies or departmental agencies (*'agentschappen'*) with result-oriented control arrangements from 1994 onwards
(27) Within several ministries, internal reallocation of decision-making competencies and the creation of structures for collective decision-making, that is the 'management boards' (*'bestuursraden'*)
(28) Strengthening the coordinating power of the Prime Minister by giving him the possibility for agenda-setting for the Council of Ministers
(29) Reshuffling of competencies regarding 'culture' between two ministries

Figure 8.3 Specialization and coordination in the Netherlands in the period 1987–94

external decentralized and, from 1994, to internal decentralized bodies or departmental agencies (*'agentschappen'*) **(26)**. These departmental agencies were in fact developed as a 'safer' alternative to devolution to ZBOs and to keep policy implementation somewhat closer to the minister. They were mainly characterized by an accrual accounting system and managerial autonomy in relation to budgetary and financial transactions. In several ministries, an internal reallocation of decision-making competencies aimed to overcome the dominance of single directorates by creating structures for collective decision-making, such as the 'management boards' (*'bestuursraden'*) **(27)**. These management boards were one way to cope with changing departmental structures and the reduced size of remaining core ministries. In some ministries they replaced the previous hierarchical system of directorates-general with a network-like steering model and decision structure, of which the secretary-general was president (Noordegraaf 1995). That was considered to be a more appropriate decision model for the smaller core ministries.

Another recommendation of the report of the secretaries-general was to strengthen the coordinating power of the Prime Minister by giving him the possibility of agenda-setting for the Council of Ministers **(28)**. The Wiegel Commission report pointed out that the interministerial coordination system (with cabinet committees, administrative commit-tees and coordinating ministers) was performing quite well, although the Wiegel Commission unsuccessfully proposed creating new-style project ministers for urgent and complicated matters. In 1994 compe-tencies regarding 'culture' were shifted from one ministry to another **(29)**. However, the Wiegel Commission argued that reorganization of the ministries was no solution for the pro-blem of coordination, since interdependence among policy areas is time-bound and ministerial mergers or splits are expensive and time-consuming (Commissie Wiegel 1993). This position was supported by subsequent cabinets (Minister voor Bestuurlijke Vernieuwing en Koninkrijksrelaties 2006: 7).

8.4   Specialization and coordination in the period 1995–2002: Cabinets Kok I and II

From the mid-1990s (Figure 8.4) the coordination strategy of the central government seemed to change. As in some other OECD countries such as the United Kingdom, the primacy of politics became the central concern to counterbalance fragmentation of the government apparatus. Several reports (for example: Commissie Sint 1994; Algemene Rekenkamer 1995) emphasized the lack of accountability of decentralized ZBOs and the resulting problems of ministerial responsibility. The design of sound steering and control arrangements for hived-off organizations was clearly a rather neglected aspect of the autonomization in the 1980s and the early 1990s (Verhoest and Van Thiel 2004). The reports questioned the appropriatedness of external autonomy and suggested creating internal agencies, similar to the Next Steps Agencies in the United Kingdom, as an alternative (Van Thiel and Pollitt 2007). Several measures were taken to streamline the organization and the accountability of the ZBOs. The government issued criteria for the creation of a ZBO, and there were restrictions for setting up new ZBOs and proposals were screened by a joint commission of the ministries of the Interior and Finance. Clearer requirements were issued on the financial and performance information that ZBOs had to provide to their minister and parliament, and the budget and accounting systems of the ZBO were regulated more strictly, compatible with the Accounting Law. Additionally, efforts were reoriented at establishing clearer result-oriented control systems for the remaining hived-off bodies, albeit again with great heterogeneity among ministries (30). Early in 2000 the cabinet submitted a draft framework law on ZBOs to parliament, at the request of the latter. However, in subsequent rounds the ambitions of this draft were limited (Verhoest and Van Thiel 2004; Van Thiel 2008). In 2003 the Cabinet Balkenende I halted the parliamentary discussion of the draft law, and demanded an evaluation of the performance and growth of ZBOs. Emphasis was however still on the creation of core departments through hiving off policy implementation (Nomden 1999: 18), but after 1995 the establishment of departmental agencies was favoured over ZBOs (31). As Table 8.1 shows, the actual consequences of these initiatives on the number of autonomous operations is somewhat unclear for ZBOs, since actual numbers differ, depending on the data sources. The number of departmental agencies clearly has increased substantially.

Table 8.1 Evolution of the number of departmental agencies and ZBOs at central level in the Netherlands

	1993	2000	2004
ZBOs	545 (607)	431 (654)	630
Departmental agencies (since 1994)	–	17	34

Note: The numbers in brackets give the maximum count of ZBOs based on the sources used
Sources: Algemene Rekenkamer (1995a); Algemene Rekenkamer (2004); Jongeneel (2005); Ministerie van Financiën (2005); Van Thiel and Van Buuren (2001); Van Thiel (2005).

Moreover, the organizational split between policy and administration created new coordination needs, which became more and more visible. A first coordination need was ensuring the feasibility of policy development initiatives for implementation. Some ministries, like the ministries of Economic Affairs and of Justice, created feasibility tests for policy design initiatives between the hived-off organizations and their mother ministries (Van Twist et al. 1996; Van Twist and Mayer 2001) **(32)**. A few ministries considered the organizational split between policy development and administration inappropriate and tried to reintegrate some policy functions (such as the Ministry of Mobility and Water Infrastructure) **(33)**. Even in 2003 the Court of Audit issued a report linking problems in policy implementation to poor policy design and poor communication between policy designers and implementers (Algemene Rekenkamer 2003; Van Oosteroom and Van Thiel 2004b). This report was never followed up, however.

Another issue arose in the coordination of control of departmental agencies and ZBOs. Several ministries coordinated the control of the individual organizations by creating new organizational interfaces such as a single control unit or account managers **(34)**. Also the 'management boards' (*'Bestuursraden'*), active in some ministeries, were potential co-ordinating platforms (Noordegraaf 1995). However, it proved that these management boards were not very succesful in increasing intraministerial coordination, for they blurred lines of control and accountability. Consequently some ministries abolished them again (Bekke et al. 1996) **(35)**. A third coordination need that arose was the need to coordinate the activities of the various agencies, ZBOs and private actors active in policy implementation. A few agencies were subjected to quasi-market forces **(36)**, like 'Senter' in the Ministry of Economics and the 'Duyvermans Computer Centre' (Ministry of Defence). Other ministries were experimenting with chain management initiatives in order to increase the legitimacy and enforcement of policies (such as in the Ministry of Mobility and Water Infrastructure) **(37)**. After 2000 chain management became more popular and is now widely used nationally (asylum, penal law, water policy) and at local levels (social services), and was applied at both the policy design and service delivery stage (Van Duivenboden et al. 2000; Van der Aa and Konijn 2001, 2002). The Ministry of the Interior facilitated and supported chain management techniques at local level. Another related evolution around the start of the new millennium was a stricter policy on commercial market activities by public organizations (Commissie Cohen 1997), resulting in some organizational splits.

The cabinet also issued a position paper on ministerial scrutiny and regulation. Ministries started to develop more coherent control policies for their policy domain (including the ZBOs). The central principles were a strict structural disaggregation between policy, implementation and scrutiny/regulation/control resulting in the creation of new regulatory and controlling agencies, as well as reducing the overlap between such bodies (Borghouts 2002; Van der Knaap 2002) (**38**). However, in 2002 the Court of Audit ascertained that many ministries still lacked a coherent policy on regulation and scrutiny.

Nevertheless, in the same year the inspection and regulation agencies in the field of social security were merged into one departmental agency. This merger was part of a drastic reform program (*'structuur uitvoering werk en inkomsten'*) for social security, which also encompassed the merger of five implementation organizations into one ZBO (Witteveen 2002) (**39**). The creation of such 'umbrella agencies' can be seen as the latest trend, according to one observer (Van Thiel 2008).

In the run-up to this reform in social security, the liberal-socialist government discussed marketization in social security and insurances (Bergsma and Van den Brink 2002). Likewise, the introduction of more competition and more choice for users in health (Maarse and Korsten 2001; Maarse 2001) and in labour policy were debated, but ultimately only reintegration activities were subjected to more market dynamics (Bergsma and Van den Brink 2002).

Another major initiative that was linked to the predominance of the primacy of politics was a major rationalization and revision of the system of external advisory bodies, which was still considered as an important cause of compartmentalization (**40**). In the new system a clear distinction was made between advice from independent experts and concertation with interest groups, whereas in the old system the influence of the interest groups was considerable but diffuse, obscuring the objectivity of the advice. The number of advisory bodies was reduced from 210 to 27 bodies (Van der Sluijs 1998). Through this reform the policy development function of the core ministries was expected to be strengthened.

A final common suggestion of the Vonhoff commission, the 1993 reports of the secretaries-general and the Wiegel report became reality in 1995 with the creation of the *'Algemene Bestuursdienst'* (**41**). This senior civil service office aimed at creating a 'grand corps' of high-ranking officials (that is, a senior executive service) of which the service became the employer. One of its main goals was reducing departmentalism by creating a more common culture and shared values and norms in central

164

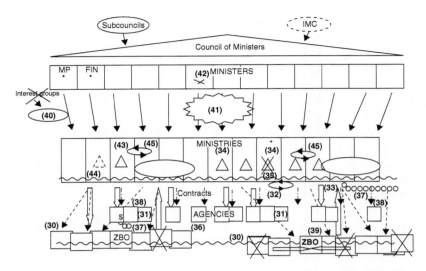

Legend IMC: Interministerial Committees; MP: Minister-President (Prime Minister); FIN: Department of Finance; Gen Aff: Department of General Affairs; ZBO: 'Zelfstandig Bestuursorgaan' – externally decentralized body; Ag: Agency.

(30) Strengthening of the uniformity of financial and performance information and the accounting system of ZBOs; some rationalization according to stricter criteria to create ZBOs and departmental reviews of ZBO statutes

(31) New departmental agencies established as a preferred form for autonomization

(32) New procedures for more intensive involvement of agencies and ZBOs in policy design (for example, feasibility tests)

(33) Integration of formerly autonomized tasks and competencies back into the parent ministry (for example, the Ministry of Mobility and Water Infrastructure)

(34) Creation of new organizational interfaces such as a single control unit or account managers within parent ministries to improve interaction with agencies and ZBOs

(35) Abolition of 'management boards' ('*Bestuursraden*') in some ministries

(36) Creation of quasi-market-like environments for some agencies

(37) Experiments with chain management in some ministries

(38) Creation of new regulatory and controlling agencies, as well as reduction of the overlap between such bodies

(39) Merger of five implementation organizations to one ZBO in the sector of social security

(40) Major rationalization and revision of the system of external advisory bodies

(41) Creation of the *Algemene Bestuursdienst* in order to create a senior executive service

(*Continued*)

(42) Substantial decrease in the number of project ministers because of unpopularity

(43) Coordination role of the Ministry of the Interior is enhanced

(44) Enhancement of the coordination role of the Ministry of Finance through initiatives to improve policy information within budgets and accounts, such as the VBTB initiative

(45) Interdepartmental peer reviews under coordination of the Ministry of the Interior

Figure 8.4 Specialization and coordination in the Netherlands in the period 1995–2002

government, using management training and rotation. As such, it aimed at strengthening the cultural coordination within central government. Initially, its coordination function was less dominant than the pure management aspects of its work, but after 2000 its effect on internal mobility of senior civil servants became substantial and created a new layer of generalist top managers (Hondeghem and Putseys 2003; Kickert 2005: 29).

During the 1990s the number of project ministers decreased substantially, making these posts rather scarce **(42)**. The coordination role of the ministries of the Interior **(43)** and Finance was enhanced, but these departments were in competition with each other for the coordination of autonomization processes across the ministries. The Ministry of Finance strengthened its position as the most powerful coordinating ministry because it was responsible for enhancing the information content of budget proposals and for monitoring of outputs, policy objectives and effects.

Launched in 1999, the VBTB initiative, integrating policy objectives with operational information, was the last major step in this evolution **(44)**. However, its rate of success in achieving its task – to improve result-oriented budgeting – was highly variable. Also, from 2001, interdepartmental peer reviews were organized and coordinated by the Ministry of the Interior in order to improve the policy design process and mutual learning **(45)**. In 2002 a new format for budgets was introduced.

8.5 Specialization and coordination in the period 2002–5: Cabinets Balkenende I and II

The first two cabinets under the Christian Democrat Prime Minister Balkenende clustered their reform initatives in the 'Different Government' programme (*Programma 'Andere Overheid'*), launched in 2003, partly as a reaction to the major political crises in the previous years, like the Scheveningen disaster and the electoral rise of the right-wing politician Pim Fortuyn. The 'Different Government' programme was an umbrella under which many bottom-up projects were launched, with the cabinet playing mainly the role of process manager (Kickert 2005). According to this programme, the national government should focus on its absolute core business, as well as performing better, reducing regulation of society and increasing the coordination and collaboration of all actors in policy networks. Politically, this programme was a reaction to the declining trust of citizens in government and politics, as the rise of Pim Fortuyn and his populist political party demonstrated very clearly. A central motive for many of the projects was the continuing departmentalism, combined with a huge proliferation of peripheral actors within policy domains and on different governmental levels (Kickert 2005; Kabinet 2003; Minister van Bestuurlijke Vernieuwing en Koninkrijksrelaties 2006). The resulting lack of interorganizational coordination was becoming highly topical because of the increased need for collaboration to solve 'wicked problems' (Langenberg and Tetteroo 2002), the need for regulatory simplification and reduction of administrative burdens (Van Dijk 2004), physical and virtual one-stop shops, Europeanization (Steur et al. 2004) and crisis management (Kabinet 2003).

With regards to the enhancement of e-government and the electronic exchange of information between public organizations, common mandatory standards were set, and a government-wide ICT programme was launched. Several large ZBOs and agencies agreed to cooperate in joint ICT platforms **(46)**. More cooperation with local and provincial authorities was laid down in intergovernmental agreements (Programma team Andere Overheid 2006). Coordination between regulatory agencies was intensified and an integration of regulatory instruments (such as licences) was pursued (see also **46**). In the context of 'Programme Youth' *('Operatie Jong')*, an interdepartmental collaboration between five ministries, which aimed at a stronger integration of policies towards youth, chain-management logics were applied to all participating inspecting and regulatory bodies in order to establish an integration control of the 'youth chain'. Similar chains were highly topical, such as in the fields of social security and integration (Kabinet 2003; Programma Team Andere Overheid 2006) **(47)**. In other sectors the introduction of demand-oriented control was discussed (such as in education, culture and safety), but measures were not implemented before the end of 2005.

However, despite these and similar changes, in 2005 interdepartmental coordination was considered as remaining weak. Departmentalism was still perceived as a major problem in central government, as several reports stated (Kickert 2005; Minister van Bestuurlijke Vernieuwing en Koningrijksrelaties 2006). A commission on the control arrangements with respect to EU matters concluded that interdepartmental coordination for European issues could be improved by a more proactive stance and more horizontal control by the Ministry of Foreign Affairs, but it did not recommend a fundamental change in coordination structure (Gemengde Commissie 'Sturing EU-aangelegenheden' 2005). However, structural changes were at the core of two 2006 reports by the secretaries-general and by the Ministry of Administrative Reform, *'Het resultaat is de maat'*, which suggested alternative reforms in order to overcome the deep-rooted problem of compartmentalism: the expansion of the agenda-setting competencies of the Prime Minister; temporary programme ministers with a budget; more flexibility in allocating personnel, by establishing government-wide pools of experts or by better secondment procedures; more involvement of implementing agencies in policy design; integration of agencies with similar tasks in different ministries in order to provide economies of scale; and better cross-cutting coordination (Minister van Bestuurlijke Vernieuwing en Koninkrijksrelaties 2006).

Concerning the management of the public services, several initiatives by the Ministry of the Interior were taken to increase interorganizational learning and collaboration. One initiative was the enhancement of innovation and diffusion of such practices by the creation of Inaxis **(48)**. This knowledge centre stimulated practices of innovation through collaboration, such as shared services, chain management and networking (www. Inaxis.nl). Moreover, a network for quality management (*'Kwaliteitskring rijksdienst'*) **(49)** for the central government, as well as interdepartmental peer reviews *('Interdepartementale visitaties')* to improve intersectoral policy design, were organized **(50)**. Government advocated shared services for management support between ministries and between agencies, for money-saving purposes **(51)** (for example, *'Gemeenschappelijk Ontwikkelingsbedrijf'*; see Kabinet 2003; Van Oosteroom and Van Thiel 2004; Programma team Andere Overheid 2006).

The debate on ZBOs continued after 2002. The 2004 Kohnstamm report (Commissie Kohnstamm 2004) stated that the delineation of ministerial responsibility for ZBOs was unclear and that hence all ZBOs, except independent regulatory bodies, should be abolished. After fierce reaction to this report from various groups (ZBOs, academics), the cabinet confirmed the huge variety of governance arrangements for ZBOs, but also considered a revision of the ZBO status in relation to particular tasks. The framework law was still under debate when the 1996 criterion for ZBOs was applied

168

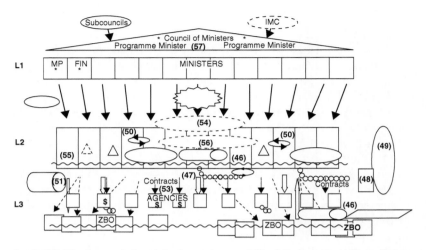

Legend IMC: Interministerial Committees; MP: Minister-President (Prime Minister); FIN: Department of Finance; Gen Aff: Department of General Affairs; ZBO: 'Zelfstandig Bestuursorgaan', externally decentralized body; Ag: Agency.

(46) Cooperation for joint ICT platforms and virtual one-stop shop between administration, autonomous bodies and local authorities
(47) More intensive use of chain management in different policy sectors (youth, safety)
(48) Establishment of Inaxis in order to enhance innovation and diffusion of innovative practices in the public sector
(49) Network for quality management ('*Kwaliteitskring rijksdienst*') for the central government
(50) Interdepartmental peer reviews ('*Interdepartementale visitaties*') to improve intersectoral policy design
(51) Shared services for management support between ministries and between agencies
(52) Initiatives to further improve the control of agencies and ZBOs in several departments (such as Justice)
(53) More agencies created
(54) Informal council of secretaries-general once again active in the context of reform and savings discussions
(55) VBTB initiative to introduce more policy-relevant budget documents failed to meet initial expectations
(56) Plans to pool policy experts across core ministries and other bodies in order to design more cross-cutting policy
(57) Plans to install programme minister (in effect in 2007)

Figure 8.5 Specialization and coordination in the Netherlands in the period 2002–5

more strictly. Several departments (such as Justice) launched initiatives to further improve the control of their agencies and ZBOs (Programma team Andere Overheid 2006) **(52)**. The number of ZBOs remained high and, depending on the source quoted, figures showed an increase or slight decrease after 2000 (see Table 8.1; Van Thiel 2005) **(53)**. In 2005 the framework law on ZBOs was finally accepted by parliament, but that did not end the discussions about agencification, such as whether ZBOs should have a constitutional basis. Toward the end of this period, the informal council of secretaries-general became active again in order to take a common stance in the ongoing reform and savings discussions **(54)**.

The VBTB initiative to introduce more policy-relevant budget documents failed to meet initial expectations **(55)**. The Court of Audit made several critical evaluations (Algemene Rekenkamer 2004–2005). Although, budget documents were to some extent more easily accessible and contained more policy information than before, the budget process became less standardized, less outcome-oriented, was implemented in a much slower time frame, and had a lower coverage rate than scheduled.

8.6   Summary and conclusion

Both before and during the period 1980–2005 the Dutch government developed a more traditional coordination system to cope with departmentalism. Shifts of competencies by ministerial merger or splits, coordinating functions, concertation bodies and financial and budgetary coordination were the mechanisms used and, over time, adjusted and fine-tuned. Clearly, some coordination mechanisms are subject to specialization and fragmentation themselves (such as the system of cabinet committees and advisory bodies). After the end of the 1980s the level of specialization increased considerably through the division of policy and implementation and the creation of core ministries. Although inter-ministerial coordination may have been reduced by these changes, new coordination needs emerged. These needs were countered by:

- the emphasis on the primacy of politics and the slowing down of the creation of external autonomous bodies;
- the reform of existing coordination mechanisms such as the budget cycle, the advisory bodies, the function of the Prime Minister and the role of horizontal ministries;
- the introduction of new coordination mechanisms such as collective decision-making bodies, cultural coordination and, to a limited extent, chain management and quasi-markets.

9
Coordination in France (1980–2005)

France is often presented as the model of the centralized, unified, and coordinated state. While like many stereotypes this one has some truth, there is also substantial overstatement, and France has had to struggle with same problems of coordination as other countries. Further, despite the appearance of unity within the public sector, there are internal divisions that pose significant problems for the would-be coordinator at the centre of government. This chapter discusses the shifts at the central level of the French Republic. Four periods are described, including 41 measures taken.

After the Second World War the French Republic wanted a strong and loyal corps of civil servants, and an end to political appointments and social inequality in recruitment. This resulted in the creation of the Ecole Nationale d'Administration (1945) and the Board of Directors of the Public Service (1947). The General Statute (1946) and the generalization of the statute of the Corps (1946) aimed at guaranteeing unified recruitment, training and statutes for civil servants (Rouban 2001). The introduction of the *'Administration de mission'* by adopting the *Commissariat au Plan* (Monnet in 1947) and the generalization of this method from 1950 guaranteed a structural form of interministerial coordination.

Administrative and financial deconcentration within the public sector resulted in a need for better coordination at the departmental level. The establishment of a coordinating responsibility as part of the regional function of the prefect (*préfet*) (1964) resulted in the prefect becoming the ultimate coordinator, as representative of the whole government. A further deconcentration of about 250 administrative decisions to the level of the prefects, between 1961 and 1969, resulted in a reorganization of the departmental *Services Extérieurs*.

The matching need for improved financial management resulted in the *Rationalisation des Choix Budgétaires* in 1968, the French version of a Planning, Programming and Budgeting System (PPBS).

9.1 The period 1981–8

In 1981 François Mitterand replaced Valéry Giscard d'Estaing as President. The French central government began the period with a strict hierarchical structure. The majority of decisions were taken within the cabinet. Within the cabinet coordination was organized along two lines. First, the central and hierarchical position of the President and the Prime Minister (in the case of 'non-cohabitation') (1) and the inter-ministerial concertation by the French system of cabinet committees – '*Comités interministériels*' (CIM), '*Réunions entre ministres*' (RdM) (2) and *Réunions interministérielles* (RiM) (3) in which the political secretariats of the relevant ministers coordinated their policy initiatives. The political level was therefore the principal level of coordination, transferring it to lower levels by a system of steering and control instruments based on both formal and informal powers.

The relations between the political level and the administrative level were ruled by two coordination mechanisms (see Figure 9.1). First, there was the formal system in which political secretariats ('*cabinets*') (4) of the ministers steered and controlled the central ministries. Second, coordination was enhanced by informal cultural links between ministers, members of the political secretariats and highly ranked civil servants, as most of them had joined a 'Grand Corps' of the state with a common education ('*Enarques*', '*polytechniciens*') (5), and a strong sense of membership and a considerable level of career mobility.

At the level of the ministries, other mechanisms in addition to the hierarchical lines of control fostered interministerial coordination. First, each change in political control of the cabinet resulted in a shift of competencies among ministries and the creation and abolition of ministries (6). As there was a one-to-one relationship between ministers and ministries, each reallocation of competencies to ministers caused shifts of competencies at the administrative level (7). Secondly, the '*administrations de mission*' (8) were temporary administrative bodies, which performed the function of advice, with their personnel drawn from several ministries. In most cases these bodies were created because of the lack of cooperation between the ministries. The '*autorités administratives indépendantes*' had a regulative and supervising role with respect to the central ministries, the deconcentrated services, and civil society (9). However, a considerable

172

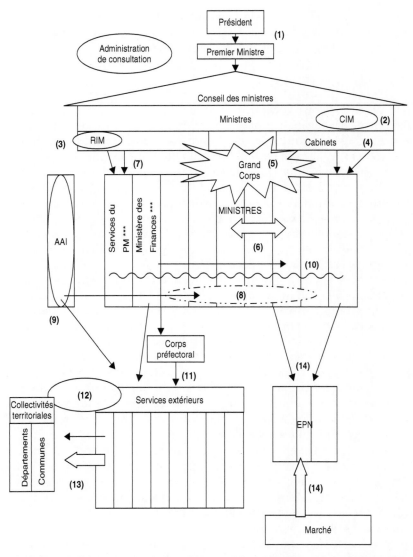

Legend CIM: Interministerial Committees; RIM: Réunions Interministérielles; AAI: Independent Administrative Authorities; PM: Prime Minister; EPN: Etablissements Publics Nationaux (National Public Bodies)

(1) President and Prime Minister
(2) Interministerial committees and reunions of ministers (CIM and RdM)

(Continued)

(3) *réunions interministérielles* (RiM)
(4) Ministerial cabinets (private secretariats)
(5) *Grands Corps*
(6) Reshuffling competencies between ministries
(7) Redirecting lines of control to keep a one-to-one relationship between minister and ministry
(8) *Administrations de mission*
(9) *Authorités administratives indépendantes*
(10) Horizontal power of the Ministry of Finance
(11) Prefect and Corps of Prefects
(12) *Conférence administrative régionale*
(13) Decentralization from *services déconcentrés* to local authorities
(14) *Commissaires* and *Contrôleurs;* nationalization of industries

Figure 9.1 Specialization and coordination in France 1981–8

departmentalism could be noted, as the power of the horizontal ministries was limited. Obviously the Ministry of Finance retained a very dominant role in steering and coordination **(10)**.

At the level of the hived-off bodies we find the *'services extérieurs'* (exterior services) of the central ministries at regional and departmental[1] level. Since 1964 these organizations existed under dual hierarchical lines: that is, their mother ministries and the *préfet* representing the cabinet. This *préfet* **(11)** had to harmonize implementation of the centrally established policy by appointing the top management of the *'services extérieurs'*, controlling the departmental finances, and leading the *'Conférence administrative régionale'* **(12)** as a concertation platform between the *services extérieurs* and the local authorities. The central position of the *préfet* in relation to the *services extérieurs* was strengthened even further in 1982. In 1983 competencies were decentralized from central ministries and their *services déconcentrés* to local authorities **(13)**. Besides the *services extérieurs* parts of policy implementation were decentralized to a large number of *Etablissements publics* (EP), which varied greatly as to their autonomy and their control by *'commissaires'* and *'contrôleurs'* **(14)**. The number of EPs increased in 1982 after the nationalization of several large private industries (Saunier-Seite 1984; Crozier 1987).

9.2 The period 1989–94

At the beginning of Mitterand's second presidential term (1981–88–95), a first large initiative to modernize the French government and administration was launched (Olivennes and Baverez 1989). A more dynamic human resource management regime combined with social peace and dialogue within the public sector was a priority (Bodiguel and Rouban 1991; Muller 1992). Also, the systematic evaluation of public policy, the accountability of civil servants, and a clearer focus on citizens as customers were key foci in government. The *Circulaire Rocard* (1989) was the start of a series of reforms. In 1992 it resulted in a series of decisions such as the *Durafour Protocol, La Charte du Service Public*, but also the *Charte de déconcentration* which caused a further deconcentration of about 315 administrative decision procedures.

One outcome of that initiative was the creation in 1990–1 of the *'centres de responsabilité'* (15) and the *Contrats de Services*. Organizations could achieve this status and gain more management autonomy by binding themselves to achieve some result norms laid down in strategic plans (*'projet de service'*) (16). A more profound reform initiative was the *'déconcentration'* of many decision-making competencies to *'services déconcentrés'* (the previous *services extérieures*) at the departmental and regional level (17). One central principle in this operation was *'interministérialité'*: the deconcentration had to enable a better coordination between the regional and departmental parts of the ministries. The coordination and leading function of the *préfet* was strengthened. A *Collège des Chefs de Service* (18) was installed within the departmental administration in order to determine common strategies. *Chefs de projet* (19) could be appointed by the *préfet* to manage short-term projects by making several *services déconcentrés* cooperate. All these mechanisms pointed at the coordination strategy of the French government which emerged: the deconcentration of services to territorial organized administrations combined with strong coordination and integration mechanisms at these levels in order to compensate for poor coordination at the level of central ministries (Crozier and Trosa 1992; Direction générale 1990, 1994). Another important evolution in this period was the privatization of several former public activities, which proceeded throughout the 1990s (20). It was embedded in an intellectual debate in which the 1994 Picq report on the responsibility and the organization of the State was a key document.

9.3 The period 1994–7

The Chirac presidency, elected in 1994, began making initiatives in 1995 (Gremion 1996). In line with the *'Comité interministériel de l'administration territoriale (CIATER)* (21) which was established as a trade-off committee between the agendas of decentralization and deconcentration, one more

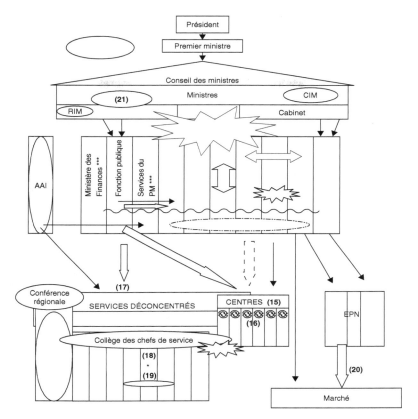

Legend CIM: Interministerial Committees; RIM: Réunions Interministérielles; AAI: Independent Administrative Authorities; PM: Prime Minister; EPN: Etablissements Publics Nationaux (National Public Bodies)

(15)   *Centres de responsabilité*
(16)   *Projet de service* (strategic service-delivery project)
(17)   *Déconcentration'* to *services déconcentrés* (previously *services extérieurs*)
(18)   *Collège des Chefs de Service*
(19)   *Chefs de projet*
(20)   Privatization (*Entreprises publiques*)
(21)   CIATER (*Comité Interministériel de l'Administration Territoriale*)

Figure 9.2   Specialization and coordination in France 1989–94

step was taken in reforming the state. The modernization of the state was somewhat reoriented as '*Réforme de l'Etat*' (Institut international d'administration publique 1996; Albertini and Silicani 1997). The *Comité interministériel pour la Réforme de l'Etat* (CIRE) **(22)** was created in 1995 at the highest level. Deconcentration of functions proceeded with the devolution of competencies concerning human resources management and the financial control on the *Etablissements Publics de l'Etat*. An initiative to strengthen the decision-making power of the prefect was blocked by the fall of the cabinet. Efforts to merge *services déconcentrés* also failed because of resistance within these structures **(23)**. In some cases *'Pôles de Compétence'* **(24)** were established (1994) between the *services déconcentrés*: these centralizing bodies encompassed the regional and departmental *services déconcentrés*, local authorities and civil society and aimed at solving problems by defining common strategies and operational plans. Again this initiative marked the importance of the level of the *services déconcentrés* in achieving a coordinated government policy.

9.4   The period 1997–2005

In 1997 the *Gauche plurielle* of Prime Minister Lionel Jospin (1997–2002) came to power. The *Réforme de l'Etat* entered its second more intensive phase. Several reports guided these reforms (Santel 1998 as director-general of DIRE; Mauroy in 2002 about decentralization; Carnenac in 2001 on e-government). These reports laid out principles for change and were the foundation for attempts at continued modernization (Fauroux et al. 2000; Institut de management public 2002). The *Comité interministériel pour la Réforme de l'Etat (CIRE)* still led the reforms and was supported by the new *Délégation interministérielle à la Réforme de l'Etat (DIRE)* **(25)**. The DIRE had highly ranked civil servants in each ministry who gathered in the *Collège des hauts Fonctionnaires de Modernisation et de Déconcentration (HFMD)* **(26)**. This concertation body had also an important role for cultural coordination within government, and was used to stimulate support for reform throughout government. Moreover networks of high-ranking civil servants were created by organizing meetings to share experiences and information. Examples of such networks were: *le réseau des modernisateurs* (modernizers' network); *l'association des hauts responsables informatiques dans l'administration* (association of key responsible individuals on e-government); *les clubs de la gestion des ressources humaines ou de la gestion publique* (management clubs on human resources, or public management), *le club de l'évaluation* (evaluation club) and others **(27)**.

E-government became a new priority. The e-administration efforts were coordinated in 1998 by the *Comité Interministériel pour la Société de*

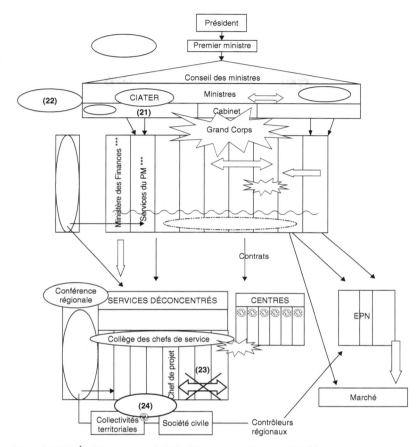

Legend EPN: Établissements Publics Nationaux (National Public Bodies); CIATER: Comité Interministériel de l'administration territoriale

(22) *Comité interministériel pour la Réforme de l'Etat* (CIRE)
(23) Failed merger of *services déconcentrés*
(24) *Pôles de Compétence*

Figure 9.3 Specialization and coordination in France 1994–7

l'Information (CISI) **(28)**. One of the first projects was the establishment of an interministerial intranet **(29)**. At the territorial level the *Système d'Information Territorial* (SIT) **(30)** was developed (2000) in order to enhance information exchange between the *services déconcentrés*. In 2001 the Carnenac Report continued to reflect upon e-government (Lasserre

178

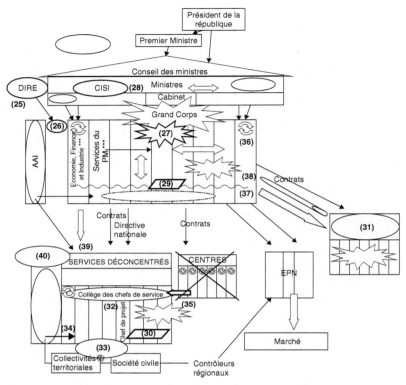

Legend DIRE: Délégation interministérielle à la Réforme de l'Etat; CISI: Comité interministériel pour la société de l'information; AAI: Independent Administrative Authorities; PM: Prime Minister; EPN: Établissements Publics Nationaux (National Public Bodies)

(25) *Délégation interministérielle à la Réforme de l'Etat* (DIRE)
(26) *Collège des Hauts Fonctionnaires de Modernisation et de Déconcentration* (HFMD)
(27) Modernization networks: *réseau des modernisateurs, l'association des hauts responsables informatiques dans l'administration, les clubs de la gestion des ressources humaines ou de la gestion publiques, le club de l'évaluation* (modernizer's network, association of key responsible individuals on e-government, management clubs on human resources, or public management, evaluation club, and others)
(28) *Comité interministériel pour la Société de l'Information* (CISI)
(29) Interministerial intranet
(30) *Système d'Information Territorial* (SIT)
(31) *Services à Compétences Nationales*

(*Continued*)

(32) *Chefs de Projets*
(33) *Pôles de Compétence*
(34) *Délégations interservices*
(35) *Centres de Responsabilité*
(36) *Programmes pluriannuels de Modernisation* (PPM, per ministry), and *Projet territorial de l'Etat* (per *département*)
(37) LOLF (*Loi Organique relative aux Lois de Finance*)
(38) ACCORD (*Application Coordonnée de Comptabilisation, d'Ordonnancement et de Règlement de la Dépense de l'Etat*) (Financial software for expenses management)
(39) *Décret relatif aux pouvoirs des préfets, à l'organisation et à l'action des services de l'Etat dans les régions et les départements* (decree to grant more power to regional and departmental prefects)
(40) *Comité de l'administration régionale*
(41) Decree creating a Directorate-General for State Modernization (*Direction de la modernisation de l'Etat DGME*) abolishing *la Délégation à la modernisation de la gestion publique et des structures de l'Etat (DMGPSE)*, *la Délégation aux usagers et aux simplifications administratives (DUSA)*, *l'Agence pour le développement de l'administration électronique (ADAE)* and *la Direction de la réforme budgétaire (DRB)*

Figure 9.4   Specialization and coordination in France 1997–2005

and Chantepie 2000). Another reform instituted shortly after the beginning of the third millennium concerned the new, more flexible, budget system: budget rules were made less strict and ministries were obliged to complement the budget cycle with the formulation of objectives and norms with respect to outputs and outcomes.

The deconcentration process was intensified by transferring numerous competencies (Sapin 2002). In 1997 a new form of organization emerged to take care of tasks at supra-departmental level, the *Services à Compétences nationales* (**31**). Such operational services were controlled by contracts and had high levels of management autonomy. In 1999 decrees defined the role of the *préfet* as the central coordinating function. These laws distinguished four mechanisms of coordination for the *services déconcentrés* (ranked from a low to a high level of integration: Projects and *Chefs de projets* (**32**), *Pôles de Compétence* (**33**), *Délégation interservices* (**34**) (the creation of a common top management for services), and the merger of organizations (including the *Centres de responsabilité* (**35**) (Cour des comptes 2003).

A last priority of the second phase of the reform was the introduction in 1998 of multi-year strategic management at the central level

(*Programmes Pluriannuels de Modernisation* (PPM) per ministry) and at the departmental level (*Projet territorial de l'Etat*) **(36)**. At the end of the period the steering powers of central ministries over the line ministries became less strict and detailed.

Finally, a crucial coordinating mechanism was the August 2001 law, called LOLF (*Loi Organique relative aux Lois de Finance*) **(37)** which is a coordinating and innovative reform programme. It took four years, from 1998 to 2001, to prepare a reform of the 1959 ordinance. Another four years, from January 2002 to 2005, were taken to implement this 'financial constitution' of the state. From January 2006, LOLF has been fully applied. LOLF follows a more transparent logic of missions, programmes and actions. It also aims at making managers more responsible (Braun 2001; Trosa and Crozier 2002; LOLF 2006; X 2006).

In January 2002 a new *Service à compétence nationale 'ACCORD' (Application coordonnée de comptabilisation, d'ordonnancement et de règlement de la dépense de l'Etat)* **(38)** was created as part of the Budget Reform Directorate. The purpose of this service (which was initially launched in 1996, but developed from 2001) was to integrate within a unified electronic environment all actors in the financial chain of expenses (managers, *ordonnateurs,* financial *contrôleurs* and accountants).

In April 2004 a crucial Decree related to the power of prefects, the organization and action of state services in regions and departments (*Décret relatif aux pouvoirs des préfets, à l'organisation et à l'action des services de l'Etat dans les régions et les départements)* **(39)** was activitated. This Decree renewed the action framework of the territorial state administration which was established following the 1982 decentralization. The implementation of LOLF resulted in new types of management dialogues between the central and the deconcentrated administration. The role of the prefect was strengthened to give tools for interservice delegation, and for managing more effectively interministerial action at the local – that is, regional and departmental – level (Rémond et al. 2002).

The regional prefect is the guardian of the coherence of state service action at the regional level. For that purpose he animates and coordinates the departmental prefects. The regional prefect decides, after having consulted the *'Comité de l'administration régionale'* **(40)**, on the strategic state action project in the region (Chaty 1997). The regional prefect is assisted by a secretary-general for regional affairs, the *'chefs de pôles régionaux de l'Etat',* and the *'chefs ou responsables des services déconcentrés des administrations civiles de l'Etat à compétence* *régionale'*. The departmental prefect decides, after having consulted the *'Collège des Chefs de Service'* on the strategic state action project in the department.

In June 2004 the new budget architecture of the state was presented by the government at the Council of Ministers. Two new interministerial missions were created. This resulted ultimately in a budget with 47 missions, of which 10 have an interministerial capacity, and 158 programmes. The general budget has 34 missions (including nine interministerial), 132 programmes and almost 580 actions. Several of these are coordinated by the regional and departmental prefects. A methodological guide for performance was developed jointly by the government, parliament, Court of Audit, and the interministerial committee for programme auditing. This document emphasised the development of a shared method (*une méthode partagée*).

In December 2005 a Decree created a Directorate-General for State Modernization (*Direction générale de la Modernisation de l'Etat* [DGME]) **(41)** within the Ministry of Economics, Finance and Industry. This DG is responsible to the minister in charge of Budget and State Reform and absorbs four existing structures in charge of reforming the state: the *Délégation à la modernisation de la gestion publique et des structures de l'Etat* (DMGPSE), the *Délégation aux usagers et aux simplifications administratives* (DUSA), *l'Agence pour le développement de l'administration électronique* (ADAE) and the *Direction de la Réforme budgétaire* (DRB). DGME coordinated, assisted and stimulated administration at the interministerial level. From 1 January 2006 LOLF was generally applied and replaced the 1959 ordinance (Documentation français 2006). In 2006 the LOLF and ACCORD projects were merged and replaced by CHORUS from 2009.

9.5 Conclusion

In 1980 the French government was organized along hierarchical lines and suffered from siloization (a system of separate vertical structures that inhibit knowledge-sharing and collaboration), which was countered by a system of cabinet committees and linked bodies. The emphasis shifted during the period 1980–2000 from the central level to the level of regions and departments. One aim of the deconcentration processes and the strengthening of the *services déconcentrés* was to enable a better coordination of centrally set and 'departmentalized' policies at the *département* and regional level. The establishment of coordinating functions (such as the *préfet*), concertation bodies, information systems and strategic management enhanced coordination at the *département* level. Through the *Réformes de l'Etat* somewhat similar mechanisms were established at the level of the ministries. Traditionally an important mechanism was cultural coordination; this mechanism was used in new forms to spread reform ideas throughout the administration. One category of fragmented bodies remained untouched by reforms: the highly heterogeneous and hard-to-control public enterprises (Dupuy and Thoenig 1985).

Several mechanisms of specialization and coordination were used. First, competencies were reshuffled, horizontally and vertically. The distribution of competencies among the ministries followed the distribution of competencies among ministers. If the distribution among ministers changed (due to a change of government, say), then the interdepartmental structure had to adapt. Central ministries lost duties in favour of the departmental *services extérieurs*, but at the same time they tried to slow this process. Mainly centralized services took advantage of the *Centres de Responsabilités*. In 1998 a hybrid form was agreed upon for services that had to remain at the national level but at the same time needed a certain degree of autonomy: the *Services à Compétences Nationales*.

A nearly continuous wave of privatization emerged from 1984 onwards. France had a long and strong tradition of governmental involvement in its economy, and the reforms beginning in the last portion of the 20th century did not end that involvement, but they certainly did reduce it. The lack of uniformity of the statutes of the *Etablissements publics* led to a situation where there was no transparency in regard to these statutes and the legislation related to them. Consequently, the central administration was *de facto* not capable of knowing what was happening in the *Etablissements public* and was unable to control them. The lack of clear arrangements led to uncontrolled conflicts of interest between and within the *Etablissements publics*.

Increased autonomy of the *services extérieurs* due to the process of deconcentration (since 1992) was also part of the change. Autonomization allowed for increasing coordination among the *services extérieurs* and thereby for an improvement of service delivery. The reforms suffered from the lack of a clear-cut separation between the deconcentrated and the decentralized government and from the lack of clarity about whether they did or did not have a hierarchical position in relation to the region and the department. This led to uncertainty and experiments going beyond the law.

Obviously control and steering have been traditionally very strong in France, again horizontally and vertically. The lines of competencies between ministers and ministries are traditionally based on a one-to-one relation. Consequently, each reallocation of competencies between ministers provoked a departmental reshuffling at the next level. The relation between the political and interdepartmental level is regulated by the political cabinets that forward the instructions of the minister to the ministry and the departments, and functions as a buffer between the minister and the administration.

The horizontal role of the horizontal ministries and services (finance and public service) is weak because of silos and compartmentalization. The ministries still have to take into account the rules and supervision recommendations of the *Autorités adminisitratives indépendantes* that are put in charge by the government of the monitoring of strict compliance with the rules of a given field. At the moment of the preparatory process of the budget, the Ministry of Finance executes an important coordination function. Due to its position of being the leader of the cabinet majority, the Prime Minister has a hierarchical position *vis-à-vis* his ministers. When there is no cohabitation, the President occupies a higher position for the same reasons. In the case of cohabitation, the President can only influence the government in relation to the issues he is qualified for. The Council of Ministers is the highest and most important body for policy coordination; coordination takes place at this level and is transferred to the ministries by guidelines and instructions.

Some ministries (not all) have secretaries-general or directors-general at their disposal who are charged with the coordination of some or all directorates of the ministries or with the direct steering and coordination of the *services externes* within the scope of a special project. The coordination within the ministry is nevertheless predominantly based on hierarchy-type mechanisms.

The *préfet* is the key position for territorial policy-making. S/he represents the French government and is charged with the coordination of the *services extérieurs*. In order to do so, s/he occupies a hierarchical position in relation to the *services extérieurs*. Moreover, since 1995 s/he is responsible for the organization of the financial control of the *Etablissements publics* (through regional inspectors). At the level of the *services extérieurs*, the prefect can appoint a project manager within the framework of a specific project, who is in charge of the coordination of the activities of several *services extérieurs*. The public companies (*Etablissements Public à Caractère Commercial et Industriel*) generally are controlled through a board, as is the case for private companies. The other EPs and *services extérieurs* fall under the authority of a chairman (the *Chef de service* of the *services extérieurs*).

France was always very hierarchical, but also emphasized the importance of advisory and consultative bodies. Despite the hierarchical position of the Prime Minister, government policy is partly prepared and established by the interministerial committees. These committees, for instance, prepared and steered the deconcentration process and the e-government policy. Meetings between cabinet members and ministers frequently take place in order to fine-tune their common activities. The government is advised by important advisory bodies such as the Council of State, the *Conseil Economique et Social*, the *Conseil supérieur de la Magistrature*, the *Conseil Supérieur de la Défence*, and others.

The *Administrations de Missions* often play an important role as consultative and advisory bodies for the project they are charged with. Nevertheless, these entities have lost a lot of their coordination power since the end of the 1970s. Nowadays, they are mostly linked to a ministry and they have a coordination function at the interdepartmental level. Most of the time, the *Autorités administratives indépendantes* were able to use substantial expertise in their sphere of action. They can be used by the ministries as a frame of reference. Obviously, each ministry makes use of its own set of advisory bodies.

At the territorial level, a broad range of advisory entities are available to the *préfet*: the *Conférence administrative régionale* that regroups all administrative services of a region; the *Collège des Chefs de Service* that encompasses all *Chefs de service* of a department or a region; and the *Pôles de Compétence*. However, it must be said that these potential coordination structures have not been used enough, nor in optimal ways, and hence coordination as this level of government has not been as strong as it might have been. The deconcentration of services to territorial organized administrations, combined with strong coordination and integration mechanisms at these levels in order to compensate for the lack of coordination at the level of central ministries, has been the dominant model in France (Maisi et al. 1991; Hoffmann-Martinot and Wollmann 2006).

France also has a considerable tradition of strategic multi-annual planning and collective strategies. The *Programmes pluri-annuels de Modernisation* (PPM) were introduced in 1998 in order to get a better overview regarding state reform at the ministerial level and to introduce the concept of strategic planning within the ministries. The PPM suffered from two major drawbacks: a vague split between the strategy of the reform programmes and the strategy for daily policy-making; and a lack of interdepartmental strategic planning for daily policy-making.

Limited trials of strategic planning have to be linked with the *Centres de Responsabilités*, where departments gained a wider management autonomy in exchange for the commitment to realise a given output. From 2000 onwards all the regions were using their *Projet territorial de l'Etat* that could develop a strategy for all regional and departmental *services extérieurs* of the region. The *Pôles de Compétence* developed a common strategy for all services and organizations involved (but this remains rather limited). LOLF was explicitly designed to link strategy and operation, and its implementation is growing.

The use of information systems as coordinating mechanisms is rather recent. The CISI (founded in 1998) developed an ambitious e-government policy and provided support for all e-initiatives within the administration. At this level its main result was putting into practice the AdEr (*Administration en Réseaux*) in 2000. At the territorial level the *Services d'Information territoriaux* were established, their main reason for existence being the exchange of information between services and the realization of a 'one-stop office'. This whole shift also had a significant legal implication. However, the direct steering of the *services extérieurs* and of the EPs (by means of guidelines and circular letters) was gradually replaced by general and yearly frameworks (*Directives Nationales d'Orientation*).

A shared professional culture is another common denominator in the French case. The corps – and especially the *Grand Corps* – guarantee a certain interdepartmental cultural coherence with their uniformity of training, recruitment and career development. These corps have saddled French administration with privileged castes, which complicates general HR management. Moreover, conflicts exist between different corps. The *Grand Corps* guarantees a certain level of peace between political and administrative spheres by using informal networks. New networks of civil servants situated around specific issues (policy evaluation, state reform, ICT) were created between 1997 and 2002 in order to facilitate the exchange of information and experiences. Even if finance and budget always were very much well-controlled, a crucial and final recent driver of reform, only recently developed, is financial and budgetary coordination through LOLF. It is not a coincidence that it is rightly called a 'financial constitution for the country'.

In conclusion, in a 25-year period (1981–2005) France has slowly, indirectly (through regions and *départements*), and in a very complex way moved from a limited number of well-controlled organizations to a system that is more fragmented at its lower levels (regions and *départements*). The level of consolidation was always safeguarded at these lower levels through the coordinating roles of councils, but also by the regional and *département* prefects. The centralized stereotype of the French system has been altered to some extent, but the perceived importance of coordination and uniformity has persisted.

10
Coordination in Belgium (1980–2005)

In Belgium after the Second World War there was a need for public administration to recover, to further develop and modernize the basic principles of the public service (uniformity, equality, legal security, independence, seniority) as expressed in the Camu Statute (1937) and the Secretariat for Permanent Recruitment (1938) (François 1998). Legislation on the issue of organizing autonomy and the control mechanisms of para-state institutions was approved in March 1954. It was applied to all institutions providing social security, but also to public banks, and to many institutions that had been granted autonomy. The initial four clear and distinct categories (A [close to the minister], B, C, and D [distant from the minister]) became blurred and resulted in a myriad of *sui generis* types of autonomy and control. However, the Statute Gilson (1964) was applied to several of these para-state organizations, for example, in 1977 to all organizations within the social security system.

Belgium is a consensual and pillarized society, and its administration is heavily politicized (Depré et al. 1966; Depré 1973; Molitor 1974; Van Hassel 1974). In many cases consultation became part of official procedures and evolved into binding advice structures. The pillarized structure of interests (Christian Democrats, socialists and conservatives) was administratively institutionalized and became part of the coordination mechanisms for policy design, decision-making, implementation and, if that was the case, evaluation. Nevertheless, many advisory boards were abolished in 1977.

Since the end of the 1970s, fiscal pressure and the irreversible shift to federalism have significantly impacted the way the public sector is organized and functions (François and Molitor 1987). In particular, most domestic service delivery functions have been moved to the regional governments, and there have been significant attempts to improve the efficiency of all public organizations.

10.1   1980–5: Static start

At a political level, decisions in Belgian government are taken by the Council of Ministers by consensus. Sensitive and important measures are discussed at the level of the 'Core Cabinet' (*Kern*) (1) comprising the Prime Minister and all the Vice-Prime Ministers. This inner cabinet acts as a coordinating nucleus and a collective decision-making body ahead of the Council of Ministers. At this level Inter-Cabinet Groups (ICGs) (2) and the Interministerial Committees (IMCs) (3), which have an official status, serve as preparatory bodies for public policies. The Council of State (*Conseil d'Etat*) (4) also has a role in coordinating new and existing legislation

Decision-making in the Council of Ministers is augmented by the wide range of Advisory Boards and High Councils (5), for example, the Central Council for Trade and Industry (*Conseil Central de l'Economie*), the Labour Council (*Conseil National de l'Emploi*), the Commission for Banking and Finance (*Commission Bancaire*). These organizations are considered 'official' advisory bodies of the government, and may play an important role as consultative bodies, including all relevant external interest groups such as trade unions and employers' organizations.

The relation between the political and administrative levels is guaranteed by large personal ministerial secretariats, almost mini-administrations, called 'ministerial *cabinets*' (6). They have a quasi-hierarchical relationship to public administration (providing guidance, decision, control and steering, and evaluation). A one-to-one steering relationship between a *cabinet* and an administrative structure is usually the rule, but because of departmental stability, co-steering and double steering (the political watchdog function of the *cabinets*) frequently occurs, also because of ministerial portfolio shifts and clustering (De Borger 1988; Suetens and Walgrave 1999; Pelgrims 2001, 2002; Brans et al. 2005).

Since 1982, ministers for the Regions (Flemish, Brussels, and Walloon) and Communities (Flemish, Francophone and German-speaking) have no longer been part of the national government. Regional and community institutions are like other parliamentary governments, including a parliament, government and administration. Numerous competencies have been transferred from the central (federal) level to the regional and community levels (which constitutionally are at the same level as the federal level), and several rounds of 'federalization' have emptied the central box of competencies, and in turn have affected the structure and functioning of the federal level (7) (Hertecant 1990; van Hoorick 1990).

Hardly any interdepartmental coordination existed in 1980. The most important coordination instrument was the budget process, especially during the period of austerity and fiscal pressure (1981–5) when budget cuts were inevitable. The budget procedure was the means *par excellence* to coordinate all measures, including savings strategies (8). For coordinated budget implementation the role of the *Inspection de Finance* (9) was very effective in enforcing horizontal controls. This austerity also included suspending recruitment, defining a yearly quota for personnel, restricting the number of top-level functions, and starting a mobility programme, a system of training and a database of civil servants (10).

In this period the Service for General Services Administration and the Directorate General of Selection and Training were transferred to the Ministry of Internal Affairs (11). The central information system, BISTEL, which coordinated and installed information management, was established in 1982 (12). The generic character of the General Statute for the civil service (Camu in 1937 and Gilson in 1964), already expanded to the para-state institutions for social security, was further refined for all civil servants (13) (François 1987) The institutions established according to the March 1954 legislation were granted different levels of autonomy and with different control mechanisms. There was an increasing level of autonomy varying from categories A (limited autonomy and tight control), to B, C and D (higher autonomy and looser control).

Institutions belonging to the A category had the most limited degree of autonomy, since the minister had full power over these institutions. The institutions in categories B, C and D were subordinated to the supervision (control and steering) of their functional ministry and the Ministry of Finance (through *Commissioners of the Government*) (14). The commissioner has the right to suspend all decisions of the institution if such a decision has violated the law, public interest, statutes or government policy. Public enterprises were then divided between categories A and B although each had a specific statute. The general legal framework was never fully and strictly applied, and many subcategories were added over time. The creation of non-profit organizations was also an effort to bypass the elaborate law of 1954.

Collaboration (consultative and advisory bodies) with the pillarized civil society was a sociological fact in the consensual system (15), especially in the fields of employment and economic policy, but services related to social security (unemployment benefits paid by trade unions; medical reimbursements paid by private *mutualité*; private risk insurances), health care (hospital services) and education (schools) also were components of a pillarized system.

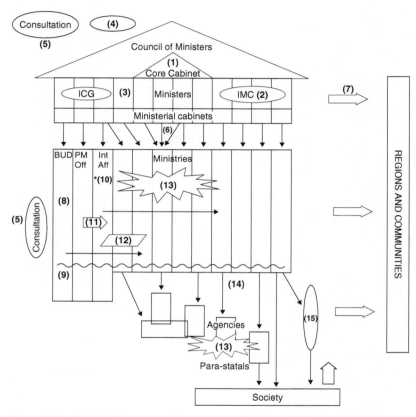

Legend IMC: Interministerial Committees; BUD: Ministry of Budget and Finances; PM Off: Prime Minister's Office; Int Aff: Ministry of Internal Affairs

(1) Core Cabinet within the Council of Ministers
(2) Interministerial Committees (IMC)
(3) Inter-Cabinet Groups (ICG)
(4) *Conseil d'Etat*
(5) Various bodies (High Councils Boards) for consultation
(6) *Cabinet Ministériel*

(*Continued*)

(7)   Devolution, transferring competencies to Regions and Communities (second round)
(8)   Minister of Budget and Budget Administration
(9)   *Inspection de Finance*
(10) Budget-driven coordination of personnel policy
(11) Transferring General Services Administration and DG Training and Selection to Internal Affairs
(12) BISTEL (ICT)
(13) Deepening and expanding the coverage of the Personnel Statute
(14) Confirming the role of *Commissaire du Gouvernement*
(15) Pillarized consultation and decision bodies

Figure 10.1   Specialization and coordination in Belgium 1980–5

10.2   1985–90: The first round of initiatives

In the first round of reform the central ministries were again involved in structural reshuffling of competencies, based on the further federalization of Belgium (third state reform, 1988–9). In 1989 the coalition partners agreed to establish the Brussels–Capital Region, meaning that the minister and ministry of the Brussels-Capital Region and the two secretaries of state disappeared from the government **(16)**. Further, competencies related to industrial policy, that is, the five so-called 'national industries' (steel, textiles, coal, glass and harbours), as well as public works, were transferred to the Regions. In 1989–90 the remaining competencies and parts of the administration of the federal Ministry for Public Works were merged with the Ministry for Post and Telecommunication into the new Ministry for Communication and Infrastructure **(17)**.

Programme budgeting was also introduced in 1985 **(18)**, and ministries had greater budgetary freedom. The reform programme, designed to quantify financially policy programmes, also intended to make the budgeting process more transparent, develop a tool for better service management, and develop a structured database that could be useful as a policy and management instrument. The programme budgets were added to the traditional budget as an appendix from 1986 until 1989. From 1989 onward the programme budget replaced the traditional budgeting format. However, the traditional budget structure did not disappear but remained pragmatically integrated, and an input-based information system and authorization was applicable. The School of the Ministry of Finance also was established.

Between 1985 and 1988 a State Secretary for Modernization and Information was added to the Prime Minister´s Office, and in 1986 the related Secretariat for Modernization and Computerization of the Public

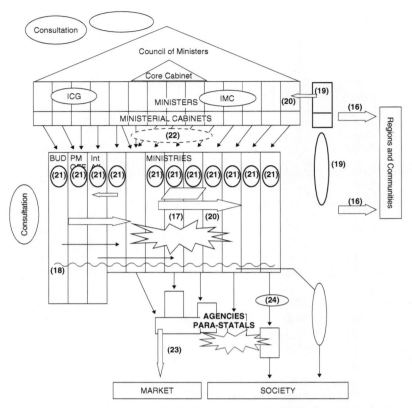

Legend ICG: Inter-Cabinet Groups; IMC: Interministerial Committees; BUD: Ministry of Budget and Finances; PM: Prime Minister; Int Aff: Ministry of Internal Affairs

(16) Devolution, transferring competencies to Regions and Communities (third round)
(17) Merging two ministries
(18) Programme budgeting and the School of the Ministry of Finance
(19) State Secretary of Modernization, State Secretariat
(20) Minister of *Fonction Publique*, transfer of competencies from the State Secretary to Internal Affairs
(21) Modernization Cells
(22) College of Secretaries-General of Ministries
(23) Privatization of airport facilities
(24) College of Administrators-General of Social Security Para-state Institutions

Figure 10.2   Specialization and coordination in Belgium 1985–90

Services was created. Initially this Secretariat of State was not an ordinary administration and was not linked to a specific line ministry **(19)**. It was a staff organization that was specifically responsible for developing modernization proposals. In the coalition agreement of Martens VI (1985–7) the goals of this Secretariat of State were to ensure a greater decisiveness of services and a higher motivation of civil servants, and to ensure higher productivity of the public services. In 1988 the Martens VIII government resigned. With the new government and coalition (Martens IX) in 1989, the Secretariat of State disappeared, and responsibility for modernizing the Public Service was transferred to the Minister of Internal Affairs. A new Minister of *Fonction Publique* was created **(20)**, however, but without a matching ministry of *Fonction Publique* (Hondeghem, 1990).

The Secretariat of State established modernization 'cells' (CMC, *Cellules de Modernisation*) in each ministry as project groups and task forces in order to provide technical assistance to civil servants for defining goals and improving management, to formulate recommendations to facilitate priority-setting, and to guide the modernization activities, evaluate them and formulate propositions in relation to managerial methods and techniques **(21)** (Legrand 1990). Another achievement of the Secretariat of State was the establishment of a college of all Secretaries-General (*Collège des Secrétaires Généraux*) **(22)**. Initially it was weak but it ultimately played an active role in modernization policy. A Royal Decree of 1989 officially recognized the College as the advisory body for the government with respect to HR (human resources)-related matters and the general administration of the state.

The entry of the Liberal Conservatives into the national government prompted discussion of privatizing public companies. However, the discussion was blocked by the resistance of the Socialist opposition and differences of opinion with the Christian Democrats. Nevertheless, the Minister of Communication succeeded in privatizing indirectly part of the Public Airway by creating BTAC Inc (Brussel Airport Terminal Company) **(23)**. This company was responsible for realizing and (particularly) financing the expansion of Brussels International Airport. Despite this, large-scale privatization was (still) out of the question. Among the para-state institutions of type D (social security), the *Collège des Administrateurs-Généraux* was created in 1989, containing the heads of these institutions **(24)**. Initially the *Collège* mainly had a representative and coordinating function in relation to the central administration and the political world.

The reforms during this period added some important coordination programmes. Most of these were procedural, especially in the budget process, but there were also some attempts to create coordinating structures. These coordination activities were to some extent in contrast to the decentralization going on at the constitutional level.

10.3   1990–5: the Tobback Plan

The new constitution of 1992 turned Belgium into a federal state. Again, competencies were transferred to the regions and communities after the *Saint-Michels* agreements (fourth reform, 1992–3) **(25)**. In 1994 the Ministry of Self-employment and the Ministry of Agriculture merged into a new Ministry of Agriculture and Self-employment **(26)**. Moreover, the number of ministers was limited to 15 by the new constitution **(27)**.

In 1993 the Minister of Internal Affairs launched a plan, the so-called 'Tobback Plan', to introduce a new job culture within the civil service. Based on a thorough audit (the Radioscopy of the Public Services) the main purposes were to introduce a new culture (management) to restructure the federal civil service and to increase efficiency. The Tobback strategy was a turning point for managing federal administration. For the first time cultural and organizational changes were discussed. Moreover, it was the first political project in Belgium that was management-oriented, and it also gave a new impetus to renewing the public service. One key decision was to streamline and create more flexibility for the elements of the Personnel Statute, resulting in the General Principles Royal Decree **(28)**. In 1994 this Royal Decree contained general principles for administrative and financial arrangements of the civil servants, and stimulated simplification of the federal civil service with limited degrees of freedom for remuneration, promotions, ranking systems and mobility (Maes 1994). In 1993 a Royal Decree strengthened the role of the *Collège des Secrétaires Généraux* **(29)** as a common management body for the federal administration.

The *Collège* became a consultative and coordinating body where different secretaries of state fine-tuned their own policies in conjunction with each other. In its first policy plan (ACTOR I in 1995), it made the following comments about the Royal Decree of 1993:

Thanks to this support the College was able to start with its new job it was assigned to by the Royal Decree of September 6th, 1993, i.e., being responsible for the interdepartmental coordination by applying all measures with respect to HR policy or the functioning of the services for which several administrations are involved. It is a real duty of management that goes beyond providing advice. (Collège de Secrétaires Généraux 1995: 5)

The *Collège* wanted to transform itself into a genuine horizontal steering body of the federal administration to design new management strategies, based on the identification of problems at the field level, to be a fully fledged platform for political authorities to formulate public management reforms and to be a strategic actor in projects with an interdepartmental dimension.

However, the *Collège* recognized that in order to fulfil these roles, a cultural change was needed, especially in the distribution of responsibilities between administration and ministerial cabinets. These cabinets, which were linked to individual ministers, were considered to inhibit the efforts towards coordination driven by the administration. In 1989, the Minister of Finance proposed introducing zero-based budgeting (ZBB) **(30)**. The ministries supported these experiments but the system was abandoned in 1991. Between 1990 and 1994 the use of memoranda was introduced, including a yearly selection of programmes that were seriously examined by the Ministry of Finance. The Ministry looked to select programmes with cross-departmental consequences and programmes with unfavourable financial results. After 1994 this instrument was gradually abandoned. Nevertheless the programme budget remained the main financial coordination instrument.

During this period, considerable efforts were made to improve HRM and ICT. In September 1991 the Advisory Board for Informatics was established **(31)**. It was made up of computer scientists and had to ensure the coordination of using ICT equipment and ICT calls for tender, of providing assistance with respect to ICT in general, and of realizing the general plan for computerization. Other initiatives were taken in order to manage information better within the federal civil service. The Cross Road Database for Social Security was established as a semi-governmental institution to coordinate all information related to social security. This institution organized information exchange between all organizations involved and the management of a general database for social security. The database connected several ministries (Social Affairs, Environment, Public Health), all para-state institutions (category D under the law of 1954) and private organizations **(32)**. In 1992 government decided to create a computerized database for civil servants. During 1993 and 1994, 83,000 individual index cards were

196

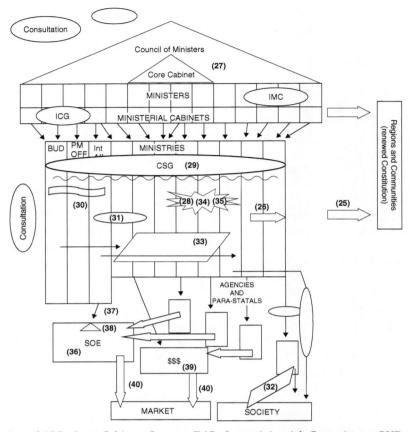

Legend ICG: Inter-Cabinet Groups; IMC: Interministerial Committees; BUD: Ministry of Budget and Finances; PM: Prime Minister; Int: Ministry of Internal Affairs; SOE: State-owned enterprises

(25) New Constitution in 1992 results in a federal state (fourth reform)
(26) Merger of two ministries (Self-employment and Agriculture)
(27) Reduction of the Council of Ministers to 15 positions
(28) Tobback Plan and General Principles Royal Decree
(29) Royal Decree strengthening the College of Secretaries-General
(30) Zero-based Budgeting and Financial Memoranda
(31) Advisory Board for Informatics
(32) Cross Road Database for Social Security
(33) Civil Servants Database
(34) Corps of Civil Service Advisers
(35) Charter for the Customer of Public Services, 1993

(*Continued*)

(36) Law establishing autonomous public companies (1991) evolving in public-law based *Société Anonyme* (1994–5)
(37) Contract management with the autonomous public companies
(38) Professionalizing the management of the autonomous public companies
(39) Law establishing financial holdings
(40) Privatization by selling shares from autonomous public companies and public banks

Figure 10.3   Specialization and coordination in Belgium 1990–5

completed with about ten items per civil servant. This database was based upon a decentralized architecture, and ministries were then charged with constructing their own computerized database and all databases were connected to the intranet. The Ministry of Internal Affairs was entitled to fulfil a controlling function, instead of completing the database itself (**33**).

In 1990 the Corps of Civil Service Advisers was established by Royal Decree and put under the Service for General Management (**34**). Its main duties, as an internal consultant, were to give advice related to the improvement of organizational and HR policy, to update instruments, methodologies or action plans in order to improve public services, and to maintain contacts with the various services, their leading civil servants and the trade unions. They became actively involved in the 1991 general audit (Radioscopy) of the federal public service, developing its methodology and monitoring its implementation. The project was compromised since it was directly linked to savings and to suspending hiring civil servants (Staes 1992; Polet 1999).

The Charter for the Customer of Public Services (**35**), established in 1993, was another initiative for cultural coordination. This charter defined the rights and duties of administration and citizens. Three fundamental features of public services were defined: transparency, flexibility and legal protection. The charter provided the operational framework ministries had to comply with when delivering public services (Berckx 1993; Bouckaert 1993; Vermeulen 1995; Franceus and Staes 1997).

Two major laws were also approved on organizing the structuring and functioning of autonomous public institutions. The first law (March 1991) applied to public autonomous companies (post, telecommunication, railways, airways) (**36**). This law was crucial because it relied on contracts (**37**). Boards and management teams were established (*conseil d'administration, comité de direction*) and business plans were required (*plan d'entreprise*) (**38**). Substantial autonomy was granted to these autonomous public enterprises on matters of personnel and industrial relations. Autonomous public organizations were also allowed to issue shares, limited by the rule that at least half of the shares and three-quarters of the voting rights remained in public hands. In 1994–5 public companies like Belgacom and the national railway company (NMBS/SNCB) could convert to a *société anonyme de droit public,* subject to commercial law.

In June 1991 government adopted another law reforming public credit and banking institutions (former category C of the 1954 law) **(39).** This law established two main holdings that regrouped all institutions around two important public credit and banking institutions (ASLK–CGER and *Crédit Communal*). These changes resulted from the start of the real political discussion about privatization. The new types of administration were intended to increase the competitiveness of public organizations in the market. In 1992 the government announced a first wave of sales of assets to the private sector. It was the start of the privatization and marketization process **(40).** A second wave of share sales took place in 1994–6.

10.4   1995–9: continuation of the efforts

In 1995 a new Ministry of Civil Service was created to introduce a new philosophy in relation to human resources management (HRM). For that purpose the Corps of Advisers of the Civil Service were turned into an internal consulting organization within the ministry but with operational autonomy (ABC, *Adviesbureau Bureau Conseil*) **(41)**. The new ministry became explicitly a horizontal ministry responsible for coordination of the activities related to HRM policies, advising government and the line ministries and line departments, developing new instruments and statutes, and delivering certain horizontal services (such as training and recruitment). However, the ministry retained one control function in relation to line departments – over compliance with statutes. A merger resulted in the creation of the Ministry of Social Affairs and Health Care in 1996 **(42)**, and in 1999 a Minister for Administrative Reform was appointed **(43)**. This marked the beginning of the Copernicus reforms. Also in 1995, at the level of the Chancellery, the existing information service INBEL was transformed into the Federal Information Service, and FEDENET, the new intranet, was installed **(44)**.

In 1997 the Minister of Civil Service, André Flahaut, announced his modernization programme. The main goal of this was to reconfirm and to put into practice the Tobback Plan (see above, Section 10.3).

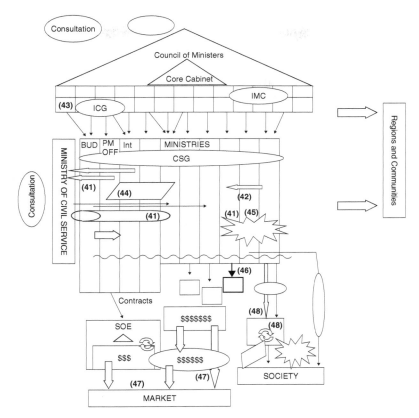

Legend ICG: Inter-Cabinet Groups; IMC: Interministerial Committees; BUD: Ministry of Budget and Finances; PM: Prime Minister; Int: Ministry of Internal Affairs; CSG: Committee of Secretary General; SOE: State-owned enterprises

(41) Establishment of Ministry of Civil Service and of *Advies Bureau Conseil* (ABC)
(42) Ministry of Social Affairs and Health Care
(43) Minister for Administrative Reform
(44) INBEL and FEDENET
(45) Plan Flahaut
(46) Agency for Administative Simplification, with Government Commissioner for Administrative Simplification; Agency for State Debt Control
(47) Federal Participation Company
(48) More autonomy and contracts for social security para-state organizations

Figure 10.4 Specialization and coordination in Belgium 1995–2000

The main accomplishments of this period were a renewed HRM strategy (recruitment, evaluation, mobility and training) and FEDENET, an updated ITC system **(45)** (Hondeghem 2000). Two agencies were created **(46)**. First, the Agency for Administrative Simplification (1998) was linked to the Prime Minister and secured a Government Commissioner in 1999; however, it had a high turnover of leadership. Second, the Agency for State Debt Control was established in 1998. Both agencies had a coordinating and horizontal scope, charged with consolidating fragmented initiatives for simplifying administrative procedures and debt management.

In the second half of the 1990s there was substantial privatization of public enterprises and public credit institutions **(47)**. The decisions were taken in 1993 and 1994 and as such the privatization operation was implemented. The Municipal Banking holding was transformed into a Federal Participation Company and was responsible for preparing the public credit institutions and the autonomous public enterprises for their privatization, a kind of 'waiting room'. De facto, the public credit institutions disappeared from the administrative scenery (either privatized or subsumed under the Federal Participation Company). Another important reform was the Royal Decree of 1997 which envisaged increasing the accountability of the Public Organizations of Social Security (former category D) **(48)**. By this Royal Decree autonomy was awarded to any para-state institution willing to enter into a management contract. The implementation of this Royal Decree remained void until 2002.

10.5   2000–5: Van den Bossche's Copernicus Plan (2000–3) and beyond

In 2000 the Copernicus reform plan was launched by Minister for the Civil Service and Modernization Luc Van den Bossche (Van den Bossche 2000). This reform foresaw drastic changes within the federal public administration (Bouckaert and François 1999; Bouckaert and Wauters 1999). At the political level, Copernicus intended to abolish the ministerial cabinets and replace them with political secretariats responsible for management and political support of the ministerial function **(49)**. A policy council, chaired by the minister, including external experts and civil servants, had an advisory function to the minister **(50)**. Policy preparation and design was transferred to an administrative cell, the *cellule stratégique*, under the direct supervision of the chairman of the board of directors of the Federal Public Service **(51)**. The minister preserved the right of injunction and appointment in relation to the members of the cell. In addition, each vice-prime minister received a 'cell for general coordination' for the different policy design cells **(52)**. The political–administrative relationships were not managed any more by political cabinets, but through direct relationships between the minister and the chairman of the Federal Public Service. In reality, however, cabinets remained since they are part of a deep-rooted political culture (Maesschalck et al. 2002; De Visscher 2003).

The minister was no longer able to prepare policy outside the administration without involving the Federal Public Service and its chairman. On the other hand the chairman had to act loyally *vis-à-vis* the minister if s/he wanted to obtain a positive evaluation. As such, this power equilibrium implies that both actors need each other and therefore are obliged to collaborate. For strategic planning, policy councils (advisory bodies) were established **(50)**. This council was scheduled to include the minister, as chair of this council, the chief of his secretariat, his Federal Public Service chairman and external experts. The purpose was to examine to what extent the minister's strategy matched reality and to check for the satisfactory strategic application of the operational plans of the Federal Public Service. A three-level strategy (short, medium and long-term) was associated with this council (strategic management).

At the central level Copernicus implied a profound reform of federal organizational structuring and functioning. It included a new division of tasks between the Federal Public Services **(53)**. There are three types of Federal Public Services (FPS) or 'ministries' – vertical, horizontal and programmatic. Three of the four horizontal Federal Public Services were established to support internal management (ICT, HR and Budget and Control) **(54)**. The fourth was the Prime Ministerial Chancellery, which focuses on supporting interministerial consultation and was responsible for following up decisions made by the 'cells for overall coordination' **(52)**. Policy preparation, design and implementation were also decentralized, to the board of directors of the FPSs. Decentralization of internal management (HR, ICT and Budget and Control) to the vertical FPSs resulted in a division of labour between the vertical and horizontal departments. The general rules and standards relating to these issues were determined by advisory groups composed of representatives of vertical FPSs. The competent horizontal FPSs were responsible only for providing backup for the consultation process and for the follow-up of the compliance with decisions taken. This resulted in a 'virtual matrix' **(55)**. The establishment of the programmatic Federal Public Services had a project ministry status. These were temporary, legislature-linked

202

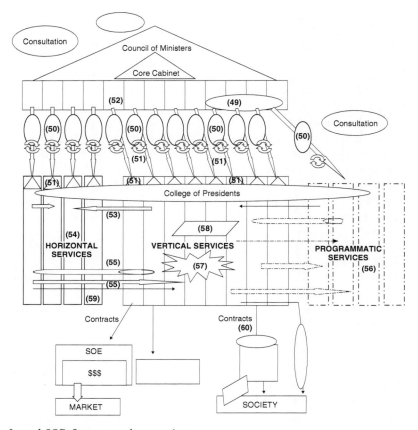

Legend SOE: State-owned enterprises

(49) Limitation of ministerial cabinets
(50) Policy Council per department
(51) Strategic capacity and board of directors per department
(52) Coordinating capacity at the vice-prime ministerial cabinet level
(53) Reshuffling of competencies between departments creating coherent packages
(54) Four horizontal departments
(55) Virtual matrix between vertical and horizontal departments
(56) Project-based Programmatic Federal Services
(57) HRM reform including mandates, evaluation, training
(58) E-government reforms
(59) Strategic plan-based financial systems with some flexibility
(60) Mandates for Social Security CEOs

Figure 10.5 Specialization and coordination in Belgium after 2000

'ministries' that either acted as a vertical FPS, coordinated actions of existing vertical FPSs, steered other FPSs or provided a service or product to other FPSs based on internal invoices (shared services) **(56)**. Finally within an FPS there was a board of directors with a chair.

Besides structural reforms, the Copernicus plan also had a considerable impact on the general coordination model. There was a thorough analysis and reform of internal processes within several FPSs the the application of Business Process Reengineering (Parys and Thijs 2003). There was a reform of HRM through the introduction of a mandate system for top-level functions, a new evaluation system and competence testing **(57)** (Nomden 2000; Parys 2001; Parys and Hondeghem 2005). A considerable effort in renewing the ICT infrastructure, the establishment of a new intranet (the Federal Metropolitan Area Network) and the launching of a new portal website (information management) was made **(58)**. On the financial-cycle side there was more emphasis on envelopes with a slight increase in flexibility. However, the internal audit function was not activated **(59)**.

The agency level was only affected because of the mandate system **(60)**. In 2002, the 1997 Royal Decree on strengthening accountability within the para-state Public Institutions for Social Security was implemented by concluding management contracts and by transferring management autonomy for ten institutions. For the remaining 'agencies' the Administrators-General (CEO) received time-limited personal mandates.

The ambitious Copernicus reform plan was intended to be realized over a three-year term. In general the new structure has been implemented, except for some key elements, including the abolition of political cabinets or installing internal audit cells. Some more flexibility has been achieved, including in HRM or envelope-based financial allocations. In short Copernicus was designed as a shock therapy for change and did result in some culture change, most notably in encouraging an openness to change in general and to re-engineering processes (Franceus 2004; Hondeghem and Depré 2005).

10.6 Conclusions

To summarize and understand the Belgian central level and its efforts in changing the system, some basic systemic features need to be taken into account. First, the politicization of the administration is significant, with ministerial *cabinets* being the major tool for coordinating the political and the administrative levels. Efforts to abolish these structures have failed and are an expression of a culture of interference and hierarchical control. A focus on the primacy of politics combined with efforts to professionalize the administrations in their capacity to propose, implement and evaluate policies. The *cabinets* remained an effective way of coordinating formal (hierarchy) and informal (network-culture) mechanisms.

Second, over the past 25 years Belgium turned incrementally into a federal system. Starting in the 1970s, several rounds of transferring competencies to the three regions (Flanders, Brussels and Wallonia) and the three communities (Flemish, Francophone and Germanophone) were realized in sometimes difficult circumstances. The viability of governments depended on the capacity to control these transfers of competencies and the related administrations and budgets. As a consequence, the Belgian central level was emptied in an ad hoc, incremental way. There was, of course, a simultaneous transfer of competencies to the European level. In many cases policy fields were spread over the central level on the one hand, and regions or communities on the other – for example, agriculture, the interior, employment. As a result, coordination problems were intrinsically part of the federalization process in two ways. First, at the federal level, the coherence of a department was increasingly reduced because of the transfer of parts of organizations according to a political rationale rather than a managerial one, or without taking policy coherence into account. Departments started looking like Swiss cheese, full of major holes. Although necessary, no solution based on merging and redesigning was politically possible. Second, regions and communities received new competencies, administrations and budgets and their newly acquired identity did not encourage them to coordinate across entities – except in Flanders, where the Flemish Community and the Flemish Region merged into one Flemish parliament, one Flemish government and one Flemish administration. The modernization dynamics of each of the six autonomous administrations (federal, Flemish, Brussels, Wallonia, Francophone and Germanophone) differed significantly (Bouckaert and Auwers 1999; Vancoppenolle and Legrain 2003; Van de Walle et al. 2005). This inhibited potential coordination between federal, regional and community entities.

Lack of external coordination became an expression of the independence and autonomy of regions and communities. In several cases the policies at the federal and the regional/community levels conflicted in their design and implementation. As a consequence, and especially during this long transition period, the system was relatively effective since it was not *'une société bloquée'*, but it was also rather inefficient, again because of difficulties of coordination.

There was and still is a high level of deconsolidation across the levels of government, for example in unemployment policy. However, the components remaining at the central level continue to be very hierarchical and consolidated. Increasingly it is perceived that the division of compentencies between central and regional/community levels is dysfunctional because of this lack of coherence of competencies (for example, repression is a federal responsibility and prevention is a community one), and because there is an increasingly diverging culture of policies and management which makes coordination almost impossible. It seems that only an 'open method of coordination' may provide some value-added.

Third, Belgium is a pillarized society where the tradition of taking consensual decisions is weakening. Coordinating different interests and groups occurred in the well-developed and institutionalized settings of advisers and councils. In some cases, such as in social security or employment policy, the government delegated competencies to make agreements and decisions. This resulted in external coordination based on networks of interest groups which are formally recognized in High Councils, Boards and Advisory Groups, but which also informally make agreements. The government and the administration facilitated these network-based coordinations. Even if the degree of pillarization is supposed to have decreased, there still exists a strong and institutionalized method of coordinating and streamlining decisions. As a consequence, service delivery for education and health remains part of a pillarized system, albeit within a competitive context. Network-based coordination resulted in building frameworks, and market-based coordination resulted in qualitative changes in service delivery.

Fourth, Belgian political and administrative elites were never very interested in managerial issues; the focus was always far more on macroeconomic and fiscal issues. This resulted in a very developed focus by the responsible politicians and civil servants on the budget department, and on the inspection of finance. At its highest the consolidated public Belgian debt was 138 per cent of GDP. The bottom-line target for federalism was the reduction of this debt. Accordingly, there was a very strict hierarchical coordination across all levels of government in relation to debt control (from local to central, including all autonomous organizations) as a macroeconomic issue. Meso-coordination (at the policy level) was difficult because of the political process of federalism. Micro-coordination was ignored as a managerial function and limited to legal requirements.

Fifth, while the focus on reforming was ever-present, it was cyclical. Reforms began rather late, were very visible in the second half of the 1980s and the beginning of the 1990s, but then slowed down. There was a second round of grand projects at the beginning of 2000 (Copernicus) which again slowed down about five years later. It is important to note that projects are linked to a government cycle and that there is a tradition in Belgium of eliminating the previous government's plan, even if the coalition remains the same. Copernicus is a good example of this. There is also a tradition of having plans for reform, with political and administrative components, but less of a tradition of implementation, let alone evaluation and the taking of corrective measures.

Sixth, fiscal stress has significantly determined the decisions taken. Taking market-type mechanisms on board in the public sector was more a matter of necessity than conviction. Apart from the EC/EU requirements to open markets, the main reason for transferring activities to the market or using MTM was fiscal stress, especially in relation to the Maastricht indicators (such as those capping consolidated debt and budgetary deficits). Improving services or changing coordination mechanisms were not determining objectives, but instead useful side-effects, of these pressures to reduce deficits and consolidated debts.

Seventh, although HTM is a crucial part of a culture of coordination, NTM is also essential, both internally for politics–administration coordination (for example, in relation to the ministerial cabinets), and externally among all the societal and pillarized actors in a governance context for the purposes of achieving consensual decision-making.

From a technical point of view the organizational setting has remained stable. There was also no movement towards disintegrating the central ministries into agencies. To a certain extent there has been an increase in the number of organizations because of the public enterprises that moved out of the ministries and were made fit for the market or, in some cases, ready for possible sale. The same applied to the social security para-state organizations where some e-government-based interface organizations were created. In all these circumstances there remained a stable, determining and high level of input and macroeconomic control. Several actors were involved at the ministerial level (Budget) – the Inspectorate of Finance, various government commissioners and the Court of Audit. The control levels were legally based and resource-focused but also included compatibility tests against government policy. Although most top civil servants have tenure and permanent functional positions, their political obedience also could guarantee strong network control. As a consequence the remaining parts of the federal administration remained stable in numbers and maintained a firm guidance function, using mostly hierarchical, but also network-based, control systems.

11
Coordination in the United States (1980–2005)

While politicians in almost any country might contest this claim, the federal government of the United States presents perhaps even more challenges to effective coordination than do governments in other countries. The American political system was designed by its founding fathers[1] to be 'all anchor and no sail'. To that institutionally divided and highly contentious political system has been added a bureaucratic system that is itself very divided, with the agencies being given a good deal of legal autonomy. These agencies also have developed sufficient political support from their clientele groups to develop and are able to maintain that autonomy (Carpenter 2001; Wolf 1997). In this administrative system some agencies are designed to be extremely independent, even though they exercise important public functions. Although almost all presidents since at least Franklin Roosevelt have sought to find ways to manage policy better from the centre (see Seidman 1998; Arnold 2000), the various coordination mechanisms that have been created rarely have been sufficiently powerful to overcome the divisions that exist within the administrative system.

Federalism must be added to the divisions that exist within the federal government itself. Although the intergovernmental dimension of government might not appear important for policy coordination, some aspects of the federal system do tend to reinforce the divisions that begin in Washington (Walker 2000). For intergovernmental politics there are even fewer means for pulling the system together than there might be for the federal government itself, although certainly presidents and Congress have sought to find means of ensuring more effective intergovernmental and policy coordination. In particular, the growth of the federal special purpose grant programmes during the 1970s and 1980s tended to integrate the various 'pickets' in picket-fence federalism, and to insulate the various policy areas from one another. Recent administrations have tended to roll those specialized grants into block grants covering broad policy areas, for example, community development, that should provide state governors greater capacity to integrate the programmes at the state level (Gamkhar 2002), but the professionalization and increased specialization of the various policy areas had already been institutionalized and horizontal policy management has remained weak.

11.1 The coordination problem: agency autonomy and iron triangles

At a superficial level, the structure of the US federal government appears similar to that of most other governments. The government has a series of cabinet departments, each headed by a politician. Beneath those cabinet-level structures is a range of agencies, bureaus, offices and other subdivisions, each responsible for a particular area of policy. In addition to these cabinet-level departments and their components there are a number of independent executive agencies responsible directly to the President, as well as a variety of public and quasi-public corporations, foundations and other organizations that deliver public services. The role of a president as an independently elected head of government is markedly different from that of a prime minister, but the basic structure of government is rather similar to other executives in democratic political systems. There are also a number of independent regulatory agencies that are designed not to be controlled by the President and the Congress, and are given collective leadership structures with long-term appointments to provide substantial independence from political control. In a very fundamental sense these regulatory organizations are not intended to be coordinated by executive action but rather are intended to exercise more independent judgement over their areas of concern.[2]

Despite the structural barriers that exist even at the constitutional level, at a superficial level it might also appear that this government would be better coordinated than most others. First, the role of the President as a leader who can wield considerable individual political power, and who can provide independent direction for policy, provides a locus for coordination and coherent policy-making. Further, the President can appoint his own loyalists to many more positions in the public sector than can most political executives (Peters 2008). The average cabinet department now has several levels of political appointees. That politicization would be significant in itself but the evidence is that an increasing number of those appointees may not have as much functional managerial responsibilities as they have responsibilities for ensuring that the actions of the organization are in conformity with the programme of the President (Light 1995). The President also has a significant personal staff, with several thousand employees in the Executive Office of the President (Hart 2000) who can assist the President in monitoring and controlling policy.

11.2 The barriers to effective coordination

The superficial understanding mentioned above that there should be higher levels of coordination in American government than in other political systems is deceptive, and a number of factors combine to reduce the coordination and control capabilities of the system. Some of the factors are constitutional, some institutional and some political, but they combine to make effective coordination almost a dream within this political system. And indeed the factors do combine and interact to accentuate the difficulties that any president, or certainly any less senior official, encounters when attempting to coordinate.

Constitutional factors

The most important constitutional factor is that the United States is a presidential system with a legislative branch that need not be coordinated with the executive, unlike that in a parliamentary system. Even when the two political branches of government are controlled by the same political party, an infrequent occurrence during the past 60 years,[3] there is no guarantee that there will be agreement between them on policy goals, and indeed some of the disputes over policy and the failures to coordinate policy are related to maintaining the prerogatives of the institutions rather than to genuine policy differences (1). A good deal of American political and policy history could be written in terms of conflicts between institutions within the federal government, and disputes over the relative powers of the central and sub-national governments.

The US Congress is perhaps the only truly 'transformative legislature' (Polsby 1975) in the world and is an active participant in governing rather than a passive rubber stamp for the executive. The desires of Congress to maintain institutional independence from presidential control and to be effective are reflected, in part, in the creation of powerful committee systems in both houses (2). These committees enhance Congressional capacities both to legislate and to exercise oversight over the executive branch and its organizations (Aberbach 1990). In many ways Congress must be understood through the committee system as much or more as through the two houses or the institutions as a whole. In terms of coordination the committee system largely mirrors the structure of the executive branch and that tends to divide Congressional considerations rather than provide an integrated vision of policy.

As mentioned above, the constitutional provision of federalism further divides government. The vertical dimensions are obvious but the power granted to the sub-national governments to administer federal programmes often means that the same divisions that exist in Washington are replicated at the state and local levels. In the original design of federalism it was expected that governors at the state level would provide some of that coordination but they often now have almost exactly the same problems as the President in integration policy and administration within their governments. Their governments are divided just as much as the federal government and the agenda of New Public Management that enhances organizational autonomy has been adopted to a greater extent in the states than at the federal level (Kaboolian 1998).

Further, it is not only isomorphism with federal organizations that creates the fragmentation of policy implementation at the state and local levels. These governments all have constitutions that create many of the divisions between the legislative and the executive branches of government. Further, although these governments have the same sorts of executive departments found in the federal government they also have a number of independent executive organizations, many of these headed by *elected* officials who are not obliged to take orders from the state governors.[4] The segmentation of state and local governments charged with implementing federal legislation may therefore exacerbate the existing divisions in that legislation.

Institutional factors

The institutions of the bureaucracy and the civil service reinforce the separations within the American political system. Although the cabinet departments are directly responsible to the President the internal structures of these departments are much more independent from their departments than might be expected from simply looking at the organograms. The departments appear to be connected directly to the presidency through the cabinet, and subject to the personal power of the President (3). Perhaps the most important factor limiting the capacity of the President and cabinet secretaries from imposing their authority is that the agency structure that exists in the federal bureaucracy (4).

Unlike agencies in the United Kingdom and other countries following the New Public Management agenda (Pollitt et al. 2005) this structure has been in place for decades. The federal bureaucracy has been built up over 200-plus years largely through the creation of agencies and the subsequent incorporation of those agencies into cabinet departments. Further, there are still a number of independent executive agencies that are not linked with cabinet departments, although they are responsible to the President and clearly perform executive functions (Seidman 1998). As well as often predating their departments, almost all the agencies have a public law basis, and can claim rights to manage, and to make regulations about, most aspects of their responsibilities. Further, each leader of the majority of these agencies is appointed by the President, so that he or she has some direct political support of their own. Their cabinet secretaries may want to control the agencies within their departments, but the leaders of the agencies often can assert their own priorities.

The powers of the agencies are reinforced through the budgetary system **(6)**. While the budgetary system does serve some coordinative functions (see below) the federal budget also recognizes the independence of agencies, by giving them their own budgets, rather than having consolidated budgets for the whole department. Even after the adoption of the Government Performance and Results Act (Radin 2000) to reform the budgetary process, the emphasis remains on the performance of the individual agency rather than the performance of departments or government as a whole.[5] Likewise, the scrutiny of budgets in Congress remains very disaggregated, so that Congress itself does not take much interest in an integrated view of the budget. The expenditure budget is not adopted as one act of Congress but rather is passed as a series of 12 or 13 appropriations acts, prepared with relatively little reference to each other. Indeed, each committee or subcommittee with authority will fight to maintain its power over an agency budget.

Unlike other industrial democracies the civil service system does not do much to help in coordinating policy and implementation **(7)**. There is a civil service,[6] but important aspects of the system limit the extent to which the personnel system cuts across government. First, the senior positions in government are political appointees rather than career public servants **(9)**. These officials come and go with the President and the cabinet secretaries, and often spend relatively short times in government (Heclo 1983; Maranto 2005). At one time these officials were very strictly political, but increasingly they are experts in the policy area for which they are responsible. That expertise is a virtue in many ways, but it does mean that they are committed to a policy area, and are not likely to be especially concerned with cooperating with experts from other policy areas. There have been some changes in the appointment of these officials, with an increasing number of the appointees not having direct line authority for programmes but rather being in place to attempt to impose political priorities.

The other aspect of the civil service system that tends to reduce the coordination of public services is that personnel in the civil service system itself tend to spend most of their career in a single department, or even a single agency. Therefore, their commitment to government is to the particular agency and its programme, and not to broader policy goals. This career pattern reinforces a pattern of recruitment that focuses on specific expertise rather than general managerial capabilities. The development of the Senior Executive Service in the late 1970s and early 1980s[7] was one attempt to create a senior civil service cadre that would be portable across the public sector and provide greater coherence and coordination in policy and administration than had been present in the past **(8)**.

As implied above, the institutions within Congress are not well designed to pursue an integrated and comprehensive view of governing. The operational strength of Congress is its committee system, rather than the plenary sessions of the two houses. There are both functional committees that mirror the structure of the executive branch and appropriations subcommittees that also track the departments and independent executive organizations (see **(2)**). While the committee system is very effective in exercising oversight over the executive branch (especially when compared to other legislative bodies), it is extremely ill-suited to developing a comprehensive view. Indeed, just as Congress may defend its prerogatives against the executive branch, the individual committees also attempt to defend their own particular areas of control.

In summary, the institutional structure of both the executive and legislative branches of government in the United States is very fragmented. There are also number of internal divisions in the bureaucracy that further fragment government and enable individual agencies to pursue their own policy objectives and to resist pressures for conformity to presidential or Congressional priorities. Indeed, one of the most important strategies for the agencies is to play the two political branches off against each other.

Political factors

The pronounced divisions within the bureaucratic structures of the federal government are reinforced strongly by the politics of policy. In particular, the infamous 'iron triangles' or 'subgovernments' in American politics (see Freeman 1955) create symbiotic relationships between an agency, a congressional committee or subcommittee, and interest groups **(10)**. These three sets of actors all have an interest in insulating the agency and its programmes from unfriendly influences, and cooperate to ensure that the interests being served by the programme will continue to be treated well by government. Heclo (1978), among others, has argued that these triangles no longer are as strong as they once might have been. The growth of public interest groups and consumer groups, and the opening up of some aspects of Congressional action to greater public scrutiny have reduced some of the insulation of these subgovernments. Still, the iron triangle idea remained a good place at which to begin a discussion of the autonomy of agencies in the federal government.

It is far from uncommon for interest groups to have strong relationships with administrative agencies, but several factors in American politics tend to facilitate these relationships. One is that the pluralistic style of interest group politics in the United States makes it easier for agencies to pick and choose which social groups they will work with, and therefore to exclude others. Likewise, the membership of committees tends to be selective and usually includes Congressmen with a direct constituency interest in the policy areas over which the committee (or subcommittee) has authority.[8]

11.3   Instruments for coordination

Having spent a good deal of space explaining the peculiar difficulties in coordination within the US federal government, we should now proceed to examine the forces that do exist to coordinate the activities of those organizations. As has been done in the other cases in this book, these will be presented as a series of snapshots, beginning in 1980. Most of the instruments that are available for coordination will persist throughout the total time period of 1980 until 2005. Indeed, the United States has undergone relatively less administrative reform during this period than have most other countries. Further, to the extent that there have been reforms they tended to be concerned (especially in the 1990s) more with increasing opportunities for participation than with attempting to enhance the efficiency of government (Peters 2001).

The majority of the mechanisms for promoting coordination in the federal government are located in the Executive Office of the President (EOP) and/or are closely connected with the presidency. If there is any part of the federal government that can pull together the various programmes it is the EOP. Three structures within this office are especially important for policy coordination. Two of these – the Office of Management and Budget (OMB) and the National Security Council (NSC) – are more or less permanent structures. The third structure – some form of domestic policy organization – has varied with the administration in office. Each President has had some body that advises him on domestic policy and does some coordination of these programmes, but the names and the exact nature of these structures has changed.

The NSC, created by the National Security Act of 1947,[9] is responsible for providing the President with independent advice on foreign and defence policy (11). This organization also plays some role in coordinating the activities of the Department of Defense and the Department of State. These latter two organizations tend to have rather different views on how to address international issues, and the NSC, and especially the National Security Advisor to the President, attempt to create a more coherent vision of policies in this area. The structure itself and the procedures used were largely unchanged from 1980 to 2005, but its success in coordination varied with the personalities and political aptitude of presidents, the two cabinet secretaries, and the National Security Advisor.

The Office of Management and Budget is responsible primarily for the budget, but President Richard Nixon also added management responsibilities to the organization in 1972 (12). The OMB has a professional staff that prepares the budget, and the Director of OMB tends to be a close confidant of the President who is responsible for imposing presidential priorities in the spending decisions of government. Given the magnitude of the budget, and the relative independence of the administrative organizations in question, this is a difficult task. The main things that the Director has as a resource is the power of the President, and the technical skills of his/her staff. Presidents do vary in the extent to which they invest their own time in reviewing the budget, and in their willingness to impose presidential control and coordination. Some presidents, such as Carter and Clinton, spent a great deal of time on details, while others were quite content with the 'big picture' of public spending.

The Office of Management and Budget also has a legislative role. It has a staff that attempts to ensure that legislation and regulation going forward from the executive branch is in conformity with the programme of the President. Although legislation must be introduced by a member of Congress a good deal of legislation actually comes out of the executive branch and is then picked up by a friendly legislator. The task of the OMB, therefore, is to ensure that this legislation agrees with the priorities of the administration, and that it is coordinated with other initiatives, as well as with existing legislation. Given the independence of many of the agencies and their ties with powerful interest groups the President does not always prevail, but there is at least some attempt to create coherence.

As well as dealing with legislation going to Congress, the Office of Management and Budget also reviews secondary legislation being proposed by the bureaucracy. In addition to the question of conformity with the programme of the President secondary legislation is also reviewed on what is essentially a cost-benefit basis, following a series of Executive Orders that have mandated increasing scrutiny of agency actions. Regulations are also reviewed for their compatibility with existing legislation, and some for their environmental consequences. In short, the Office of Management and Budget is a major clearing house for presidents to be able to impose their own priorities on government and, if used with enough vigour, these powers can also enforce a good deal of coordination across government.

The third office within the Executive Office of the President that can have substantial impact on policy and coordination is (in the Bush administration) the Domestic Policy Council, although analogous organizations have existed under a variety of different names in previous administrations (13). Different administrations have addressed the problem of coordinating domestic policy differently, although the general pattern has been to have some mechanism that parallels the National Security Council. The difficulty in domestic policy, however, is that instead of having two major departments to coordinate, there are now a dozen, along with several dozen independent executive agencies. These departments and agencies all have their own priorities and their own visions of what good policy is, and are often competitors for budgets and policy power. At the domestic level the problems and the solutions may be less agreed upon that at the international level, and hence the coordination problems in the domestic council may be more difficult.

Presidents also vary in the extent to which they use the cabinet as a mechanism for coordination and policy control. In general, however, the cabinet is more of a ceremonial body than a working body, and the important relationships are bilateral, between an individual cabinet secretary and the President, rather than collective (14). Few if any significant decisions are made in cabinet, although the ability to use the meetings for apparent collegial governance is important for media purposes. That having been said, the meetings of the full cabinet do provide an opportunity to discuss issues that affect more than one department, and to provide some coordinated views on policy. If nothing else the cabinet may remind its members of the existence of other departments and the possible interactions of one programme with others. Further, several presidents (see below) have used committees and councils composed of members of the cabinet to coordinate at least parts of the domestic policy agenda.

Although we may think of the presidency as an institutionalized structure, it varies across time as each President attempts to find a structure and a set of procedures for imposing his stamp on policy and implementation (see Burke 1992). The structures serving the President also are not themselves always well integrated, and there may be personal and organizational conflicts that limit the capacity of the office to perform its task. In particular, there may be conflicts between the White House staff and the more institutionalized elements of the Executive Office of the President, with the latter being considered by the former almost a part of the permanent bureaucracy rather than members of the presidential staff (Wyszomirski 1982).

Congress

As noted, Congress also tends to work in a very decentralized manner, but it does have two organs that provide some coordination to policy and administration. These two organizations are the Congressional Budget Office (CBO) and the Government Accountability Office (GAO).[10] The CBO was formed in 1974 to provide Congress with some capacity to contest the domination of the President (and OMB) in budgeting (15).[11] It provides independent analysis and advice on budget issues and tends to monitor broader issues of overall budget control, such as the deficit. Over the past several decades the CBO has become more respected in relation to these budget numbers than the OMB, in part because it must serve both parties in Congress while OMB is more politically controlled. The CBO is also a major player in the development of the Reconciliation Act each winter that brings together the revenue and expenditure side of the budget.

The GAO started its existence as simply an auditing organization, used by Congress to assess the fiscal probity of the executive branch (16). Over time the GAO has, like many other public sector auditing organizations (see Leeuw et al. 1994) into a more analytic organization that also examines the efficiency of actions. Much of the work of the GAO is now assessing the impacts of federal legislation and monitoring its implementation. In the process of that monitoring it also identifies many cases in which federal programmes are not well coordinated, either at the policy or the administrative levels, and can make recommendations to Congress about how to improve the coherence among public programmes.[12] Indeed the number of instances of poor coordination among organizations that are identified by the GAO appears to be increasing.

To some extent the more informal substructure of Congress does provide some means of pressing cross-cutting issues throughout the full range of public policies. For example, the various caucuses based on race, gender, region or particular policy concerns tend to examine all legislation through those particularistic lenses. These caucuses certainly do not ensure that those cross-cutting issues will be successful or that policies will be changed to conform to the needs and demands of these groups, but they do ensure that those broader issues will be considered and brought to the attention of the leadership.

Although there are these two institutions in Congress perhaps the major change in Congress promoting policy coordination has been the increasing level of party domination over policy. Beginning with the 1994 election and the influx of the Gingrich Republicans and their 'Contract with America', Congress has become dominated by more responsible political parties, much in the style of European parliamentary democracies. Whereas before that time policy tended to be made by changing coalitions around individual pieces of legislation, the advent of stronger and more ideological parties has tended to produce more integration of policy. The parties (particularly the Republicans) may not always coordinate the fine details of policy, but they do ensure the ideological consistency of the policies adopted.

11.4   The phases of coordination

The above description of the structures of government in the United States emphasizes the peculiarities of this political system when compared to the parliamentary regimes that make up the rest of the 'sample' of countries in this book. This description further has identified the numerous forces that create autonomy for organizations and programmes, and that thereby create the need for mechanisms of coordination. We will now identify the principal mechanisms that can provide coordination, beginning like the other chapters with a baseline in 1980, and examining snapshots of changes during the various presidencies until 2005. While there have been some changes in public administration over this time period, in some ways the most remarkable feature of the system has been the persistence of patterns, and the absence of the types of major upheavals found in almost all the other countries in this collection.

Coordination in 1980[13]

The government that Ronald Reagan inherited when he was sworn into office in 1981 could not be characterized as a showpiece of effective coordination. There had been several attempts to build in more effective coordination devices during the Johnson (1963–8) and Nixon (1968–74) administrations, but these were largely abandoned by the time that the Ronald Reagan came to office. In particular, the Program Budgeting Program (PPBS), introduced first by Robert McNamara in the Department of Defense and then spread to the rest of government by the Johnson White House, was an attempt to utilize the budget as a means of examining the broad goals of government and then to allocate resources toward those goals rather than to individual programmes (for the continuing impact in the Department of Defense see Thompson and Jones 1994). Likewise, Management by Objectives in the Nixon administration (see Rose 1976) also attempted to identify central government objectives and then to relate those broader objectives to the individual programme goals.

The Carter administration (1977–81), following the rather technocratic preferences of the President, had undertaken some attempts to rationalize, and in a limited way, to coordinate programmes in the federal government. One such attempt at reform was the Civil Service Reform Act of 1978 and with it the creation of the Senior Executive Service (SES) (see (8)). The career opportunities for federal civil servants had previously been largely within a single organization but the SES created a cadre of senior managers that could be moved around across the range of organizations. While this style of change in the civil service system is hardly a sure means of producing coordination, the SES did in practice provide people at the top of the system with broader knowledge of what government as a whole does. The creation of the SES also provided another form of coordination, though political means, because it created another set of appointments for the President that could be used for coordination.[14]

The basic divisions in the system identified above persisted, but so too did the limited number of coordination devices. The budget process is carried out in a largely piecemeal fashion, but still there was some consideration (at least within the Office of Management

220

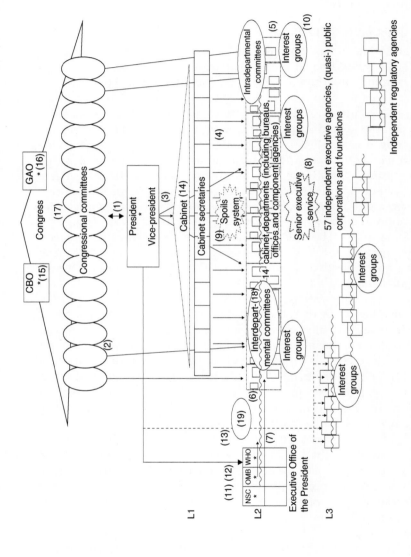

Legend CBO: Congressional Budget Office; GAO: General Accounting Office; NSC: National Security Council; OMB: Office of Management and Budget; WHO: White House Office

Situation in the early 1980s: mostly rather stable elements of specialization and coordination that last throughout the period 1980–2005

(1) (Potential) policy conflict between President and Congress
(2) Committee structure in Congress mirroring structures at the executive level Federalism
(3) Personal presidential power through Cabinet over departments
(4) A one-to-one correspondence of cabinet secretary to department
(5) Fragmented departmental structure with agencies with public law basis and direct political support and several independent agencies outside departments
(6) Budgetary system with emphasis on budgets for individual agencies and limited consolidation by appropriation acts
(7) Central control by Office of Personnel Management over civil service systems rules, leading to one civil service, but with low levels of mobility between organizations ('single career cones'). Central standardization and coordination of procurement by General Services Administration
(8) Senior Executive Service (losing its coordinating capacity during the next presidencies)
(9) Spoils system, by which senior positions are politicized (gaining increasing importance during next presidencies)
(10) Symbiotic relationships from agencies with interest groups and congressional committees ('iron triangles')
(11) National Security Council, which coordinates activities of Department of Defense and State Department
(12) Office of Management and Budget with coordination role concerning budget preparation and review of legislation in order to assess conformity with the Presidential programme and to coordinate it with other initiatives.
(13) Structures for coordinating domestic policy, which tries to coordinate to some extent a large number of departments and agencies
(14) Cabinet is mainly a ceremonial body with high emphasis on bilateral relations between President and cabinet secretaries. Coordinating function is rather limited.
(15) Congressional Budget Office (CBO) monitors overall budget control (through the Reconciliation Act)
(16) Government Accountability Office (GAO), which increasingly assessed implementation and impact of programmes, pointing to problems of coordination
(17) Informal coordination within Congress and by party dominance (has increased over time)
(18) Large number of interdepartmental and intradepartmental committees
(19) Regulatory Analysis and Review Group consisting of OMB officials and line departments

Figure 11.1 US government under the Carter administration (1977–81)

221

and Budget and the Congressional Budget Office) of the total amount being spent and the possible connections of spending categories. Major administrative processes such as personnel (Office of Personnel Management) and procurement (General Services Administration) were highly standardized and coordinated. Beneath the iceberg of departmental structures a large number of interdepartmental and intradepartmental[15] committees were engaged in the daily grinding work of attempting to make programmes more compatible **(18)**.

One procedural innovation at the end of the Carter administration, the Regulatory Analysis and Review Group, was an attempt to coordinate the legislative activities of the federal government **(19)**.[16] The federal bureaucracy issues thousands of regulations each year (Kerwin 2004) and given the number of cross-cutting issues that exist in this or any government naturally some of those regulations may be in conflict with one another. The Regulatory Review procedures brought together OMB officials with high-level officials from the line departments to review the proposed regulations coming from the bureaucracy. This was in large part to assess their economic costs but also identified regulations that were not in conformity with the programme of the President and those that were in conflict with other regulations. As noted this legislative review function had been performed for Congressional legislation for some time, but the addition of regulations to that activity enhanced the coordination and control capacity significantly. This process was later strengthened with Executive Order 12044 from President Carter.

The Reagan presidency

The Reagan administration did not adopt many new coordination devices, but it did use existing procedures with some vengeance to impose its own priorities.[17] For example, the previously mentioned Congressional Budget Act provided for two reconciliation acts as a part of the budget process to bring together the entire budget for review.[18] Especially in its first year in office the Reagan administration used this Omnibus Reconciliation Act as a means of altering the priorities of government and of imposing its own stamp on government. Likewise, the Reagan White House used the powers of legislative clearance within the Office of Management and Budget even more vigorously than had previous administrations, and were able to impose a programme of deregulation on the economy.

One coordination device that the Reagan administration did create early in its time in office was a series of Cabinet Councils that brought together the Cabinet-level officials with policy officials from the Executive Office of the Presidency in order to address significant policy issues, and especially those that cut across conventional departmental lines (20). Relatively quickly there were seven of these councils operating as a means both of resolving potential conflicts among departments and also as a means for the key actors in the White House to impose their own strategic vision on policy (Heclo 1983). By the second term of the administration these seven councils had been collapsed into two, one focusing on the economy and the other on domestic policy.[19]

The Reagan administration also undertook two more general reform efforts as part of their 'Reform 88' initiative. One was the Grace Commission (21), made up of private-sector managers, that reviewed the entire federal government and made suggestions for saving money. Most of the efforts of this Commission were applied to individual programmes but there were some cross-cutting initiatives as well. In the end, however, this project was extremely unsuccessful, largely because the private-sector members of the Commission did not appear to understand government and made numerous recommendations that were unfeasible (Savoie 1994).

The second component of Reform 88 was the President's Council on Management Improvement (22). Like most of the other initiatives in this administration the focus was on saving money in particular programmes rather than enhancing coordination. The principal impact on coordination was through the emphasis on the President's (or perhaps his staff's) strategic objectives and the use of political power to attempt to enforce those objectives.

By 1985 and its second term in office, the Reagan administration had much greater experience in government and was able to create somewhat greater coordination on management and on policy. Much of the effort of the administration was directed at specific pieces of legislation, rather than coordination, and it was able to create substantial policy change in areas such as social welfare and the environment. There were, however, some attempts to utilize coordination programs both to create other opportunities for policy change and to improve the efficiency of government. For example, the President's Management Improvement Council brought together a number of top managers in the public sector in an attempt to improve management, including coordination.

Although it might be considered a central element in good management, the limited reform efforts of the Reagan administration did not focus to any appreciable sense on coordination. The emphasis in this administration was on improving – and also eliminating – individual programmes rather than on looking at government as a whole and attempting to make it work together more effectively. The emphasis

224

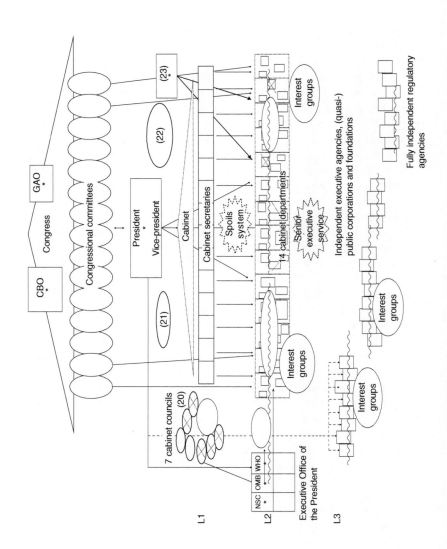

Legend CBO: Congressional Budget Office; GAO: General Accounting Office; NSC: National Security Council; OMB: Office of Management and Budget; WHO: White House Office

Not represented on figure

(20) Extensive use of the procedures to control the consolidated budget and to use the powers of legislative clearance to impose Presidential programme (OMB)

Creation of seven Cabinet Councils consisting of Cabinet-level officials and policy officials of the Executive Office of the Presidency, later reduced to two councils.

(21) Grace Commission, which was rather unsuccessful in coordination of savings

(22) President's Council on Management Improvement with a focus on savings on individual programmes, based on the President's strategic objectives

(23) Introduction of a 'Drugs Czar' coordinating agencies involved in anti-drugs operations

Figure 11.2 US government under the Reagan administrations (1981–9)

on individual programmes and agencies did, if anything, reduce levels of coordination. Individual managers had to focus more closely on their own priorities and could not afford to worry too much about requirements to coordinate. Further, if programmes considered themselves under threat, as many did, then they were unlikely to invest in coordinating with other programmes.

The First Bush presidency

The first President Bush inherited a presidency that had been shaped by eight years of the Reagan administration and its general disdain for the public sector. George H. W. Bush, on the other hand, had spent almost all of his working life in government and generally regarded civil servants much more positively than had most of the previous administrations. Rather than attempting to downsize government as the only solution to the problems of governing, the first Bush administration sought also to improve the quality of governing. George Bush was also more involved personally than had been Ronald Reagan, so that the priorities that were implemented tended to be somewhat more a product of his concerns rather than those of the White House staff.

The style of this administration was also markedly different from that of the Reagan years. In particular, the White House did not have the strictly hierarchical policy management that had characterized the Reagan administration. The President liked to have 'scheduled train crashes' in which advocates of various policies would debate the virtues of various positions before settling on the final policy (Porter 1991). This rather informal style was compensated for by an extremely powerful Chief of Staff (John Sununu) who was capable of coordinating activities once a decision had been made. The two large councils of cabinet secretaries were retained as other mechanisms for producing reform.

As was to be true some years later for the Government Performance and Results Act, the quality improvement programme initiated in the Bush administration had an indirect impact on coordination **(24)**. By discussing means of improving quality and performance in individual programmes and the negative interactions among programmes this reform identified areas in which the lack of coordination was a source of poor quality of services delivered. While the quality initiative was relatively weak compared with many attempts at government reform, and did not survive the change of administrations, it was another attempt to produce better service delivery that had at least some impact on the desire, if not always on the ability, to coordinate more effectively.

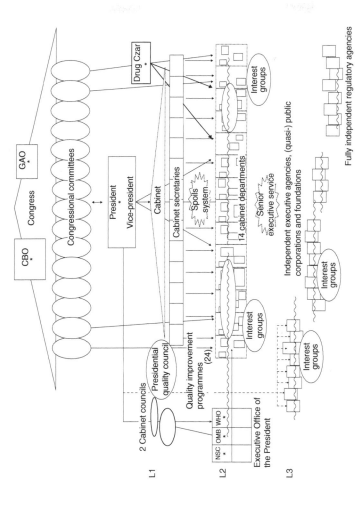

Legend CBO: Congressional Budget Office; GAO: General Accounting Office; NSC: National Security Council; OMB: Office of Management and Budget; WHO: White House Office

Not represented Informal mechanisms of coordination within cabinet ('scheduled train crashes') and a powerful Chief of Staff on the figure

(24)　　　Programmes but with some effect on coordination between programmes

Figure 11.3 US government under the George H. W. Bush administration (1989–93)

228

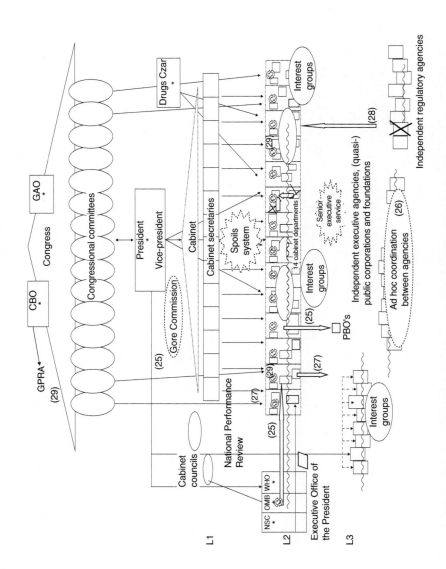

Legend CBO: Congressional Budget Office; GAO: General Accounting Office; GPRA: Government Performance and Results Act of 1993; NSC: National Security Council; OMB: Office of Management and Budget; WHO: White House Office; PBO: Performance-based Organizations

(25) Gore Commission and National Performance Review resulting in reform within some departments and a focus on 'high-impact agencies'. Devolution of management autonomy to 'Performance-based Organizations' (PBOs) (self-funding) (in subsequent administrations they were reintegrated in the cabinet departments)

(26) Ad hoc initiatives for coordination between agencies and programmes, initiated by individuals

(27) The Social Security Administration was taken from the Department of Health and Human Services in the late 1990s and made independent. It became an independent agency in the executive branch by the Social Security Independence and Program Improvements Act of 1994 (42 U.S.C. 901), effective 31 March 1995.

(28) The Interstate Commerce Commission – an independent regulatory agency – was terminated in 1995 and much of its function transferred to the newly created surface transportation board within the Department of Transportation

(29) Government Performance and Results Act (1993), helping to identify cross-cutting issues and linking programmes to overall indicators of performance. Strategic plans are integrated in the budget process for each individual agency

Figure 11.4 US government under the Clinton administrations (1993–2001)

The Clinton administration

After 12 years of Republican presidents the Clinton administration came to office in 1992 with an agenda for substantive policy change, but also with stated goals for reforming the management of the federal government. The management agenda was initially a version of the rather familiar set of statements by politicians about the failings of the Washington bureaucracy, but then evolved into a more detailed set of proposals for change. These changes were to be a product of the National Performance Review, otherwise known as the Gore Commission (Kettl and DiIulio 1995). This commission was unlike many others that have been utilized to create reform in the United States and elsewhere in that it was made up primarily of members of the civil service itself who saw the need for change from the inside of government, rather than from the perspective of businessmen or academics.

Like much of the managerial thinking about government at that time the Gore Commission focused on improving management in individual organizations more than on government as a whole, and hence dealt little with problems of coordination (25). To the extent that reform issues were addressed they tended to be primarily within individual cabinet departments rather than across departments. In some cases, such as the Department of Agriculture or the Department of Defense, those problems of internal coordination were significant, but larger coordination issues tended to be ignored. One of the elements in the National Performance Review that had some positive impact on coordination was the identification of 'high-impact agencies' and associated management problems that could have implications that exceeded the bounds of the one organization.[20]

There were relatively few programmatic changes in the Clinton administration that could produce improved coordination. That having been said, some individual members of the administration did press for coordination of programmes (26). For example, Carol Browner, as administrator of the Environmental Protection Agency, attempted to link the environmental agenda with a broader public health agenda (Samet and Burke 2001). Other skilful policy entrepreneurs in the administration sought to bring together programmes so that the administration could provide more coherent and more effective programmes, but individual action rather than structural or procedural remedies were the principal mechanism (Aberbach 1999).

One of the most important programmes for policy coordination begun in the time of the Clinton administration had little to do with the administration, but rather was an initiative of Congress. This was the Government Performance and Results Act of 1993 (GPRA) **(29)**. Although much of the emphasis of GPRA is on individual programmes and the improvement of performance within them, there were some elements that did facilitate coordination. If nothing else GPRA helped the federal government to identify programmes that have cross-cutting clienteles and cross-cutting goals and to begin to consider means of better linking programmes with each other, and with indicators of performance that were being adopted (USGAO 2000a; 2000b). For example, the overlaps in the more than 90 federal programmes offering early childhood services were identified and some reforms were introduced (Saldarini 1999).

The George W. Bush administrations

In many ways the time period covered by this book ends before some of the more important reforms directed at policy coordination in the United States began. Although it had a number of manifest policy and administrative failures, the administration of President George W. Bush did begin to address the problem of coordination. Although articulating the familiar Republican litany about terminating programmes and eliminating departments, this administration also began to use managerialist techniques to improve coordination.[21,22] One of the more important of these techniques was the use of cross-cutting performance indicators and developing some cross-cutting programmes to emphasize the ways in which programmes interact **(30)**. These indicator systems were rather modest in comparison to those used in New Zealand and several other countries, but they did represent a significant improvement in the coordination potential in American government.

The other major attempt at coordination during the George W. Bush administrations was the creation of the Department of Homeland Security **(31)**.[23] Soon after the September 11, 2001 terrorist attacks the administration created a massive new department, bringing together more than 20 organizations and programmes into this single cabinet department. Part of the stated logic of this reorganization was to better coordinate the actions of the various organizations that had some responsibility for national security (Kettl 2004). Likewise, after some debate over the wisdom of consolidation, an 'intelligence czar' was appointed in an attempt to better integrate intelligence collection and analysis. Interestingly, however, the Department of Homeland Security had minimal connection with this new office, and perhaps even less with the Department of Defense **(32)**.

232

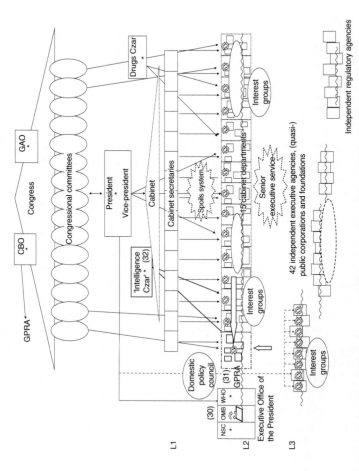

Legend CBO: Congressional Budget Office; GAO: General Accounting Office; GPRA: Government Performance and Results Act of 1993; NSC: National Security Council; OMB: Office of Management and Budget; WHO: White House Office

(30) Cross-cutting performance indicators
(31) Creation of the Department of Homeland Security
(32) Creation of an 'intelligence *czar*'

Figure 11.5 US government under the George W. Bush administrations (2001–5 [and to 2008])

11.5 Summary and conclusions

American government is not well-designed to produce effective policy coordination. Beginning with the constitutional system and going through to the political linkages that support the autonomy of individual organizations in the public bureaucracy, the structure of the system does not make creating policy coherence easy. This fragmentation is in part by conscious design and is in part a product of politics, but it is a very real aspect of governing. Perhaps most remarkably, very little of the past two and a half decades of administrative reform has been directed at improving coordination. Moreover, compared to other countries, administrative structures have been extremely stable[24] with rather constant levels of autonomy during the period under review.[25] Some organizations have been moved out of cabinet departments, and some terminated, but the basic structure has remained stable. The major exception to that generalization was the creation of the Department of Homeland Security.

In this system the power of the presidency is perhaps the central source of policy coordination, and the institutions of the presidency in the Executive Office of the President have been created to provide some general direction to government. That having been said, individual presidents have been committed to varying degrees to utilizing that power for coordination. When most presidents have engaged in the process of administrative reform they have been more concerned with eliminating 'fraud, waste and abuse' than with generating coherence. The major concern for coherence has been that presidents want to use their power and their staffs to impose a particular set of policy priorities over the permanent parts of government. That task of implementing priorities has been made extremely difficult by the structure of government, and few presidents have been able to claim great success in that endeavour.

Whether presidential or not, the dominant style of coordination is hierarchical. Markets play a limited role in coordination because so much direct service delivery is performed by individual state and local governments. Likewise, although the complex linkages among committees, agencies and interest groups can be seen as a type of network, in essence these structures tend to exclude rather than include many actors, and hence do not provide much of a coordinating function within the society.

As in many other countries the crucial role of policy coordination has become more evident in the past several years. In part because of reactions to terrorist threats and in part because of the increasing recognition through performance management techniques of the interaction of programmes, the federal government has introduced additional structural and procedural mechanisms for coordination. While these instruments are largely subordinate to measures concerned with the management of individual programmes, they do represent some increased attention paid to the need to make government more coordinated and more coherent.

Part 3
Cross-Country Comparison

12
Specialization and Coordination in Seven Countries: Findings and Discussion

In this chapter we summarize some of the general findings over 25 years for seven countries (New Zealand, United Kingdom, Sweden, the Netherlands, France, Belgium and the USA).

First, we describe what actually happened in the seven countries, by presenting their trajectory from 1980 to 2005 at the general level of central government. This results in three clusters of countries with divergent trajectories. Next, we compare the coordination strategies in the seven countries with respect to the drivers for coordination, the nature of the reform and changes in the coordination mechanisms used. We also investigate to what extent the traditional emphasis on hierarchical coordination methods shifted during the period 1980–2005 towards an emphasis on market- and network-based mechanisms. We conclude with a discussion of the main findings and formulate some elements for a future research agenda.

12.1 The central hypotheses: a recapitulation

The starting hypotheses of this book were as follows:

1) Following NPM doctrines, OECD countries have increased levels of specialization within their public sector (position 2 on Figure 12.1);
2) Fragmentation of management and policies increase because of higher levels of specialization, and lower levels of coordination and consolidation;
3) Fragmentation is reduced by increasing the levels of coordination and introducing new coordination mechanisms (position 3, Figure 12.1);
4) New coordination mechanisms based on NTM and MTM rather than strict HTM were introduced to match the new state structure, to

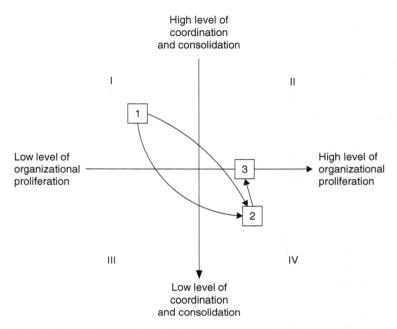

Figure 12.1 Specialization and coordination of organizations and policy cycles: the assumed general trajectory in OECD countries

combine some merits of specialization with the benefits of coordination, and to avoid the dysfunctions of specialization and autonomy.

The assumed trajectory of specialization and coordination (Figure 12.1) was described in Chapter 1. The following research questions are central:

1) To what extent have countries increased the coordination of management and policy as a reaction to too high levels of specialization and fragmentation?
2) To what extent have countries indeed introduced new coordination mechanisms (more markets and networks rather than hierarchies) to cope with the negative consequences of increased specialization?

We will summarize in general terms the trajectory of the central public sector in the seven countries in terms of specialization and organizational proliferation on the one hand and of consolidation and coordination on the other. Essentially, what we will do is to present the trajectory of each country on the two-axis scheme, which displayed the basic argument of this article (see Figure 12.1).

A crucial research question for comparing the countries in this book concerns the kind of coordination mechanisms (HTM, NTM, MTM) dominant in each period and the changes over time. In part we make a judgement on which coordination mechanism(s) prevails in a certain period, based on links between coordination instruments and the coordination mechanisms they refer to. So, we look for the *dominant* coordination mechanism or mechanisms in a specific period, in order to detect *changes* in coordination strategies. The way we make judgements on the dominant coordination mechanisms is mainly *shifts in emphasis*.

12.2   What has happened in reality? Trajectories of specialization and coordination in seven countries

There are three country clusters in our analysis. First, four countries (New Zealand, the UK, the Netherlands and Sweden) follow reasonably well the hypothesized trajectory as predicted in Figure 12.1. Second, two countries (France and Belgium) have an alternative trajectory which does have some elements in common with the first cluster. Third, there is the *sui generis* position of the USA.

United Kingdom (UK)

The coordination trajectory of the UK shows a number of clear tendencies (Figure 12.2). Its initial position in 1979 is characterized by a situation in which the different layers of the central government functioned in a relatively centralized, consolidated and only slightly proliferated way. The Prime Minister, the Cabinet Office and the Treasury were the main actors for coordinating all actors, in a predominantly hierarchical way, supplemented with a cabinet committee structure and ministers without portfolio (Seldon 1990; Moran 2005). Think thanks like the Central Policy Review Staff sought to provide capacity development for planning and coordination of governmental policy, in order to reduce departmentalism and to focus on governmental rather than departmental goals (Klein and Plowden 2005; Bogdanor 2005). This was embedded in an 'Oxbridge culture' among senior ranks of civil service (Bogdanor 2005, Hood 2005: 32). However, this is not to say that the UK central government did not suffer from 'departmentalism'

United Kingdom

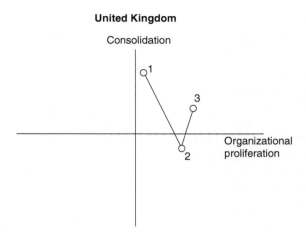

Figure 12.2   Specialization and coordination of organizations and policy cycles: the trajectory in United Kingdom

(Bogdanor 2005: 4–5; Page 2005: 139–46). Moreover, even at that time, numerous non-departmental public bodies were active in the periphery of government (Hogwood 1997).

During the 1980s and the first half of the 1990s, a strong movement towards a more proliferated administration – combined with decoupling the different policy stages – was apparent. First, a large number of independently functioning 'Next Steps agencies' and other autonomous bodies were created in order to disaggregate policy implementation from policy design structurally (Hogwood 1997). Second, large parts of the public sector were privatized. At that time, coordination was largely assured by introducing a broad range of market-based instruments, such as privatization, purchaser–provider splits, quasi-markets, market testing, compulsory competitive tendering, contractualization and financial incentives (Le Grand and Bartlett 1993; Bogdanor 2005). However, the hierarchical position and coordination power of the Prime Minister was strengthened further in this period by abolishing think tanks such as the CPRS (Peele 1995) and by creating informal committees, which bypassed the existing cabinet committees. Central entities such as the Cabinet Office remained important for coordination. However, by the mid-1990s, it became clear that organizational proliferation, the strong emphasis on clear objectives and performance targets for individual agencies and public managers, as well as on market-like values, had diminished the capacity of central government to deal with cross-cutting issues and 'wicked problems' (Pollitt 2003; Bogdanor 2005).

Since the second half of the 1990s governments have emphasized joining up actors involved at the central and other levels of government. Initiatives oriented towards creating an integrated information system, or a government-wide system of comprehensive spending reviews, underlined the renewed attention for a more consolidated, holistic approach (Ling 2002). Since 1997 there has been a major emphasis on interorganizational collaboration by 'joining-up' initiatives and network-like cooperative structures between organizations. New instruments for financial management (like joint budgets) and strategic management (like the Public Service Agreements) tried to reconcile organizational accountability with incentives for collaboration (Bogdanor 2005; 6 2004; James 2004a).

However, also in this period, the coordinating power of the centre, and in particular of the Prime Minister, was enhanced even further by the creation of several coordination units within the Cabinet Office that focused on cross-cutting issues (like the Performance and Innovation Unit) (Bogdanor 2005: 12–13; 6 2005: 72–3). Moreover, more attention was directed towards coordination among the central units and agencies, which all have a role in coordination (such as by the creation of the Delivery and Reform Team). Government also strengthend the strategic role of line departments in linking the public, private and voluntary sectors. Reviews of the *non-departmental public bodies* (NDPBs) and quangos resulted in only a small decline in their numbers. There was an increased reluctance to create non-department public bodies outside ministries but at the same time there was a continuing, although slowing, agencification in Next Steps agencies. Although a variety of public organizations continued to exist, the consolidation of public services became a high priority and cross-organizational performance was emphasized.

New Zealand (NZ)

In New Zealand, combined with a different starting position, a similar pattern emerged, but it was more radical. In 1984, organizational proliferation was already quite substantial, with 36 ministries, several non-core departments, various public corporations and Crown-owned companies and a raft of other public bodies (boards, tribunals) (Boston et al. 1996: 77–8). However, the centrifugal tendencies of departmentalism and proliferation was to some extent counterbalanced by strong line departments, an extensive system of cabinet and interdepartmental committees and effective interdepartmental coordination and strong input control by central agencies like the State Service Commission (SSC) and the Treasury. This makes the starting position in quadrant IV near the centre, with proliferation but effective coordination.

From 1984, the slide to the outer corner of quadrant III started. The creation of a large number of Crown Entities, state-owned enterprises, and more and small ministries reshuffled in an ad hoc way created a loose and fragmented organizational space of autonomous entities. This was exacerbated by splitting policy design, which occurred in these small ministries, from implementation. Purchaser–provider links were constructed through market-type-mechanisms (Mulgan 1997; Pallot 1991). Emphasis was on narrow organizational objectives and on contractual accountability within the individual minister–chief executive relationships, to the detriment of cabinet–chief executive relations and horizontal relationships among chief executives. At the same time, existing coordination mechanisms at the politico-administrative interface and at the interdepartmental level were weakened (Boston 1992) by an erosion of the cabinet committee system and strong changes in the regulatory powers or structure of central agencies. Also, the Senior Executive Service failed as a CEO platform (Schick 1996: 50). The turning point was in the beginning of the 1990s. Although there was some coordination effort at the governmental and interministerial level in the early 1990s, the focus was on market-type-mechanisms (MTM) for the agencies, which appeared insufficient.

The period from 1990 to 1995 was a push-and-pull stage. There was a further push for specialization, thorough purchaser–provider splits, increased competition and further hiving off (Schick 1996). However, at the same time there was a coordination pull effort: cabinet committees and ad hoc interdepartmental working committees were revamped or restructured, and interdepartmental consultation was stimulated. As a response on the observed lack of strategic management capacity (Steering Group 1991), the government introduced a system of cross-portfolio Strategic Result Areas, to which the departmental objectives and targets were linked. Moreover, the central agencies regained more coordinating powers. The SSC coordinated the Result Areas and harmonized the Minister–CEO performance agreements and the Treasury increased budgetary coordination. The Prime Minister strengthened his position with the Department of the Prime Minister and Cabinet (DPMC).

At the end of the 1990s and the beginning of the millennium there were concerns about the 'whole of government strategic capacity (...), problems of excessive structural "fragmentation" and "siloization",

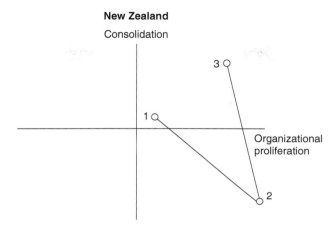

Figure 12.3 Specialization and coordination of organizations and policy cycles: the trajectory in New Zealand

the weakening of longer-term executive and managerial capability and the attenuation of a coherent state sector ethos' (Gregory 2006). Therefore, ministers chaired Strategic Result Area Committees in order to strengthen the strategic management system, and an Integrated Performance System was established. The 'Review of the Centre' initiative emphasized cross-portfolio and cross-unit cooperation, and strengthening uniformity (Gill 2002) and coordination between agencies and other units using mechanisms of hierarchy (HTM), and networks (NTM). The vertical accountability of Crown Entities to the Minister of State Services or portfolio minister was enhanced, as well as cross-agency brokerage of human resources (Gregory 2006; Boston and Eichbaum 2005). Some policy ministries and operational departments were reintegrated, and three major departments were merged. Central government capacity (such as through the SSC) was strengthened. Quasi-markets were largely rolled back in the health sector as a coordinating mechanism (Gauld 2001).

All this resulted in decreased organizational proliferation and a significant reconsolidation of the whole machinery, resulting in a position of consolidation much higher than New Zealand's initial starting position 20 years earlier (Figure 12.3).

Sweden

The initial position of Sweden was one of a relatively high level of organizational proliferation, combined with strong coordination between departments. The high level of organizational proliferation was mainly due to the dual structure of the Swedish administrative system, with a large number of large, mostly multifunctional agencies, with constitutionally enshrined autonomy, versus a limited number of small departments. At that time policy coordination was guaranteed by strong informal networks (partially based on political affiliation to the ruling Social Democratic party), ad hoc mechanisms, common policy preparation committees and procedural means like the system of mandated inter-departmental consultation (OECD 1992; Larrson 2002). Inter-policy coordination was particularly strong because of the small centre with strong informal linkages (Dahlberg 1993). Intra-policy coordination between departments and agencies was already problematic, despite informal links and joint policy preparation committees, because central control of agencies was predominantly focused on inputs.

In the period between 1985 and 1995 there was a double shift. Large-scale initiatives of decentralization, deregulation, corporatization, privatization and devolution of managerial competencies increased the level of specialization. Specifically, the devolution of managerial competencies towards agencies increased their heterogeneity. However, on the other hand, the decentralization and deregulation process, which changed the tasks of agencies, resulted in mergers and abolition of several agencies, reducing their total number. With respect to coordination and consolidation, the ongoing devolution during that period adversely affected intra-policy coordination, since the result-management instruments did not function well enough to provide strategic control (Molander et al. 2002). However, a budgetary crisis drove a stricter central control of government expenditure through the introduction of expenditure ceilings, and some joint initiatives between agencies emerged to create economies of scale.

From 1995, more initiatives to strengthen coherence were introduced. The government emphasized joint initiatives based on networking, for issues like e-government, regional coordination and training (see Niklasson 2004). New initiatives were taken to strengthen consolidation of information and to link financial with performance information (for example, VESTA; see Blöndal 2001). After that, the need for more central hierarchical control was felt, resulting in increasingly hands-on control of agencies from the centre, mergers of departments and centralization of coordination power with respect to e-government, EU policy and public administration reform. However, the small ministries continued to lack strategic control capacity for steering agencies (Molander et al. 2002). This resulted in an end-position in which macro consolidation

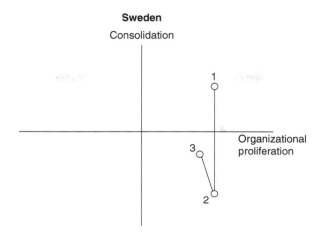

Sweden

Consolidation

1

3

2

Organizational
proliferation

Figure 12.4 Specialization and coordination of organizations and policy cycles: the trajectory in Sweden

was again somewhat strengthened, although intra-policy coordination remained relatively weak (Figure 12.4).

The Netherlands

Around 1980 the Netherlands had a clear departmentalism at its ministerial level which was further strengthened by a one-to-one relationship between minister and department, a weaker Prime Minister, and weaker central horizontal departments (except for Finance). As a starting position the Netherlands suffered from a high degree of 'departmentalism' at the level of ministries. 'Departmentalism' characterizes ministries as 'stovepipes', resulting in an administration as a loosely coupled cluster of 'sectoral islands'. There were some coordinating committees and ministers, but they did not dominate. A consensual tradition still existed.

The shift away from the first quadrant to the fourth quadrant started in the 1980s (Figure 12.5). The booming number of agencies and the strengthening of ZBOs resulted in a high level of specialization at the agency/ZBO level. The criteria for creating agencies were the capacity to measure output, and having a cost accounting system. Although there was an initial effort for coordination at the governmental and interministerial level in the 1980s and the first half of the 1990s (coordination of policy design), there was still a perceived loss of control over these agencies/ZBOs. Devolution of HRM competencies was one element of this loss of control.

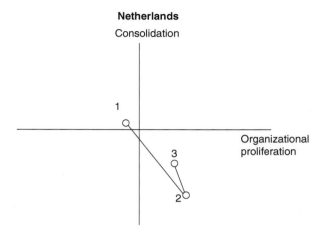

Figure 12.5 Specialization and coordination of organizations and policy cycles: the trajectory in the Netherlands

There was a clear option to split policy design (within small core departments) and implementation. One assumption was that agencification of policy implementation would facilitate coordination at the core. A critical study of the audit office (Rekenkamer) found that the central executive had lost control over its agencies and ZBOs reversed this trend.

This resulted in reconsidering the policy in relation to agencies and ZBOs. It also resulted in the strengthening of coordination at the level of agencies after the second half of the 1990s (coordination of implementation). The strenghtening of the Prime Minister's role, a shift to results-based management (up to outcomes), reintegration of some organizations within their ministry, a focus on departmental agencies rather than on ZBOs, a stronger horizontal role for the Interior and Finance, a shift towards more uniform structures and management systems, and the creation of a kind of pooled senior executive service were all elements of a reverse of the trend in the direction of the second quadrant.

This end position still remains in the fourth quadrant since the intentions were stronger than the realities. The performance-based budget process (VBTB) was less standardized, less outcome-oriented, was implemented in a much slower time frame, and had a lower coverage rate than was scheduled. Also the pooled senior executive service never really worked properly. The move to a cost-based uniform system for accrual budgeting and accounting was very ambiguous. So called 'coordinating chain-management initiatives' were more theoretical than practical. In general, the number of autonomous organizations changed only slightly.

These four countries appear to follow the same analytical trajectory. The starting point has a certain number of autonomous organizations. This evolved through further creation of new agencies (except if the number was already very high), combined with decoupling the policy cycle and relaxing control systems. In a third step, there was a correcting mechanism, a U-turn, to reconsolidate the policy, or the related contract or financial cycles, without necessarily recentralizing.

The second cluster, France and Belgium, differs from the first one.

France

France follows a different trajectory. In 1981 there was a strict hierarchical organizational structure, including deconcentration, which was strongly controlled. This was combined with a coherent policy cycle controlled by state professionals and strong executive politicians. Between 1981 and 1985 government began a cautious and very complex transfer of competencies to lower levels of government (more to *service extérieurs,* from *services déconcentrés* to local governments, more to *Etablissements publics,* especially after nationalizations in that period), without losing control over budgets and operations through strong prefects and platforms such as the *Conférence administrative régionale.* This first round of changes was slowed down by economic problems and the political challenge of cohabitation.

From 1989 to 1994 there was a major and visible reform programme, beginning with the *Circulaire Rocard* (1989). There were some guiding charters (on quality, on deconcentration). But again, each complex transfer of power was matched by a complex set of measures to guarantee control. External services became deconcentrated, but not decentralized. There were 'responsibility centres', service contracts and project leaders but control loss was avoided by strengthening the prefects, and creating the *Collège des Chefs de Service.*

During the period 1994–7 a complex trade-off began between deconcentration and decentralization. A key interministerial committee was created which prepared further reforms beyond administrating territories. This was almost an intermezzo prior to a second stage in the continuation of the reform.

From 1997 until 2005, the next reforms were implemented. Again, each complex set of measures to place activities or organizations at a distance was compensated by equally complex measures to keep control.

There were, for example, numerous bottom-up initiatives, electronic communication, strengthening centres for (national and other) competencies, and other projects. A College of Higher Civil Servants was created. New decrees strengthened the position of prefects (regional and departmental), and within the Ministry of Finance a directorate-general centralizing budget reform, administrative simplification, management, and electronic administration was created. A logical next step from a required multi-annual modernization programme was all-encompassing financial legislation. The LOLF was considered the financial constitution and aimed to ultimately guarantee the coherence of reforms, following the logic of missions, programmes and actions, including some horizontal programmes. Its ambition was to create a more efficient and democratic budget process.

The French specificity is that public management reform is even beyond reform of administrations or institutions. It is State reform. And improving coordination at the central level happens mostly through the sub-central level (*régions* and *départements*). There was no significant increase in agencies at the central level (except for the *centres de responsabilité,* which are a kind of temporary departmental agencies) and except for the creation at the sub-central level of regions, and *services à compétences nationales* (services with national competencies). Public enterprises remained largely untouched. It meant there was a higher level of organizational proliferation at a deconcentrated lower level of government. It also meant that the coordinating combined capacity of the regions, the departmental prefect, the 'concertation' bodies, and strategic planning and financial coordination kept a stable consolidated control and steering capacity for more autonomous deconcentrated activities. Hence, Figure 12.6 shows a dotted line.

In the 25-year period covered (1980–2005) France slowly, indirectly (through regions and departments), and in a very complex way, moved from a limited number of well-controlled organizations to a more fragmented system at its lower levels (*régions and départements*). The level of consolidation was safeguarded at these lower levels through the coordinating roles of councils and official networks, but also by the regional and departmental prefects (hierarchy). Hence the moderate slope from quadrant I to quadrant II.

Belgium

In Belgium (Figure 12.7), the starting position at the end of the 1970s was defined by a strong central state, a strong political control and coordination capacity by ministers and political parties, and strong consultation

France

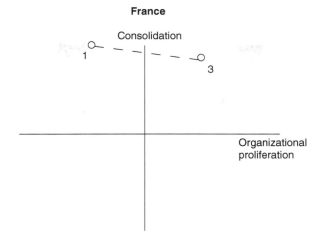

Figure 12.6 Specialization and coordination of organizations and policy cycles: the trajectory in France

within civil society which was also connected to political parties. There was some variation in the organizational spectrum in categories A (close to the minister) to D (high autonomy and looser administrative and political control), based on the 1954 law. However, this was a limited category. Hence, the starting position is clearly in quadrant I.

What follows is an atypical pattern, for typically Belgian reasons. First, moving organizational parts away from the ministerial departments did not happen because of managerial or policy reasons, but because of the very political process of creating regions and communities as separate constitutional entities. Second, this transfer was not a vertical one, as in decentralization, but a horizontal one. Federal, regional and community institutions are at the same constitutional level. Regional and community levels (parliament, government, and administration) are not subject to the federal level, but at the same level.

This resulted in a constitutionally established juxtaposition of several political and administrative institutions, even if there was a shift from 'executives and councils' to 'governments and parliaments'. As a result, coordination and consolidation issues arise not so much between parts, but within new and smaller parts, and within a smaller existing central part of the country.

A possible solution could have been a political coordination based on elite consensus.

In the next stages, it was more of the same, that is, transferring competencies from the federal level to regional and community levels. As a result, the federal administration had to cope with 'empty' parts in the organization, which created a movement towards mergers, and renewed coordination and consolidation. This was combined with an explicit intention to modernize, starting in 1985 with a State Secretary. Many of the measures taken, however, were purely procedural and formal. The paradox is that a smaller entity required more focus on coordination and consolidation.

After the fourth state reform in 1992, there was an explicit focus by Tobback on a new managerial culture. The General Principles Royal Decree was an expression of this. However, the problem for coordination between administration silos at the federal level was still dominated by the political cabinets that preferred direct and vertical political steering. Nevertheless, there was more network and cultural coordination (internal consulting, quality charter), more market coordination for public companies (even if the reason was fiscal pressure and European requirements rather than managerial improvement), with a remaining strong hierarchical control inspired by fiscal pressure (for example, from the enormous consolidated state debt).

This leads to Copernicus, the most comprehensive and consistent reform programme. It resulted in more autonomy for redesigned ministries (strategy, budget, mandates). However, there was a solid coordination of

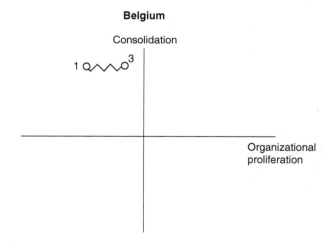

Figure 12.7   Specialization and coordination of organizations and policy cycles: the trajectory in Belgium

the vertical departments through the establishment of four horizontal ones and by programmatic ones. Also, there was an effort to reduce the impact of political cabinets and to give more autonomy to administrations, including a coordination of policy design. Finally, there was an effort to link resources and objectives, and a virtual matrix, colleges of top civil servants and redesigned procedures (such as a strategic plan) also tried to coordinate a slightly higher number of actors in the policy cycle. A massive creation of agencies did not occur at all, even if there was an evacuation of marketized entities. For all these reasons there was a prudent shift to more actors, but an equally solid effort not to lose control of a much smaller federal administration.

The United States (USA)

The USA forms a third cluster in itself, due to the particularities of its trajectory with respect to specialization and coordination. The levels of coordination and specialization in the United States varied little during the time period we were investigating. Therefore, in the descriptive format we are using, the trajectory is rather short. The executive branch of the federal government has had significant organizational proliferation for decades, with a large number of major agencies and other organizations. The autonomy enjoyed by these organizations is also significant, and the level of coordination imposed on the organizations is relatively slight. There were some subtle increases in the autonomy of agencies during the second Bush administration, but many of these fell outside the time period considered in our research. The institutions that might be expected to provide some coordination are themselves highly differentiated, mirroring the complexity of the federal government. For example, the Executive Office of the President is capable of providing some coordination through its National Security Council and Domestic Policy Council.[1], but the degree of coordination actually created may depend on the President. Some, such as Carter and Clinton, were intimately concerned with the details of policy while others took a much more *laissez-faire* attitude. The budget has been a central coordination instrument, managed through the Office of Management and Budget, but it was heavily influenced by the agencies and by the subcommittees of the Appropriations Committees in Congress. In addition, the internal structure of Congress mirrors the structure of the executive branch. This structure is good for oversight, but much less good for coordinating organizations and policy. There was a shift toward more consolidation through initiatives such as, for example, GPRA (standardized financial and performance information), a focus on government-wide indicators through the Performance Analysis and Review Program (PAR) in the Office of Management and Budget, and a reconsolidation of policies through 'czars' and the creation of at least one superdepartment (Homeland Security). That said, however, the hands-off management style of the Bush administration tended to create more autonomy.

The second and third cluster of countries clearly show that the straightforward mechanism of creating too many agencies with too much autonomy, which then need to be conditioned within a recoordination framework using hierarchy, markets and networks, has not really emerged in these countries.

The number of organizations and the level of their autonomy is not increasing (USA), or only slightly (Belgium), or is an epiphenomenon at another level of government (France). Second, coordination capacity remains high and stable, or increases slowly. Third, all seven countries are moving to the second quadrant on the scheme with a focus on a consolidated capacity and a stable number of organizations.

12.3   Some further comparison of the trajectories of seven countries

In this part we compare several features of these trajectories in these seven countries in more depth. First, we analyse the role of specialization

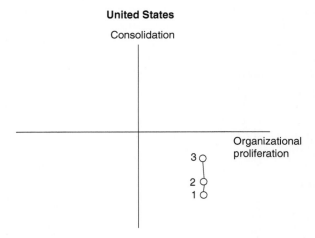

Figure 12.8   Specialization and coordination of organizations and policy cycles: the trajectory in the United States

as a driver for increased coordination. Does specialization increase the need for coordination or are other drivers more important? Second, we focus on different aspects of the coordination strategy as (a set of) reform initiative(s) in each of the countries. Do coordination strategies in countries, for example, differ with respect to their intensity and comprehensiveness? Third, we compare the coordination strategies with respect to the dominant coordination mechanisms and the changes over time in that respect. Is there really a shift towards the increased use of MTM and NTM, and a decline of traditional HTM?

12.3.1 Specialization as a driver for increased coordination?

For almost all of the countries, there appears to be a link between the extent of their coordination initiatives and the degree of specialization and/or fragmentation they face within their central government. For instance, the 1991 Logan Report in New Zealand identified the focus on outputs as one of the main factors inhibiting their ability to meet the strategic objectives of government and called for a connection between outputs and outcomes. Dutch reports (such as Commissie Sint 1994; Algemene Rekenkamer 1994) focused on the subordination of politics because of the lack of governmental oversight and control over quangos and the large influence of interest groups in policy design and advice. Departmental analyses pointed to the problems stemming from the organizational disconnection of policy design and implementation.

At different times, all countries appear to link their coordination efforts with the emergence of specialization/fragmentation (Verhoest and Bouckaert 2005):

- the UK and New Zealand, with unambiguous attempts to increase coordination after waves of agencification;
- the Netherlands, where vertical specialization by devolution and delegation of tasks was initially considered as an appropriate means to improve coordination at the remaining small central ministries, but where these efforts resulted in an even stronger need for new coordination mechanisms, both at (inter)ministerial level and agency level;
- Sweden, with relatively stable coordination efforts tackling historical processes of specialization, which were aggravated by increasing managerial autonomy of agencies after the late 1980s;
- France, with a gradual increase of coordination simultaneous with a growing proliferation because of '*déconcentration*';

- in the Belgian Copernicus plan, with the vertical specialized federal services designed in the context of four horizontal federal public services and a variable number of programmatic and project-based federal services that have a coordinating capacity;
- the United States, which differentiated its administrative system some decades ago and then experienced fewer pressures from specialization.

These findings support the assumption, central in organization theory, that specialization increases the need for coordination. Peters (Peters and Savoie 1996: 295–6; Peters 2003) states that some NPM changes have increased the capacity of individual programmes and organizations to resist coordination efforts. These changes include the use of performance indicators for evaluation, more demands for accountability, decentralization, autonomization and the involvement of non-governmental actors in service delivery. They are strongly linked to the issue of specialization. Indeed, agencification may increase the danger of redundancy, lacunae and incoherence within and between policy programmes.

Countries developed coordination strategies at two levels in order to deal with problems of 'departmentalism' on the one hand and the dysfunctional effects of vertical specialization on the other. First, there is the government-wide or interministerial level. The second level is within the range of agencies. Some examples may illuminate this point. For instance, in France, the coordination efforts at the second level were meant to compensate for the lack of coordination at central (inter)ministerial level. In New Zealand, the reinforcement of the coordination at government or interministerial level was necessary because of the failure of MTM, oriented mainly at the level of agencies. In the Netherlands, vertical specialization by devolution and delegation of tasks was considered an appropriate means to improve coordination at the remaining small central ministries. The Netherlands developed two partially linked strategies at the two levels. In the Dutch case the coordination problems at the (inter)ministerial level were tackled by the reform of the concertation structure, the installation of coordinating ministers, and vertical specialization. The latter required new coordination mechanisms such as organizational recentralization (revision of ZBOs), revised existing coordination mechanisms (a result-oriented budget cycle, the role of horizontal ministries and the Prime Minister), and experiments with new coordination mechanisms such as collective decision-making, chain management and quasi-markets (Verhoest and Bouckaert 2005).

However, it is probably wrong to consider specialization in itself as being the main and sole driver for coordination in these countries. In the 1990s, the need for coordination also seemed to increase because of other factors. In the country studies, we found a large number of such evolutions and challenges for coordination, including:

- internationalization, especially the influence of EU membership (such as in Sweden, the Netherlands);
- implementation of ICT and e-government (such as in Sweden, New Zealand and Belgium);
- deregulation – regulatory reform (such as in Sweden and the Netherlands);
- the importance of horizontal policy objectives such as equal opportunities, sustainable development, environmental policies, minority policies (for example, in New Zealand, Belgium and the United States);
- the need for more cooperation and collaboration at service delivery level in order to deal with 'wicked' societal problems (such as in the United Kingdom and New Zealand);
- increased emphasis on effectiveness of policy rather than savings and efficiency as a priority (for example, in New Zealand, the United Kingdom, the Netherlands with chain management structures and VBTB);
- homeland security threats and emergency management – crisis management (USA)
- restoring/strengthening primacy of politics (such as in the United Kingdom, the Netherlands and the United States);
- intransparency of structures and management of agencies and control problems (such as in New Zealand and the Netherlands);
- loss of corporate or common culture because of devolved HRM policies (such as in the United Kingdom, New Zealand and the Netherlands);
- traditional factors increasing the need for coordination include political risks in coalition governments (such as in Sweden and Belgium).

These emerging challenges for coordination are in most cases unrelated to an increased level of specialization (except perhaps for the last three), but the organizational proliferation provides a more challenging context for dealing with these evolutions. Organizational proliferation may make it harder to pursue common strategies and objectives within the public sector, since hierarchical control mechanisms are attenuated. For most drivers, specialization can probably be considered as a mediating variable aggravating the need for interorganizational coordination.

12.3.2 Coordination strategies as reform initiative

Table A.1 in the Appendix lists some features of the coordination strategies in the seven different countries. The coordination strategies in the seven countries differ with respect to the extent that they are embedded in politically explicit initiatives or public sector reform programmes.

New Zealand and the UK have both been characterized by strategies that seemed to be a radical break from previous approaches. Both their specialization initiatives through large-scale agencification programmes, and their coordination reforms were quite drastic, at least rhetorically. During the 1980s and early 1990s both countries relied quite heavily on MTM as a coordination mechanism in the public sector. With the Strategic Management Initative in the 1990s and the Review of the Centre initiative after 2000, the New Zealand government emphasized other mechanisms of coordination, while (partly) rolling back MTM. Similarly, the UK has had a Joined-up Government policy since 1997.

With these initiatives, both countries pursued the most politically explicit coordination strategies of the seven countries. Moreover, the most recent coordination initiatives in both countries were meant to be comprehensive in their application, although Joined-up Government should be considered more as an umbrella for fragmented initiatives. To some extent, this could even be said for the New Zealand Review of the Centre initative.

Initiatives were also rather top-down, as they were initiated by strong central actors taking the lead for the development and implementation of this strategy (the State Service Commission for New Zealand and the Prime Minister and the Cabinet Office for the UK). However, both the Review of the Centre initiative and the Joined-up Government initiative tried to foster 'spontaneous' initiatives for coordination and collaboration between public sector organizations at the ground level (such as cross-circuit breaker teams in New Zealand, and integrated service delivery initiatives).

Both Sweden and France show a somewhat more continuous, less extreme approach in the design of their coordination strategy that presents more a mix of different types of coordination instruments (hierarchy/market/network-based) throughout the period 1980–2005, compared to New Zealand or the UK.

France, as a country of our second cluster, holds a middle position between New Zealand and the UK on the one hand, and Sweden on the other hand. France launched a relatively comprehensive, mainly top-down coordination strategy, with a specific focus on tackling emerging coordination needs, related to the *déconcentration* process. However, its coordination strategy was not to bring about radical change from the past. Instead, France increased its coordination capacity, mainly at regional level, in a gradual way, accompanying the different steps in the deconcentration process. In this respect, France was the first of the seven countries to explicitly focus on the strengthening of coordination in combination with (and not as a reaction to) decentralization.

In the case of Sweden, the degree of political explicitness appears to be lower compared to that in New Zealand or the UK. Moreover, the initiatives seemed to be more fragmented and there was no dominant actor throughout the period under study (especially before 2000). The central problem for the Swedish government in this period was how to formulate common answers to new challenges in a context of highly autonomous agencies and relatively weak parent departments. Forced by its dual administrative system, the Swedish government deployed a somewhat more bottom-up-driven coordination strategy, with an important emphasis on joint initiatives and support from the agencies. However, these bottom-up initiatives were increasingly encapsulated in or used to enhance central government agendas.

When it comes to the nature of its coordination initiatives as reform strategies, the Netherlands are situated somewhere between UK and New Zealand on the one hand and Sweden on the other. Although several technical commissions studied the problem of coordination during the period, no politically explicit, encompassing reform strategies focusing on coordination were launched. The sole exception was perhaps the 'Other Government Programme', which was also an umbrella for many different initiatives and which was rather limited in its success. However, new coordination instruments were introduced throughout the whole period, with a combination of some central top-down-imposed measures on the one hand and diverse departmental initiatives on the other hand. The continuous efforts for better coordination in the Dutch central government were historically determined because of the large extent of departmentalism, based on the principle of individual ministerial responsibility. However, renewed attention and more intensive efforts are noticeable since the mid-1990s, when the large-scale hiving-off of tasks to ZBOs was more and more criticized for its negative proliferation effects.

Typical of the Netherlands was not only the enduring efforts at coordination, the proliferated nature of its efforts (both concerning their field of application as their focus), but also the limited success of most coordination initiatives. The most recent discussions point to the emergence of a more encompassing and concerted view on coordination in the Dutch central government.

In Belgium, initially, coordination was ad hoc and disconnected, the measures taken were rather procedural and formal, and therefore 'empty' of content. Colleges were established (for secretaries-general and administrators-general), or ICT platforms were put in place. Only under Copernicus did coordination become part of a broader reform picture.

Also, coordination in Belgium was in general top-down, especially if public finances were involved. However, the Modernisation Cells were a very bottom-up attempt to stimulate a culture of reform.

For the United States the linkage with the sub-national level of service delivery was one of the major movements toward coordination. Specifically the use of block grants for a range of social services and community development has forced more coordination among these programmes. Likewise, the development of one 'superdepartment' (Homeland Security) and consolidation of a number of border protection services has tended to produce a more coordinated range of services.

Countries also differ as to the extent that they relied on legal changes to increase coordination between actors. France and Belgium showed a clear tendency towards a *de jure* implementation of its coordination initiatives. The UK and Sweden appear to have been more oriented towards a *de facto* implementation. This could be linked to the respective legal traditions and the role of administrative law in these three countries, with France and Belgium following the 'State of Law' model, the UK referring to the public interest model, and Sweden holding a middle position between both legal traditions.

New Zealand seems to be an exception, as many of its important reforms were enshrined in subsequent laws, although its legal tradition is based on a public interest model (Pollitt and Bouckaert 2004; Beuselinck 2006). The Netherlands seems to be somewhere in between the two traditions.

12.3.3 Dominant coordination approaches and mechanisms over time

A first question is: *To what extent do countries differ in their reliance on managerial or structural instruments for coordination* (for a list of coordination instruments, see Table A.1 in the Appendix)?

The coordination strategies differ in the seven countries under review (see Table A.2 in the Appendix). Both the UK and New Zealand emphasize quite strongly individual and organizational incentives in order to enhance interorganizational coordination. This is obviously the case with MTM, but surprisingly also with NTM, where organizations and individual senior managers get rewards in performance contracts and financial management systems when they collaborate with other organizations to achieve cross-organizational objectives. A major question in both countries is how to foster responsibility for such cross-organizational objectives in administrative systems which build on one-to-one accountability relationships (James 2004b). Moreover, both countries rely quite heavily on strategic planning tools, performance indicators and other managerial instruments like cross-portfolio budgets in their coordination strategies (6 2005: 72–5). Information systems are important, but mainly to allocate responsibility and incentives, not to coordinate. Considering the comprehensiveness and top-down direction of coordination initiatives, the coordination strategies in these two countries seem to be predominantly *rationalistic and instrumental* although cultural, informal coordination and structural forms of coordination are not totally absent. Sweden with its dual administrative system has another approach to coordination, which is much more *participatory*, emphasizing joint ownerships, collegial steering and negotiation bodies, and platforms for reforms. Historically, informal forms of coordination are dominant, and managerial instruments for coordination are less dominant.

France seems to have a *mixed* approach to coordination, with a heavy emphasis on structural forms of coordination (mergers and splits, coordinating functions, reform platforms and negotiation bodies), combined with traditional forms of informal cultural coordination (for example, ENA). Recently, more managerial instruments have been used, such as strategic planning and financial management reforms (for example, LOLF). The Netherlands shows a heavy reliance on structural forms of coordination. These structures for coordination traditionally involved hierarchical means like the shift of competencies through departmental mergers and splits, changes in control lines, with a strong reliance on coordinating functions (at the ministerial level), as well as formal NTM through an extended system of cabinet committees. During the period under review these traditional coordination structures were revised or reused (for example, revision of ZBOs, new-style programme ministers, a stronger role for horizontal ministries and the Prime Minister), and new coordination mechanisms such as collective decision-making, chain management and quasi-markets, were introduced. Only since the mid-1990s has there been an increased use of more managerial forms (such as financial consolidation by the VBTB initiative or cultural management through the *Algemene Bestuursdienst*).

In Belgium, the political dominance of the cabinets, with their direct line of hierarchy to the administration, has prevented well-functioning administrative coordination. Pure structural coordination tools, such as the colleges of secretaries-general or administrators-general, initially were just an opportunity for collaboration. However, the cross-road databank for social security was a successful NTM-based way of coordinating all actors involved. Programme budgeting to materialise its coordination capacity was never developed. However, debt and deficit management were perfectly and extremely hierarchically organized.

Somewhat paradoxically, the USA has relied more on hierarchical methods than many of the other countries. Although there were some market and network-based mechanisms, these tended to be backed by hierarchy. For example, while the creation of the Senior Executive Service was designed as an NTM, its enforcement was strongly backed by the powers of the President and of the Office of Personnel Management. Also, the implementation of the Government Performance and Results Act had some MTM characteristics, but again was backed by the powers of Congress.

A second question is: *What coordination mechanisms (HTM, MTM, NTM) were dominant in the coordination strategies in the seven countries from 1980 to 2005?* Overall, and certainly within the control lines between minister, department and agencies, HTM has been weakened since the late 1980s, and has shifted away from detailed input control. However, since the late 1990s HTM seem to have been revamped, with mergers, reintegration, uniformization and strengthened regulation of agencies. Simultaneously, some centralization of coordination in the Prime Minister's office or in central agencies has taken place. This general pattern holds for all countries, albeit to different extents.

New Zealand fits this general picture very well, as does the UK. However, the UK had stronger centralization of coordination power by the Prime Minister and the Cabinet Office throughout the period of 1980–2005 (Bogdanor 2005; Hood 2005; Richards and Smith 2006).

For Sweden, hierarchical coordination was overall rather weak due to the position and size of agencies. However, the Swedish government seemed to develop a more 'hands-on' approach towards agencies and with some more recent centralization of coordination power. Even then, HTM in Sweden remain rather 'implicit' and 'hidden'. In Belgium coordination has been quite hierarchical. There were mergers and transfers, and new portfolios have been established (a state secretary for modernization, and the ministry of *fonction publique*).

France shows the most widespread hierarchical coordination throughout the period 1980–2005, as organizational mergers and splits and coordinating functions (such as prefect) gained importance.

The Netherlands traditionally applied HTM within the ministerial departments, but for interministerial and interdepartmental coordination, mergers and splits were quite often used as well as all kinds of coordinating functions, the latter mainly at the ministerial level. Although since the mid-1980s departmental mergers and splits were considered to be too costly and time-consuming, ten years later the reshuffling of competencies by mergers again became more popular, both at the level of departments and of agencies. The Netherlands continued to experiment with new or renewed coordinating functions, like project or programme ministers, stronger central departments as well as a stronger Prime Minister and secretaries-general. Since the late 1990s, there was also the rationalization and stricter control by ministers of ZBOs.

Both New Zealand and the UK appeared to emphasize market-based coordination, through large-scale initiatives of privatization, quasi-markets, competitive tendering and incentive-based management systems. This market-type coordination was particularly strong in the mid-1980s and early 1990s in both countries. Although they were less emphasized after the mid-1990s, they remained significant in several sectors. Sweden, France and Belgium showed a much more limited use of market-based coordination; France to an even lesser extent than Sweden. Also in the Netherlands, market-type coordination remained limited to the privatizations in the 1980s, some quasi-markets for agencies in the 1990s and the introduction of market principles in some social sectors after 2000.

Several countries, such as New Zealand and the Netherlands, traditionally relied on committee structures for interministerial and interdepartmental coordination, which were in some cases rationalized or revised during the period under review. Sweden seems to be the major exception in that respect since no committee structure existed for implementation. The analysis of the countries indicates a shared tendency to increase their use of new-style *formal* network-based coordination instruments during the 1990s (early 1990s for France and the Netherlands, mid-1990s for New Zealand, Sweden, late 1990s for the UK, and the mid-1980s and early 1990s in Belgium). All countries created collegial steering bodies or negotiation bodies and platforms for coordinating reforms, sometimes complemented by management instruments for sharing information and fostering collaboration.

After the late 1980s, France and Sweden, especially, appeared to use informal forms of network-type coordination, based on shared cultures within the public sector. In Sweden the importance of consensual decision-making, as well as the role of traditional political party dominance, possibly stimulated an informal, network type of coordination. For France this network type of coordination was encouraged by the shared culture among the main actors (the ENA and *Grand Corps*). The more informal cultural networks that were important at the beginning of the 1980s in both New Zealand ('Wellington village culture') and the UK ('Oxbridge culture') disintegrated to some extent in the 1980s and early 1990s because of the stronger emphasis on competitive attitudes in the civil service system (Gregory 2003; Bogdanor 2005: 13) and, at least in the case of the UK, more adversarial relationships between civil servants and politicians. In Belgium, the strongest networks and cultures were the political cabinets, which ultimately turned into hierarchies.

In these two countries, as well as in the Netherlands, more formal NTM, such as a senior executive service, and common training and behavioural standards were developed in order to enhance or re-strengthen a common culture in the civil service.

As noted above, the USA has relied on HTM, although the stereotype has been that it is a market-based society. The standard approach to any coordination question has been to invoke hierarchy. The analogue of a network of senior public servants found in many other countries was being created alongside the 'in and outers' (political appointees), but was then undermined seriously by a return to more politicized selection of those positions. There may now be better political coordination but somewhat less satisfactory policy coordination.

A third question is: *Did MTM and NTM, instead of HTM, become the dominant coordination mechanisms during the period 1980–2005? (see Table A.3 in the Appendix)*

Overall, in the early 1980s these countries were dominated by traditional HTM (input control), combined with some, mainly informal, NTM. Since the mid-1980s HTM were weakened because of devolution, deregulation or decentralization, and more emphasis has been placed on MTM, albeit to a widely varying extents. However, after

1995 MTM declined in importance, even in New Zealand and the UK. At that time, all countries experimented with various forms of formal NTM. But, as we mentioned before, these formal NTM were combined, especially after 2000, with a more rigorous use of HTM. These HTM were mainly used to reduce the level of organizational proliferation by reintegrating and merging organizations on the one hand and by restoring uniform organizational forms on the other. As evident from our country discussions, the administrative systems did not return to their initial position in quadrant I of Figure 12.1, and the level of organizational proliferation was still quite high in these four most explicit countries. In most cases, the organizational autonomy of agencies was regulated more strongly, but not reversed. Besides the few cases in which reintegration and mergers occurred, the revival in use of HTM tried to reconcile better strategic control of the state apparatus with flexibility and autonomy for service providers (see Richards and Smith 2006).

In the Belgian case, HTM always remained a dominant mechanism. Since hierarchy shifted from the purely structural to a more managerial one, networks also shifted from a more structural type of network (such as colleges) to a more managerial type (such as cultural).

The pattern for the USA is not dissimilar to that of the larger cluster of four, except that there was less experimentation with MTM and even with NTM. The continuing paradox is that hierarchy dominated. That paradox is in part explicable by the distrust that most Americans have for government (especially the bureaucracy), as well as by the power of interest groups to control their own policy areas.

12.3.4 Explaining country-specific patterns

In general there seems to be a mixed pattern. Some countries intentionally reduced HTM whereas others wanted to keep them (and perhaps change their nature slightly), or others only wanted to reduce them in a slow way. All added NTM and MTM. However, some wanted a lot of MTM, others only a limited amount; all tried to combine it with NTM, moving from informal to formal types.

Finally some countries developed corrective actions following the next principles: keep NTM if it is effective, reduce MTM if it is ineffective, and increase or keep HTM to rebalance the coordination mix.

There is a range of reasons why countries have specific patterns:

- There was an evolution to NTM coordination because of the increased autonomy of agencies and a changed role for horizontal/central departments. The use of NTM also depended on politico-administrative traditions: such as in Sweden (agencies), or France (ENA).

- The influence of ministerial versus collegial responsibility is also important; compare the Netherlands with Sweden.
- It is clear that understanding the influence of ministerial political secretariats on policy coordination is crucial (for example in relation to ministerial 'cabinets' in Belgium and France).
- The historical role and position of central/horizontal departments is also important (New Zealand: centralized; Sweden: decentralized).
- The size of a country plays a role.
- 'Below the agencies' there are different relationships between specialization and coordination: for example, in France there is a specialization and transfer to *départements* to increase coordination at that level; in New Zealand, the UK, Sweden and the Netherlands, specialization increases the need to coordinate at the level of agencies.
- The *type* of agencification is also important. There may be single-objective or single-task agencies as in the UK, New Zealand and the Netherlands, or multiple-objective agencies such as in Sweden and France.
- Obviously the relationship between politics and administration is important since it determines the level on which policy coordination mainly occurs and influences the importance of administrative instruments for coordination. For example, because of the existence of ministerial cabinets in Belgium there is a devaluation of administration's role in policy design and coordination, while the college of secretaries-general has only an advisory and concertation function. The ENA in France and its mixed careers result in the establishment of a lot of commissions. In Sweden informal concertation between ministers and civil servants is crucial. In New Zealand separate careers or in the Netherlands the technical expertise of their civil servants result in the important role of policy advice and administrative preparatory committees.

12.4   Pending issues for further research

1. There are different starting positions for countries. However, there are three clear clusters of comparable trajectories. There is an NPM cluster which consists of New Zealand, the UK, the Netherlands and Sweden. They take the format of a 'detour trajectory', making a clear U-turn. The second and third cluster are 'linear trajectories' and differ because of their starting position.

There is a second cluster which consists of a continental European set: Belgium and France. There is a third and *sui generis* cluster which consists of the USA.

Further research questions: Are there other types of trajectories? How will other OECD countries be mapped?

2. There is a mechanism of action–reaction for NPM countries (from quadrant I to IV and then to II), and a more linear pattern for non-NPM countries (from quadrant I to II).

It is likely that NPM countries demonstrated a very coherent set of actions and a coherent set of reactions, resulting in these 'extreme' patterns of trajectories. Obviously Belgium and France also have action–reaction mechanisms but with a different time perspective, and perhaps also in a more combined and simultaneous way, especially in France.

This cautious linear pattern gives an impression of immobility or slowness, whereas the NPM cluster demonstrates an almost hyperkinetic movement and initiative.

Further research questions: What will be the next action–reaction patterns? Is there a point of stability, or is it a predominantly unstable equilibrium which requires an action and a reaction?

3. There seems to be an attractiveness for all countries to the second quadrant (more autonomy, but coordinated). The general principle here is to have sufficient autonomy for a sufficient number of organizations, but also a solid level of consolidation. There is a preference to have functional specialization and a matching level of coordination. Specialization will only trigger a bonus if there is sufficient coordination.

Further research questions: How do we know that there is optimal coordination? Who is in charge of the coordination of coordination?

4. A key question relates to the cost-benefit analysis (CBA) of these trajectories. It is clear that first reforming the public sector by dismantling large organizations and disconnecting policy cycles has been a massive and costly exercise. It also resulted in a significant policy capacity loss for several policy fields. It became clear that costs were not matching benefits, which were perhaps not always or not yet visible. Corrective measures had to be taken, not just from a political control point of view, but also because the ultimate consolidation exercise, the budgetary consolidation, is an economic requirement. It became clear that the potential loss of this control was the bottom line since it had an impact on deficits and consolidated debt levels.

Further research question: Is an ex-ante CBA possible? Why is there no ex-post CBA of these transformations? What have been the costs and the benefits of these shifts?

5. Are short cuts possible for NPM countries? Is there a learning cycle?

Obviously these are theoretical and hypothetical questions for the countries in this study, especially for New Zealand, the UK, the Netherlands and Sweden. It is clear that slow, more linear and cautious shifts in Belgium and France, but also in the USA, belong to a reality which seems not to require extreme reactions to land in more 'reasonable' zones on the map of possibilities.

It seems that learning was more within clusters than between clusters, and that the learning between clusters was very conditional.

Obviously, the learning between the 'Anglo Saxon NPM' cluster was more single-loop learning, or an imitation of an internationally promoted standard.

The continental cluster understood the importance of creating some degrees of freedom for strict management purposes, but also to keep control over policy-related issues in a consolidated sense.

Further research questions: How can we organize all levels of learning? Especially for countries in Central and Eastern Europe, having joined the EU, how can they learn from these experiences? Can they control and develop a 'detour trajectory' or a 'linear trajectory'? How can Latin America, Africa and Asia learn from these experiences?

6. A normative question is related to a 'final' and 'optimal' position. Also, what are the strategic and a tactical meanings of a trajectory? Is the reaction position a 'failure' or a tactical move?

Describing trajectories over 25 to 30 years is difficult. It is even more difficult to understand, explain, let alone predict or prescribe trajectories.

Obviously, a 'final' position is not thinkable unless one accepts an 'end to history', and 'optimal' is always contingent and dependent upon existing or perceived disequilibria which sometimes are made intentionally unstable. It is clear that coherent strategies and tactics may at first view be very disconnected, even incompatible, when they are implemented. However, it is not always made explicit what the strategies are, nor what the tactics could be. The feasibility and desirability of options are crucial. And sometimes failures which are corrected are politically reintegrated in a rhetorical way, almost as if it were the initial intention to cause the 'failure' in order to be able to make a 'correction' that was initially impossible.

Further research questions: Do reform initiatives have tactical and strategic levels? How long is a long-term strategy?

7. What is the next step? And why? Is it a cyclical story?

Especially for the NPM countries there seems to be a question of a next step which would follow a cyclical pattern. It could mean that there are shifts to recentralization – which has happened in Australia – and of further reconsolidation of policies.

An extreme position would be that the next step results in the starting position of three decades ago (in quadrant I). The key question is whether that really constitutes the same position because of the influence of learning cycles.

It seems that returning to quadrant I is an upgraded position compared to the initial one. Output and effect information have substituted for input and activity information to drive the whole system. Returning to quadrant 1 means a consolidation and coordination of a limited number of organizations. However, this would be driven by outputs, outcomes, efficiency and effectiveness, and responsibility and accountability.

Further research questions: Is this kind of research useful for scenarios? Is it possible to extrapolate trajectories?

8. There is an increase in the complexity of the systems. Hierarchies are complemented with market and network mechanisms. It is impressive to see the growing complexity of the systems. This is surprising since the objective of transparency is also one of the objectives of reform. Increased complexity is never an intended objective. It seems to be an unintended side-effect which even requires meta-decisions such as selecting coordinating coordination instruments.

Especially in the NPM cluster, in the reaction stage, markets and networks were reduced in their development and influence. HTM remains dominant, MTM is limited in its applicability, and NTM is in most cases weak and not sustainable.

Further research questions: Under what conditions could MTM – which were much propagated by the OECD – and NTM become more functional?

9. The practice of the three groups of countries studied is that they use in their coordination strategy a mix of coordination mechanisms (MTM, HTM and NTM). Under what conditions did this mix result in synergies and a better policy coordination capacity (Figure 12.9)? It is still unclear what determines the effectiveness of a policy capacity coordination mix. Effectiveness may depend on the capacity requirements

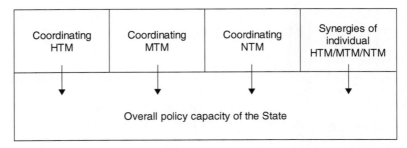

Figure 12.9   Effects of coordination mechanisms on the policy capacity of the State
Source: Verhoest and Bouckaert (2005).

for successful implementation (see Peters 2003); the contingencies of the instruments may also be important; and finally, the combined capacity is crucial.

Our argument is that countries deliberately choose a mix of coordination mechanisms for four reasons. First, a combined use of coordination mechanisms enables countries to compensate for the potential negative effects and dangers of an exclusive use of one separate coordination mechanism (see Table 12.1). A variety or a mix of policy coordination instruments is optimal.

Not every mechanism is appropriate for use in a certain situation or environment. If one wants to retain the merits of specialization, an extensive use of certain HTM is not possible. In that case MTM and NTM will be more likely. For instance, in highly fragmented administrative systems, the coordinating role of horizontal ministries (Finance, Personnel, services of the Prime Minister) is enhanced by restricting regulation to a minimum set of general rules (fewer HTM), by setting up structures for support and concertation with the other quasi-autonomous ministries (NTM) and by sourcing their implementing services in regulated internal markets (MTM). Moreover, in countries where HTM are used, their nature is more moderate so that they can be combined with a certain degree of vertical specialization (for example, Flemish ministerial holdings or Australian mega-departments). MTM can only be applied in settings where a market can be created and can function optimally (such as internal markets for support services for management). NTM need some degree of interdependency and trust among participating organizations.

Table 12.1 Some potential advantages and disadvantages of coordination mechanisms

	Potential advantages	Potential disadvantages
HTMs	Firmness and speed (such as in times of crisis) Potential equity and objectivity Clear responsibilities	Lack of legitimacy and ownership Large organizational structures lack fit with a complex environment Overload and bottlenecks
MTMs	Incentives to perform Contractual clarity Supply equals demand	Overemphasis on organizational self-interest and competition between organizations Fostering instability of system Potential loss of economies of scale One-sidedness of information (as in tendering for policy advice)
NTMs	High level of legitimacy of decisions taken High level of validity of decisions because of shared information Fostered by information technology Emphasis on internalization of shared norms	Slow and difficult processes (such as in decision-making) Lack of clear responsibilities Lack of enforcement capacity

Source: Verhoest and Bouckaert (2005).

Another merit of using a mix of coordination mechanisms is that the availability of different resources needed to build coordination capacity can fluctuate over time and sectors (Peters 2003). Mixes enable compensating policy capacities.

Finally, new and renewed coordination mechanisms and their mix enable governments to combine substantial specialization (with its merits related to its result-orientedness) with a higher coordination capacity. To a large extent, the countries under scrutiny retain the specialization in their administrative systems and develop a coordination system which can deal with a high level of specialization (like NTM).

Further questions: What, theoretically, is an optimal mix of HTM/MTM/ NTM?

10. This analysis is generic and perceived from the central level. No distinctions have been made for policy-specific fields. Two questions emerge here. What is the degree of variance within a country at the policy field level? In this study countries have been taken as units of

analysis. A complementary set of studies should be made within a country for a range of policy fields, and also for one policy field between countries. A second issue is to what extent measures are taken as top-down and generic, or contingent, policy determined, and driven by some strong line departments and ministries. In explanatory research this should also be taken into account.

Further research question: What is the coordination variance within a country between policy fields?

11. Theoretical implications and tempting explanations. It will be essential to use different families of theories (administrative, managerial, economic) to understand and explain these shifts. Possible candidates include all types of (neo)-institutionalism (economic, sociological and historical), bounded rationality, imitation and learning theories (leaders and followers), and (administrative) cultural theories (see Beuselinck et al. 2006).

Further research question: What theories can help us to describe, explain and predict the similarities and differences in the dynamics of trajectories in various countries?

12.5   Conclusions

This book has examined the tension between specialization and co-ordination in public organizations. What had become the conventional wisdom for the public sector, reflected in the development of autonomous agencies, created a number of managerial problems for government and seems to have provoked a number of responses. As we examined the pattern of development of organizational autonomy in seven countries, we suggested a series of related research questions.

A naïve assumption might be that all countries would respond to the ideas of New Public Management in the same manner. For New Zealand, the UK, the Netherlands, and partly in Sweden that assumption was confirmed. For France and Belgium it was not. The USA remains a *sui generis* system. Three countries clearly responded to the idea of significant and increased organizational autonomy, but then found that they had gone somewhat too far and therefore reimposed some coordination over those organizations. France, however, tended to maintain a balance between autonomy and coordination, so that the centre always had substantial capacity to steer the actors in the public sector.

The background research on these patterns of change indicates that the increasing specialization and autonomy of public organizations in response to the NPM ideology was a major driver of the subsequent attempts at coordination. Specialization, however, was not the only driver, and factors such as the perceived need to enhance coordination in the face of pressures such as the mobilization of clientele groups, globalization and increased linkage of policy domains also played roles in these changes. Further, the desire on the part of political leaders to reassert the primacy of political control also was significant.

We also found that when national governments attempted to reassert their control over autonomous organizations, most used a range of instruments. Market and network instruments were used especially when the civil service was reliable as an institutionalized network to promote better coordination. There was also a clear use of rather conventional hierarchical instruments, particularly those associated with the Prime Minister and central agencies, as well as reintegration and strengthening of the vertical accountability of these autonomous bodies. However, at least in the Anglo countries, the centralization of coordination power in the Prime Minister and in the central agencies was strongly supported by the use of new performance-oriented instruments (such as cascades of objectives and targets, budgets and performance-oriented incentives).

In summary, although the pendulum between specialization and coordination of organizations and programmes has been swinging for several decades, the movement continues. During the last several decades many governments have gone a long way in the direction of specialization, only to discover the dysfunctions created by an excessive concern with one of the standard principles of organization. The attempt to balance the autonomy and fragmentation created by specialization created a return to more integrated organizational structures, and the use of a number of instruments for improving coherence and coordination. This, however, almost certainly will not be the last set of movements, as governments continue to find organizational solutions to their governance problems.

APPENDIX
COMPARATIVE TABLES

Table A.1 Features of coordination strategies as reform initiatives in seven countries

Features of coordination strategies	New Zealand	United Kingdom	Sweden	The Netherlands	France	Belgium	USA
Politically explicit initiative/implicit	Politically explicit to a high extent	Politically explicit to a very high extent	Politically explicit to a limited extent (on specific elements)	Some initiatives politically explicit to some extent (*Programma Andere Overheid*)	Politically explicit to some extent (*interministérialité*)	Explicit initiative but implicit implementation	Limited political Involvement
De jure or *de facto* implementation	Most important reforms based on laws, others without law	*De facto* implementation (codes, guidelines, executive decisions)	Some overarching laws, most decisions without legal change	Combination of *de jure* and *de facto* implementation	Mainly *de jure* implementation (except for modernization networks)	*De jure*	Mainly *de facto* except for building superministries
Comprehensive or fragmented	Comprehensive overall programme with several initiatives	Rather fragmented initiatives within overall coordination programme (JUG)	Rather fragmented initiatives (e-gov, EU, no overall coordination programme)	Rather fragmented initiatives (more comprehensive in last period)	Comprehensive when addressing deconcentration; completed by other initiatives	Fragmented initially; with Copernicus much more coherent	Fragmented, ad hoc
Principal change agents	Main actor is State Service Commission but power struggle is centralized to some extent	Main actor is Prime Minister and Cabinet Office, very centralized	Main actor depends on issue (several central agencies involved in coordination); some centralization after 2000	Main actors are ministers of Interior and of Finance, but also other actors	Main actors are President, Prime Minister and interministerial committees; some changes over time	Budget and Finance ministers and ministries, and also *Fonction Publique*	Multiple actors, including Congress

Top-down or bottom-up (extent of involvement of agencies in development of the coordination strategies)	Rather top-down	Rather top-down	Rather bottom-up or at least joint development by departments and agencies	Rather top-down but variety between ministries	Rather top-down	Predominantly top-down	Mixed top-down and bottom-up
Sequence of specialization/proliferation and coordination (Verhoest and Bouckaert 2004)	Coordination emphasized after major increase in specialization/proliferation	Coordination emphasized after major increase in specialization/proliferation	Coordination emphasized within context of historical specialization/proliferation	Traditionally coordination already problematic because of departmentalism, but increased after specialization	Gradual increase of coordination, simultaneously with increase in level of specialization/proliferation	Initially partly disconnected, then, with Copernicus, connected	Throughout the period somewhat more emphasis on coordination in a proliferated governmental landscape. Overall limited change of coordination efforts
Start of major coordination initiatives in time (within period 1980–2005)	Mid-1990s	End 1990s	Mid-1990s	Coordination initiatives throughout whole period 1980–2005, increased since second half of the 1990s	Early 1990s (inter-ministerialité)	Ad hoc since 1985; systematic and systemic since 2000	Stable except for reactions to 9/11

Table A.2 Coordination approach and mechanisms in six countries (except USA)

Features	New Zealand	United Kingdom	Sweden	The Netherlands	France	Belgium
0. Main approach/ main instruments	Approach is rather rationalistic-instrumental because of strong emphasis on planning, incentives and other managerial instruments for cooperation. Strategic management cycle and information are central (late 1990s cultural coordination more important)	Approach is rather rationalistic-instrumental because of strong emphasis on planning and incentives for cooperation. Performance indicators, planning documents and reviews	Approach is based on involvement and joint efforts (less rationalistic-instrumental). Joint ownerships, collegial steering bodies and negotiation bodies	Predominantly structural coordination instruments (both hierarchical and networks). Some managerial coordination instruments applied since late 1990s for cultural and financial coordination	Approach is rather mixed, relying on organizational forms of coordination, cultural coordination and some managerial instruments Cultural coordination, organizational reforms and coordinating functions are crucial; lately more emphasis on strategic and financial management reforms	Predominantly hierarchy and networks. Political and administrative platforms for consultation. From 2000 also management instruments

1. Use of hierarchy-based instruments

Extent	Initially HTM not so strong from PM to departments but strong central agencies and strong HTM within departments. HTM (both within and outside departments) seriously weakened in the 1980s. HTM only from 1995 moderately and after 2000 strongly reinforced	Remained strong throughout the period 1980–2005, with respect to HTM by Prime Minister and Cabinet Office towards rest of government. HTM within ministries is reduced and only strengthened to some extent at the end of the period	HTM traditionally quite weak (except for input control)	Initially HTM mainly within departments – interdepartmental coordination through mergers/splits and coordinating functions; HTM (both within and outside departments) weakened in the 1980s, with some reinforcement since mid-1990s	Traditionally HTM in the form of input control and political control quite strong	Always political. Very strict input control. Procedural and ad hoc for other measures. Since Copernicus: strong hierarchy, but with virtual coordination

Kind/ vehicle	Mainly mergers, reintegration, more direct control of agencies and stronger central agencies; strategic planning mid-1990s to some extent HTM	Coordinating functions and entities are crucial (Ministers without portfolio, coordinating entities within Cabinet Office)	Traditionally input control (result control of agencies remained problematic); since 2000 by more 'hands-on' approach towards agencies and some centralization. Some HTM in first half of the 1990s because of restructuring of agencies and savings. HTM becomes stronger after 2000, but remains 'implicit', 'hidden' and consensual'	Traditionally departmental mergers and coordinating functions. Departmental mergers/splits not p,referred strategies since mid-1980s, but increasingly used since late 1990s (reintegration and mergers of agencies, new mergers of departments). Collective decision-making bodies, coordinating functions and ministerial control of agencies have renewed importance	Traditionally input control and political control; traditional coordinating functions strengthened	Mergers, transfers, new entities. Cascading of strategic plans. Input focus for financial management
Timing of corrective measures	After 2000 strongly reinforced with respect to departments and agencies (before 2000 with strategic planning some strengthening of coordination capacity over ministries)	HTM by the Prime Minister/Cabinet Office remains important and becomes increasingly strong. HTM by departments only restrengthened to some extent after 2000	Some correction after 2000 because of difficult coordination of agencies and in first half of the 1990s because of savings	Second half of 1990s reinforced with respect to departments and agencies	During 1980–2005 traditional input control decreases and restrengthened traditional coordinating functions (préfet) introduced	Incremental until 2000. Systematic vision for Copernicus reforms

(Continued)

Table A.2 Continued

Features	New Zealand	United Kingdom	Sweden	The Netherlands	France	Belgium
2. Use of market-based instruments						
Extent	To a very high extent from mid-1980s onwards	To a very high extent from mid-1980s onwards	To a moderate extent mainly during early 1990s	To some extent from mid-1980s (privatization) onwards	To some extent from mid-1980s (privatization) till mid-1990s	Not within the public service
Kind	Privatization, competition between State bodies, quasi-markets, purchaser-provider. MTM also strongly reflected in use of incentives for organizations and individuals	Privatization, compulsory competitive tendering, market testing, quasi-markets. MTM also strongly reflected in use of incentives for organizations and individuals	Privatization, deregulation, quasi-markets. Organizational and individual incentives not strongly emphasized	Privatization, quasi-markets for agencies, introduction of market principles in specific policy fields	Privatizations. Organizational and individual incentives not strongly emphasized	Shift to privatization for major public companies. Even where there is a programme budget, there is no results orientation. No quasi-markets
Timing of corrective measures	MTM less emphasized after 1995 and rolled back to some extent after 2000 (however, incentives for organizations and individuals remain important)	MTM less emphasized after mid-1990s, but not really rolled back	Less emphasized after 1995	MTM limited emphasis since late 1980s, not a dominant strategy during the whole period	No emphasis after 1995	Privatizations, mainly late 1980s and some late 1990s

3. Use of network-based instruments

Extent	Initially some informal NTM ('Wellington village culture') and elaborate committee structure. Weakened after mid-1980s (SES failed), but strongly emphasized since mid-1990s	Initially some informal NTM ('Oxbridge culture') and a committee structure. Weakened in the 1980s and early 1990s. Cultural coordination by codes since early 1990s. Since late 1990s strong emphasis on instrumental forms of NTM	Initially rather strong informal NTM (partially because of political party dominance). After decrease in early 1990s, NTM by joint ownership and forums strongly emphasized after mid-1990s	Initially formal NTM through extended committee structure, which was later rationalized. Increasing emphasis on formal NTMs (departmental management boards, senior executive service, shared services, platforms for knowledge exchange)	Initially and later strong informal NTM (ENA and *Grand Corps*) and committee structure. Increasing emphasis on *collèges* and platforms for exchange	Informal political networks strong; increasing emphasis on formal networks
Kind	Emphasis mainly on formal NTM through strategic planning, committees and cooperation, information systems, with cooperation fostered by incentives (rather instrumental and rationalistic)	NTM emphasized by creation of task forces, JUG structures, financial management reforms stressing joint initiatives, joint information systems (rather instrumental and rationalistic)	Much informal, ad hoc negotiation and concertation. No formal structure of cabinet committees. Strong emphasis on involvement and joint efforts through joint ownership, collegial steering bodies, negotiation bodies, and forums for reforms	From early 1990s increasing emphasis on collective decision-making bodies in departments, cultural coordination, shared services and platforms for knowledge exchange, especially after 2000	Initially formal (in committee structure) and informal (*Grand Corps*). NTM remain important throughout period. Networks mainly us0ed as forums to stimulate reforms and negotiation bodies	Strong political culture and party networking. Administrative networks but slowly implemented and ad hoc. Collegial types, except for social security: shared information data base

(Continued)

Table A.2 Continued

Features	New Zealand	United Kingdom	Sweden	The Netherlands	France	Belgium
Timing of corrective measures	Strongly emphasized since mid-1990s. Since middle/end of the 1990s revived emphasis on joint civil service culture	Strongly emphasized since late 1990s. Since early 1990s emphasis again on cultural coordination (managerialism and civil service culture)	Strongly emphasized since mid-1990s. Since late 1990s more coordinated leadership policy	From early 1990s increasing emphasis, particularly after 2000	From early 1990s increasing emphasis on platforms, forums next to cultural coordination	No explicit pattern over time

Table A.3 Chronological overview of coordination tendencies in seven countries

	NZ	UK	Sweden	The Netherlands	France	Belgium	USA
Starting position: early 1980s	HTM Mainly informal NTM ('Wellington village culture') MTM largely absent	Strong coordination by HTM (very strongcentre) Some predominantly formal NTM (committees) (some informal through 'Oxbridge culture') MTM largely absent	HTM (input controls) Mainly informal NTM and some formal NTM (political affiliation, informal discussions, procedural means) MTM largely absent	Moderate HTM (mainly within ministries – individual ministerial responsibility; coordinating ministers; departmental mergers and splits) Extended formal NTM (through committee structure) MTM absent	Strong HTM Formal (committee structure) and informal (*Grand Corps*) NTM MTM absent (from 1986 onwards some privatization)	Strong HTM (political and financial administration) Strong political NTM No MTM	Primarily HTM Input controls Budget
Period 1: early to mid-1980s		HTM with centralization of power with Prime Minister (also merger but some central offices weakened) From 1988 HTM weakened within departments because of large-scale agencification NTM not emphasized (informal NTM reduced by reforms) MTM more and more emphasized by privatizations and incentives		Moderate HTM (withinministries; rationalization of coordinating ministers; introduction of weak project ministers; mergers and splits) Rationalization of formal NTM (through rationalized committee structure) Some MTM in early privatizations	Idem	Idem	Idem

(Continued)

Table A.3 Continued

	NZ	UK	Sweden	The Netherlands	France	Belgium	USA
Period 2: mid-1980s to early 1990s	HTM seriously weakened NTM seriously weakened MTM strongly emphasized		HTM weakened because of devolution, deregulation and decentralization (some management by results) Mainly informal NTM and some formal NTM (political affiliation, informal discussions, procedural means) MTM largely absent	HTM weakened by devolution and agencification Some new formal NTM (departmental 'Management boards') and informal NTM (consultation of secretaries-general) MTM by privatizations at the end of the 1980s	Idem	HTM amended (not weakened) Administrative NTM (top-down: colleges; bottom-up: modernization cells)	Idem
Period 3: early 1990s to mid-1990s	HTM somewhat reinforced (e.g. role of horizontal departments) Formal NTM introduced MTM strongly emphasized	HTM with centralization of power with Prime Minister and Cabinet Office HTM *within* departments severely weakened by agencification Some cultural coordination by codes (NTM) MTM strongly emphasized	HTM moderate because combination of devolution, deregulation on the one hand and some restructuration, savings on the other hand Less informal NTM and some formal NTM MTM emphasized	Idem	HTM reduced to some extent because of *centres de responsabilité* and *déconcentration*, combined with new and restrengthened traditional coordinating functions Some NTM (in the form of *collèges* and committees) MTM to some extent by privatization	Stronger HTM: mergers, fewer ministers, contract management; Combined with stronger NTM (databases, internal consultants, charters) MTM: shifts to privatization	Gore reforms: pushing more toward NTMs GPRA also adds some coordination

Period 4: mid-1990s to early 2000	**Some HTM** (through mergers, for example) **Formal NTM strongly emphasized MTM less emphasized**	From 1997 onwards **HTM strengthened** by creating numerous coordinating cells close to the Prime Minister, review of NDPBs **NTM strongly** emphasized by creation of task forces, JUG structures, **Some MTM**	**HTM still relatively weak,** some strengthening **Formal NTM strongly emphasized MTM to limited extent**	**HTM more strongly** emphasized (by stricter control or reintegration of ZBOs, preference for departmental agencies, new organizational interfaces, stronger central departments) **New NTM and cultural coordination** (chain management and Senior Executive Service ABD, departmental peer review). **Traditional NTM rationalized** (advisory bodies) Limited MTM experiments (quasi-markets for agencies)	From 1993 **traditional HTM reduced by** *déconcentration* combined with **new and restrengthened** traditional coordinating functions **NTM emphasized** by creating of networks, committees, *Pôles de Compétence* and SIT **MTM not emphasized**	Idem	Bush administration performance management adds **system-wide indicators**
Period 5: early 2000s to 2005	**HTM strongly emphasized** (merger, reintegration, more direct control, central agencies) **Formal NTM still strongly** emphasized **MTM rolled back**	**HTM through** strengthening coordination role of departments, coordination by Cabinet Office, coordination of coordination **NTM emphasized** by creation of JUG structures, financial management reforms stressing joint initiatives, joint information systems **Some MTM**	**HTM more strongly** emphasized (but rather hidden – some centralization and reshuffling of compentencies) **Formal NTM still strongly emphasized** Less MTM	**HTM** (rationalization and mergers of agencies; stricter control of agencies; VBTB) **Strong emphasis on formal and informal NTM** (shared services, cooperation for ICT and innovation; networks; informal consultation of secretaries-general; more intensive chain management) **Limited MTM experiments**	**Traditional HTM reduced by LOLF** (less input control, more output control) combined with **restrength-ened** traditional coordination functions, strategic management and merger) **NTM emphasized** by creating many networks, committees and information networks **MTM not emphasized**	**Keep level of HTM Add NTM** (project-based Federal Public Services; boards of directors; policy councils with externals)	Idem

References

General

6, P. (2004) 'Joined-up Government in the Western World in Comparative Perspective: A Preliminary Literature Review and Exploration', *Journal of Public Administration Research and Theory*, 14, 103–38.

6, P. (2005) 'Joined-up Government in the West beyond Britain: A Provisional Assessment', in V. Bogdanor (ed.), *Joined-up Government* (Oxford: Oxford University Press).

6, P., D. Leat, K. Seltzer and G. Stoker (2002) *Towards Holistic Governance: The New Reform Agenda* (Basingstoke: Palgrave Macmillan).

Alexander, E. R. (1995) *How Organisations Act Together. Interorganisational Coordination in Theory and Practice* (Amsterdam: OSA).

Alter, C. and J. Hage (1993) *Organisations Working Together* (Newbury Park: Sage).

Anderson, G. (1996) 'The New Focus on the Policy Capacity of the Federal Government', *Canadian Journal of Public Administration*, 39 (4), 469–88.

Appleby, P. (1949) *Policy and Administration* (University: University of Alabama Press).

Bache, I. and M. Flinders (eds) (2004) *Multi-level Governance* (Oxford: Oxford University Press).

Bardach, E. (1996) 'Turf Barriers to Interagency Collaboration', in D. F. Kettl and H. B. Milward (eds), *The State of Public Management* (Balitmore: Johns Hopkins University Press), 168–92.

Bardach, E. and C. Lesser (1996) 'Accountability in Public Service Collaboratives: For What and To Whom?', *Journal of Public Administration Research and Theory*, 6, 197–224

Bardach, E. (1998) *Getting Agencies to Work Together: The Practice and Theory of Managerial Craftsmanship* (Washington DC: Brookings Institution Press), 19–49.

Bennet, C. J. (1991) 'What is Policy Convergence and What Causes It?, *British Journal of Political Science*, 21 (2), 215–33.

Beuselinck, E. (2006) 'Restructuring Donors' Aid Administration: A Comparative Perspective on Shifting Coordination Initiatives, Assessing the Relevance of a Historical and Sociological Neo-institutional Framework.' Paper presented at the EGPA Conference, Milan, 6–8 September.

Beuselinck, E. and K. Verhoest (2005) 'Patterns of Coordination in OECD–Public Organisations: Towards an Understanding of Underlying Causes.' Paper presented at the 21st EGOS-Colloquium: 'Unlocking Organizations', Berlin.

Beuselinck, E., K. Verhoest and G. Bouckaert (2007) 'Reforms of Central Government Coordination in OECD Countries: Culture as Counterforce for Cross-national Unifying Processes?', in K. Schedler and I. Proeller (eds), *Cultural Aspects of Public Management Reforms* (Amsterdam: Elsevier).

Bogdanor, V. (ed.) (2004) *The British Constitution in the Twentieth Century* (Oxford: Oxford University Press).

Bogdanor V. (ed.) (2005) *Joined-up Government* (Oxford: The British Academy in association with Oxford University Press).

Börzel, Tania. (1998) 'Organising Babylon – On the Different Conceptions of Policy Networks, *Public Administration*, 76 (2), 253–73.

Boston, J. and C. Eichbaum (2005) 'State Sector Reform and Renewal in New Zealand: Lessons for Governance.' Paper prepared for the conference on 'Repositioning of Public Governance – Global Experiences and Challenges', Taipei, 18–19 November.

Bouckaert, G. (2003) 'La Réforme de la Gestion Publique: Change-t-Elle Les Systèmes Administratifs?', *Révue Française D'Administration Publique*, 105/106, 39–54.

Bouckaert, G., K. Verhoest and A. Wauters (2000) *Van effectiviteit van coördinatie naar coördinatie van effectiviteit*, Overheidsmanagement nr. 10 (Brugge: die Keure).

Bouckaert, G., W. Van Dooren, B. Verschuere, J. Voets and E. Wayenberg (2002) 'Trajectories for Modernising Local Governance – Revisiting the Flanders Case', *Public Management Review*, 3 (4), 309–42.

Bryson, J. M. (1988) *Strategic Planning for Public and Non-profit Organizations: A Guide to Strengthening and Sustaining Organisational Achievement* (San Francisco: Jossey-Bass).

Cabinet Office (2000) *Wiring It Up: Whitehall's Management of Cross-cutting Policies and Services* (London: Performance and Innovation Unit).

Campbell, C. and G. Szablowski (1965) *The Superbureaucrats* (Toronto: Macmillan of Canada).

Campbell, J. L. (2001) 'Institutional Analysis and the Role of Ideas in Political Economy', in J. L. Campbell and O. K. Pedersen (eds), *The Rise of Neoliberalism and Institutional Analysis* (Chicago: University of Chicago Press).

Chan, A. and S. Clegg (2002) 'History, Culture and Organizational Studies', *Culture and Organization*, 8 (4), 259–73.

Chisholm, D. (1989) *Coordination without Hierarchy: Informal Structures in Multiorganizational Systems* (Berkeley: University of California Press).

Christensen, T. and P. Lægreid (eds) (2001) *New Public Management – The Transformation of Ideas and Practice* (Aldershot: Ashgate).

Christensen, T. and P. Laegreid (eds) (2006a) *Autonomy and Regulation. Coping with Agencies in the Modern State* (Cheltenham: Edward Elgar).

Christensen, T. and Laegreid, P. (2006b) 'The Whole-of-Government Approach: Regulation, Performance and Public Sector Reform.' Paper presented at 'A Performing Public Sector: The Second Transatlantic Dialogue', Leuven, 1–3 June.

Christensen, T. and P. Laegreid (2006c) 'Balancing the State: Reregulation and the Reassertion of the Centre', in T. Christensen and P. Laegreid (eds), *Autonomy and Regulation. Coping with Agencies in the Modern State* (Cheltenham: Edward Elgar), 359–80.

Coleman, W. (2005) 'Globality and Transnational Policy-Making in Agriculture: Complexity, Contradictions and Conflict', in E. Grande and W. Pauley (eds), *Complex Sovereignty* (Toronto: University of Toronto Press).

Coulson, A. (ed.) (1998) *Trust and Contracts. Relationships in Local Government, Health and Public Services* (Bristol: Policy Press, University of Bristol).

Crozier, M. (1964) *The Bureaucracy Phenomenon* (Chicago: Chicago University Press).

Davis, G. (1996) *A Government of Routines: Executive Coordination in an Australian State* (Melbourne: Macmillan).

Davis, H. and B. Walker (1998) 'Trust and Competition: Blue-Collar Services in Local Government', in Andrew Coulson (ed.), *Trust and Contracts. Relationships in Local Government, Health and Public Services* (Bristol: Policy Press, University of Bristol), 159–82.

De Bruijn, J. A. and E. F. ten Heuvelhof (1999) *Management in netwerken* (2nd edn) (Utrecht: Lemma).

Döring, H. (1995) *Parliaments and Majority Rule in Western Europe* (Frankfurt: Campus).

Dyckman, L. J. (2004) *Federal Food Safety and Security System: Fundamental Restructuring Is Necessary* (Washington, DC: US General Accountability Office).

Egeberg, M. (2003) 'How Bureaucratic Structure Matters: An Organizational Perspective', in B. G. Peters and J. Pierre (eds), *Handbook of Public Administration* (London: Sage).

Finer, S. E. (2007) *The History of Government from the Earliest Times* (Oxford: Oxford University Press).

Furubotn, E. and S. Pejovich (1974) 'Introduction: The New Property Rights Literature', in E. Furubotn and S. Pejovich (eds), *The Economics of Property Rights* (Cambridge: Cambridge University Press),1–9.

Galbraith, J. R. (1973) *Designing Complex Organizations* (Reading MA: Addison-Wesley).

Galbraith, J. R. (1977) *Organization Design* (Reading MA: Addison-Wesley).

Gouldner, A. (1954) *Patterns of Industrial Bureaucracy* (Glencoe IL: The Free Press).

Gregory, B. (2006) 'Theoretical Faith and Practical Works: De-autonomizing and Joining-up in the New Zealand State Sector', in T. Christensen and P. Laegreid (eds), *Autonomy and Regulation: Coping with Agencies in the Modern State* (Cheltenham: Edward Elgar), 137–61.

Greve, C., M. Flinders and S. van Thiel (1999) 'Quangos – What's in a Name? Defining Quangos from a Comparative Perspective', *Governance: An International Journal of Policy and Administration*, 12 (2), 129–46.

Gulick, L. (1937) 'Notes on the Theory of Organization', in L. Gulick and L. F. Urwick (eds), *Papers on the Science of Administration* (New York: Institute of Public Administration), 1–45.

Gulick, L. and L. Urwick (1937) *Papers on the Science of Administration* (New York: Institute of Public Administration).

Hall, R. A., J. C. Clark, P. V. Giordano and M. V. Rockel (1976) 'Patterns of Interorganizational Relationships, *Administrative Science Quarterly*, 22 (3), 457–74.

Halligan, J. (2003) 'Leadership and the Senior Service from a Comparative Perspective', in B. G. Peters and P. John (eds), *Handbook of Public Administration* (London: Sage), 98–108.

Halligan, J. (2006) 'The Reassertion of the Centre in a First Generation NPM System', in T. Christensen and P. Laegreid (eds), *Autonomy and Regulation: Coping with Agencies in the Modern State* (Cheltenham: Edward Elgar), 162–80.

Hart, J. (1998) 'Central Agencies and Departments: Empowerment and Coordination', in B. G. Peters and D. J. Savoie (eds), *Taking Stock: Assessing Public Sector Reforms* (Montreal: McGill–Queen's University Press).

Hedström, P. and R. Swedberg (1998) *Social Mechanisms: An Analytical Approach to Social Theory* (Cambridge: Cambridge University Press).

Heffron, F. (1989) *Organisation Theory and Public Organisations – the Political Connection* (Englewood Cliffs: Prentice Hall).

Hegner, F. (1986) 'Solidarity and Hierarchy: Institutional Arrangements for the Coordination of Actions', in F. X. Kaufmann, G. Majone and V. Ostrom (eds), *Guidance, Control and Evaluation in the Public Sector* (Berlin: de Gruyter), 408–29.

Hertin, J. and F. Berkhout (2003) 'Analysing Institutional Strategies for Environmental Policy Integration', *Journal of Environmental Policy and Planning*, 5, 192–216.

Hjalager, A-M. (1999) 'Interorganisational Learning Systems', *Journal of Strategic Marketing*, 8 (2), 121–38.

Hofstede, G. (2001) *Culture's Consequences: Comparing Values, Behaviors, Institutions and Organizations across Nations* (Thousand Oaks: Sage).

Holmqvist, M. (1999) 'Learning in Imaginary Organizations: Creating Interorganisational Knowledge, *Journal of Organizational Change Management*, 12 (5), 419–38.

Hood, C. (1991) 'A Public Management for All Seasons?', *Public Administration*, 69 (1), 3–19.

Hood, C. (2005) 'The Idea of Joined-up Government: A Historical Perspective', in V. Bogdanor (ed.), *Joined-up Government* (Oxford: Oxford University Press).

Hood, C. and A. Dunsire (1981) *Bureaumetrics* (Westmead: Gower).

Hooghe, L. and G. Marks (2001) *Multi-level Governance and European Integration* (Lanham: Rowman and Littlefield).

House, R. J. and P. J. Hanges (eds) (2004) *Culture, Leadership and Organizations: The Globe Study of 62 Societies* (Thousand Oaks/London: Sage).

Huber, J. D. and C. R. Shipan (2002) *Deliberate Discretion?: The Institutional Foundations of Bureaucratic Autonomy* (Cambridge: Cambridge University Press).

Hudson, B., B. Hardy, M. Henwood and G. Wistow (2002) 'In Pursuit of Inter-agency Collaboration in the Public Sector: What Is the Contribution of Theory and Research?', in S. Osborne (ed.) *Public Management: Critical Perspectives*, vol. II (London: Routledge and Kegan Paul), 325–51.

Hult, K. (1987) *Agency Merger and Bureaucratic Redesign* (Pittsburgh: University of Pittsburgh Press).

Huxham, C. and S. Vangen (2005) *Managing to Collaborate: The Theory and Practice of Collaborative Advantage* (London: Routledge).

Itoh, P. (1992) 'Cooperation in Hierarchical Organizations: An Incentive Approach', *Journal of Law Economics and Organizations*, 8, 321–35.

Jacob, K. (2004) 'Institutions and Instruments for Government Self-Regulation: Environmental Policy Integration', *Journal of Comparative Policy Analysis*, 6, 207–33.

James, O. (2004a) 'Executive Agencies and Joined-up Government', in C. Pollitt and C. Talbot (eds), *Unbundled Government: A Critical Analysis of the Global Trend to Agencies, Quangos and Contractualisation* (New York: Routledge).

James, O. (2004b) 'The UK Core Executive's Use of Public Service Agreements as a Tool of Governance', *Public Administration*, 82 (2), 397–419.

James, O. and A. Moseley (2006) 'Co-ordinating Public Services from the Top Down or Bottom-Up? Assessing the Implementation of Joined-up Government by Street-level Bureaucrats in Homelessness Services in England.' Paper presented at the EGPA Conference, Milan, 6–8 September.

Jennings, E. T. K. and D. Krane (1994) 'Coordination and Welfare Reform: The Quest for the Philosopher's Stone', *Public Administration Review*, 54 (4), 341–48.

Jensen, M. C. and W. H. Meckling (1976) 'Theory of the Firm: Managerial Behaviour, Agency Costs and Ownership Structure', *Journal of Financial Economics*, 3 (4), 305–60.

Jensen, L. (2003) 'Aiming for Centrality: The Politico-Administrative Strategies of the Danish Ministry of Finance', in J. Wanna, L. Jensen and J. de Vries (eds), *Controlling Public Expenditure: The Changing Roles of Central Budget Public Organizations – Better Guardians?* (Cheltenham: Edward Elgar).

Jerome-Forget, M., J. White and J. M. Wiener (eds) (1995) *Health Care Reform Through Internal Markets* (Montreal: Institute for Research on Public Policy).

Kassim, H., A. Menon, B. G. Peters and V. Wright (eds) (1999) *Coordination in the European Union: The Brussels Dimension* (Oxford: Oxford University Press).

Kaufmann, F. X., G. Majone, and V. Ostrom (eds) (1986) *Guidance, Control and Evaluation in the Public Sector* (Berlin: de Gruyter).

Kettl, D. F. (2004) *The Department of Homeland Security's First Year* (New York: Century Foundation).

Kickert, W. J. M. and Jan L. M. Hakvoort (2000) 'Public Governance in Europe: A Historical–Institutional Tour d'horizon', in O. Van Heffen, W. J. M. Kickert and J. J. A. Thomassen (eds), *Governance in Modern Society: Effects, Change and Formation of Government Institutions* (Dordrecht: Kluwer).

Kickert, Walter J. M., E-H. Klijn and J. F. M. Koppenjan (eds) (1997) *Managing Complex Networks: Strategies for the Public Sector* (London: Sage).

Klein, R. and W. Plowden (2005) 'JASO Meets JUG: Lessons of the 1975 Joint Approach to Social Policy for Joined-up Government', in V. Bogdanor (ed.), *Joined-up Government* (Oxford: The British Academy in association with Oxford University Press).

Klijn, E. H. and J. F. M. Koppenjan (2000) 'Public Management and Policy Networks: Foundations of a Network Approach to Governance, *Public Management*, 2 (2), 135–58.

Kooiman, J. (ed.) (1993) *Modern Governance: New Government–Society Internations* (London: Sage)

Kooiman, J. (2003) *Governing as Governance* (London: Sage).

Lægreid, P., V. W. Rolland, P. G. Roness and J-E. Ågotnes (2003) 'The Structural Anatomy of the Norwegian State 1947–2003.' Paper presented at the seminar on organizational forms, autonomy and control in the public sector, Bergen 1–2 December.

Lalenis, K., M. de Jong and V. M. Mamadouh (2002) 'Families of Nations and Institutional Transplantation', in M. de Jong, K. Lalenis and V. M. Mamadouh (eds), *The Theory and Practice of Institutional Transplantation* (Dordrecht: Kluwer), 33–52.

Lane, J. E. (1983) 'The Concept of Implementation', *Statsvetenskapliga Tidskrift*, 86, 17–40.

Lawrence, P. R. and J. W. Lorsch (1967) *Organisation and Management: Managing Differentiation and Integration* (Cambridge MA: Harvard University Press/ Graduate School of Business Adminsitration Press).

Legrain, A. and K. Verhoest (2004) 'Le secteur public en France et en Belgique: de la coordination hiérarchique à la coordination par réseaux', *Politiques et Management Public*, 22 (3), 163–91.

Le Grand, J. and W. Bartlett (1993) *Quasi-markets and Social Policy* (London: Macmillan).

Levinson N. and A. Minoru (1995) 'Cross-national Alliances and Inter-organisational Learning', *Organizational Dynamics*, 24 (2), 50–64.

Lijphart, Arend (1999) *Patterns of Democracy: Government Forms and Performance in Thirty-six Countries* (New Haven: Yale University Press).

Lindblom, C. E. (1965) *The Intelligence of Democracy* (New York: Free Press).

Ling, T. (2002) 'Delivering Joined-up Government in the UK: Dimensions, Issues and Problems', *Public Administration*, 80 (4), 615–42.

Linder, S. H. and B. G. Peters (1987) 'A Design Perspective on Policy Implementation; The Fallacy of Misplaced Precision', *Policy Studies Review*, 6 (Feb), 459–75.

Lipsky, M. (1980) *Street-level Bureaucracy: Dilemmas of the Individual in Public Services* (New York: Russell Sage Foundation).

Lowndes, V. and C. Skelcher (2002) 'The Dynamics of Multi-organizational Partnerships: An Analysis of Changing Modes of Governance', in S. Osborne (ed.), *Public Management: Critical Perspectives* (London: Routledge and Kegan Paul), 302–23.

Lynn, L. E., C. J. Heinrich, and C. J. Hill (2001) *Improving Governance: A New Logic for Empirical Research* (Washington DC: Georgetown University Press).

Malone, T. W. and K. Crowston (1994) 'The Interdisciplinary Study of Coordination', *ACM Computing Surveys*, 26, 87–118.

March, J. C. and H. A. Simon (1958) *Organizations* (New York: Wiley).

Massey, A. (1997) 'In Search of the State: Markets, Myths and Paradigms', in Andrew Massey (ed.), *Globalization and Marketization of Governement Services* (Basingstoke: Macmillan), 1–16

Metcalfe, J. L. (1976) 'Organizational Strategies and Interorganizational Networks', *Human Relations*, 29 (4), 327–45.

Ministry of Finance (2003) *Final Report of the Ministerial Working Group* (Helsinki: Ministry of Finance).

Mintzberg, H. J. (1979) *The Structuring of Organizations: A Synthesis of the Research* (Englewood Cliffs: Prentice-Hall).

Moore, M. H. (1995) *Creating Public Value: Strategic Management in Government* (Cambridge MA: Harvard University Press).

Mulford, C. L. and D. L. Rogers (1982) 'Definitions and Models', in D. A. Whetten and D. L. Rogers (eds), *Interorganizational Coordination* (Ames: Iowa State University Press).

Mulgan, G. (2005) 'Joined-Up Government: Past, Present, and Future', in V. Bogdanor (ed.) *Joined-Up Government.* British Academy Occasional Paper 5 (Oxford: Oxford University Press).

Niklasson, L. and J. Quist (2007) *Joining-up for Regional Development. How Governments Deal with a Wicked Problem, Overlapping Policies and Fragmented Responsibilities* (Stockholm: Statskontoret).

Niskanen, W. A. (1971) *Bureaucracy and Representative Government* (Chicago: Aldine-Atherton).

Oden, H. W. (1997) *Managing Corporate Culture, Innovation and Entrepreneurship* (Westport: Quorum Books).

Office of Management and Budget (2003) *Government Wide Performance Indicators* (Washington DC: OMB).

O'Toole, L. (1997) 'Treating Networks Seriously: Practical and Research-Based Agendas', *Public Administration Review*, 57 (1), 45–52.

OECD (1993a) *Market-type Mechanisms* (Paris: Public Management Committee, OECD).

OECD (1993b) *Managing With Market-Type Mechanisms* (Paris: OECD).

OECD (1996) *Building Policy Coherence: Tools and Tensions*, PUMA Occasional Papers No. 12 (Paris: OECD).

OECD (1999) *Integrating Financial Management and Performance Management*, PUMA/SBO (99)4 Final (Paris: OECD).

OECD (2002) *Distributed Public Governance. Agencies, Authorities and Other Government Bodies* (Paris: OECD).

Osborne, S. (2002) 'Managing the Coordination of Social Services in the Mixed Economy of Welfare: Competition, Cooperation or Common Cause?', in S. Osborne (ed.) *Public Management: Critical Perspectives* (London: Routledge and Kegan Paul), vol. 2, 253–72.

Ostrom, E. (1990) *Governing the Commons: Institutions for Collective Action* (Cambridge: Cambridge University Press).

Ouchi, W. G. (1980 'Markets, Bureaucracies and Clans', *Administrative Science Quarterly*, 25 (1), 129–41.

Page, E. and V. Wright (eds) (1999) *Bureaucratic Elites in Western European States: A Comparative Analysis of Top Officials* (Oxford: Oxford University Press).

Painter, M. A. and B. G. Peters (2010) *Administrative Traditions and Administrative Reform* (Basingstoke: Palgrave Macmillan).

Peters, G. B. (1998) 'Managing Horizontal Government: The Politics of Co-ordination', *Public Administration*, 76 (2), 295–311.

Peters, G. B. (2001) *The Politics of Bureaucracy* (London: Routledge).

Peters, G. B. (2003) 'The Capacity to Coordinate.' Paper presented at the Workshop on Policy Capacity, Hong Kong.

Pierre, J. and B. G. Peters (2000) *Governance, Politics and the State* (Hong Kong: Macmillan).

Pierson, P. (2000) 'The Limits of Design: Explaining Institutional Origins and Change', *Governance*, 13 (4), 475–99.

Plug, P., M. Van Twist and L. Geut (2003) *Sturing van marktwerking: de bestuurlijke gevolgen van liberalisering en privatisering* (Assen: Van Gorcum).

Pollitt, C. (2003) 'Joined-up Government: A Survey', *Political Studies Review*, 1 (1), 34–49.

Pollitt, C. and G. Bouckaert (2004) *Public Management Reform: A Comparative Analysis* (Oxford: Oxford University Press).

Pollitt, C., K. Bathgate, J. Caulfield, A. Smullen and C. Talbot (2001) 'Agency Fever? Analysis of an International Policy Fashion', *Journal of Comparative Policy Analysis: Research and Practice*, 3 (3), 271–90.

Pollitt, C. and C. Talbot (eds) (2004) *Unbundled Government. A Critical Analysis of the Global Trend to Agencies, Quangos and Contractualisation* (London: Routledge).

Pollitt, C., C. Talbot, J. Caulfield and A. Smullen (2005) *Agencies: How Governments Do Things through Semi-autonomous Organizations* (Basingstoke: Palgrave Macmillan).

Powell, W. (1991) 'Neither Market nor Hierarchy: Network Forms of Organization', in G. Thompson, J. Frances, R. Levacic and J. Mitchell (eds), *Markets, Hierarchies and Networks: The Coordination of Social Life* (London: Sage).

Pratt, J. W. and R. J. Zeckhauser (1991) 'Principals and Agents: an Overview', in J. W. Pratt and R. J. Zeckhauser (eds), *Principals and Agents: The Structure of Business* (Boston: Harvard University Press).

Pressman, J. and A. Wildavsky (1974) *Implementation* (Berkeley: University of California Press).

Richards, D. and D. Kavanagh (2000) 'Can Joined-up Government Be a Reality? A Case Study of British Labour Government 1997–2000.' Paper presented to the Australian Political Studies Association 2000 Conference, 4–6 October.

Richards, D. and M. Smith (2006) 'The Tensions of Political Control and Administrative Autonomy: From NPM to a Reconstituted Westminster Model', in T. Christensen and P. Laegreid (eds), *Autonomy and Regulation: Coping with Agencies in the Modern State* (Cheltenham: Edward Elgar), 181–202.

Rogers, D. L. and D. A. Whetten (1985) *Interorganizational Coordination: Theory, Research and Implementation* (Ames: Iowa State University Press).

Röber, M. and E. Schröter (2006) 'Big City Government – The Problem of Horizontal and Vertical Co-ordination.' Paper presented at the EGPA Conference, Milan, 6–8 September.

Rouban, Luc (2003) 'Politicization of the Civil Service', in G. B. Peters and P. John (eds), *Handbook of Public Administration* (London: Sage), 310–19.

Sabatier, P. A. and H. Jenkins-Smith (1993) *Policy Change and Learning: An Advocacy-Coalition Approach* (Boulder: Westview).

Salamon, L. M. (2002) *The Tools of Government: A Guide to the New Governance* (Oxford and New York: Oxford University Press).

Savas, E. S. (2000) *Privatization and Public–Private Partnerships* (New York: Chatham House Publishers).

Scharpf, F. W. (1994) *Games Real Actors Play* (Boulder: Westview Press).

Sciolino, E. (2004) 'A Campaign to Drink Another Glass of Wine for France', *The New York Times*, 23 July.

Schermerhorn, J. R. (1975) 'Determinants of Interorganization Cooperation', *Academy of Management Journal*, 18 (4), 846–56.

Seidman, H. B. (1998) *Politics, Power and Position: The Dynamics of Federal Organizations* (New York: Oxford University Press).

Sharpe, L. J. (1985) 'Intergovernmental Policy-making: The Limits of Subnational Autonomy', in F. X. Kaufmann, G. Majone and V. Ostrom (eds), *Guidance, Control and Evaluation in the Public Sector* (Berlin: de Gruyter), 159–81.

Thelen, K. (1999) 'Historical Institutionalism in Comparative Politics', *Annual Review of Political Sciences*, 2, 369–404.

Thompson, J. D. (1967) *Organizations in Action* (New York: McGraw-Hill).

Thompson, G. H. (2003) *Between Hierarchies and Markets: The Logic and Limits of Network Forms of Organization* (New York: Oxford University Press).

Thompson, G., J. Frances, R. Levacic and J. Mitchell (1991) *Markets, Hierarchies and Networks: The Coordination of Social Life* (London: Sage).

Van Duivenboden, H., M. van Twist, M. Veldhuizen and R. in 't Veld (eds) (2000) *Ketenmanagement in de publieke sector* (Utrecht: Lemma).

Van Heffen and P-J. Klok (2000) 'Institutionalism: State Models and Policy Processes', in O. Van Heffen, Walter J. M. Kickert and Jacques J. A. Thomassen (eds), *Governance in Modern Society: Effects, Change and Formation of Government Institutions* (Dordrecht: Kluwer).

Verhoest, K. and G. Bouckaert (2005) 'Machinery of Government and Policy Capacity: The Effects of Specialisation and Coordination', in M. Painter and J. Pierre (eds), *Policy Capacity* (Basingstoke: Palgrave).

Verhoest, Koen (2005) 'The Impact of Contractualisation on Control and Accountability in Government–Agency Relations: The Case of Flanders (Belgium)', in G. Drewry, C. Greve and T. Tanquerel (eds), *Contracts, Performance Measurement and Accountability in the Public Sector* (Amsterdam: EGPA/IOS Press), 135–56.

Verhoest, K., A. Legrain and G. Bouckaert (2003) *Over samenwerking en afstemming: Instrumenten voor een optimale beleids- en beheerscoördinatie binnen de publieke sector* (Brussels: Academia Press, DWTC ism Instituut voor de Overheid).

Verhoest, K., B. Verschuere, G. B. Peters and G. Bouckaert (2004) 'Controlling Autonomous Public Agencies as an Indicator of New Public Management', *Management International/International Management/Gestion Internacional*, 9 (1), 25–35.

Vosselman, E. G. J. (1996) *Ontwerp Van 'Management Control' – Systemen. Een Economische Benadering* (Deventer: Kluwer Bedrijfswetenschappen).

Walsh, K. (1995) *Public Services and Market Mechanisms: Competition, Contracting and the New Public Management* (Basingstoke: Macmillan)

Waterman, R. W. and K. J. Meier (1998) 'Principal–Agent Models: An Expansion?, *Journal of Public Administration Research and Theory*, 8 (2), 173–202.

Weber, M. (1947) *The Theory of Social and Economic Organization* (New York: The Free Press).

Weick, K. E. (1994) 'Organizational Culture as a Source of High Reliability', in H. Tsoukas (ed.), *New Thinking in Organizational Behaviour* (Oxford: Butterworth-Heinemann), 147–62.

Walsh, K. (1995) *Public Services and Market Mechanisms: Competition, Contracting and the New Public Management* (Basingstoke: Macmillan).

Waterman, R. W. and K. J. Meier (1998) 'Principal–Agent Models: An Expansion?', *Journal of Public Administration Research and Theory*, 8 (2), 173–202.

Webb, A. (1991) 'Coordination: A Problem in Public Sector Management', *Policy and Politics*, 19 (4), 229–41.

Williamson, O. E. (1993) 'Calculativeness, Trust, and Economic Organization', *Journal of Law and Economics*, 36 (1), 453–86.

Williamson, O. E. (1985) *The Economic Institutions of Capitalism: Firms, Markets, Relational Contracting* (New York: Free Press).

Winter, S. (2003) 'The Implementation Perspective', in B. G. Peters and J. Pierre (eds), *The Handbook of Public Administration* (London: Sage).

Wollman, H. (2003) *Evaluation in Public Sector Reform. Concepts and Practice in International Perspective* (Cheltenham: Edward Elgar).

Country Chapter: New Zealand

Boston, J. (1992) 'The Problems of Policy Coordination: The New Zealand Experience', *Governance*, 5 (1), 88–103.

Boston, J. and C. Eichbaum (2005) 'State Sector Reform and Renewal in New Zealand: Lessons for Governance.' Paper prepared for the conference on 'Repositioning of Public Governance – Global Experiences and Challenges', Taipei, November.

Boston, J., J. Martin, J. Pallot and P. Walsh (1996) *Public Management: The New Zealand Model* (Oxford: Oxford University Press).

Cabinet Committee on Government Expenditure and Administration (2002a) *Review of the Centre – Paper Three – Improving Alignment: Crown Entities*, December 2002, Wellington.

Cabinet Committee on Government Expenditure and Administration (2002b) *Review of the Centre – Paper Four – Departmental Accountability and Reporting Arrangements*, December 2002, Wellington.

Cabinet Committee on Government Expenditure and Administration (2002c) *Review of the Centre – Paper Two – Integrated Service Delivery*, December 2002, Wellington.

E-government Unit (2004) *Achieving E-government 2004: A Report on Progress towards the New Zealand E-government Strategy* (Wellington: State Service Commission) Available at: www.e-government.govt.nz/docs/ready-access-2004/index.htm.

Gauld, R. (2001) *Revolving Doors: New Zealand's Health Reforms* (Wellington: Institute of Policy Studies).

Gregory, B. (2006) 'Theoretical Faith and Practical Works: De-Autonomizing and Joining-up in the New Zealand State Sector', in T. Christensen and P. Laegreid (eds), *Autonomy and Regulation: Coping with Agencies in the Modern State* (Cheltenham: Edward Elgar), 137–61.

Gill, D. (2002) 'New Zealand', in OECD (ed.), *Distributed Public Governance: Agencies, Authorities and other Government Bodies* (Paris: OECD), 133–60.

Millar, L. (2004) 'Networking Government: E-Government in New Zealand', *Public Sector Journal*, 27 (4), 1–10.

Minister of State Services (2002) *Current Problems in Public Management, 9 October 2002* (Wellington: State Service Commission).

Minister of State Services (2004a) *Update: Integrated Service Delivery Programme. May 2004*, published 20 July 2004 (Wellington: State Service Commission).

Minister of State Services (2004b) 'Consolidation of Regulatory and Dispute Resolution Services Concerned with Housing and Building.' Media release, 30 June 2004, Wellington.

Mulgan, R. (1997) 'Restructuring – The New Zealand Experience from an Australian Perspective.' Paper prepared for the Public Policy Program, ANU, Canberra.

National Party (1993) *Manifesto '93: Stepping Out on the Path to 2010: The Spirit of Recovery* (Wellington: National Party).

Norman, R. (2004) 'Recovering from a Tidal Wave: New Directions for Performance Management in New Zealand's Public Sector', *Public Finance and Management*, 4 (3), 429–47.

OECD (1993) *Public Management: OECD Country Profiles* (Paris: OECD).

OECD (2000) *Issues and Developments in Public Management: New Zealand – 2000* (Paris: OECD).

Pallot, J. (1991) 'Financial Management Reform', in J. Boston, J. Martin, J. Pallot and P. Walsh (eds), *Reshaping the State* (Oxford: Oxford University Press).

Putseys, L. and A. Hondeghem (2003) *Contracten met leidende ambtenaren: Internationaal vergelijkend onderzoek naar de contractualisering van de sturings- en arbeidsrelatie*. Overheidsmanagement no. 15 (Brugge: die Keure).

Schick, A. (1996) *The Spirit of Reform* (Wellington: State Service Commission).

SSC (State Service Commission) (1997a) *Strategic Management in the Public Service: A Review of the Implementation of Key Result Areas 1994–1997 – Stakeholder Perspectives* (Wellington: State Service Commission).

SSC (State Service Commission) (1997b) *Strategic Human Resource Capability Issues in the Public Service* (Wellington: State Service Commission).

SSC (State Service Commission) (1998a) *New Zealand's State Sector Reform: A Decade of Change* (Wellington: State Service Commission).

SSC (State Service Commission) (1998b) *Assessment of the State of the New Zealand Public Service*. Occasional Paper No. 1 (Wellington: State Service Commission).

SSC (State Service Commission) (1998c) *State Service Commission Strategic Social Policy: How Significant is Machinery of Government?* Unpublished paper, March 1998 (Wellington: State Service Commission).

SSC (State Service Commission) (1998d) *A Better Focus on Outcomes through SRA Networks*. Occasional Paper No. 3 (Wellington: State Service Commission).

SSC (State Service Commission) (1999b) *Essential Ingredients: Improving the Quality of Policy Advice*. State Service Commission Occasional Paper No. 9 (Wellington: State Service Commission).

SSC (State Service Commission) (1999c) *Improving Accountability: Developing an Integrated Performance System*. Occasional Paper No. 11, August (Wellington: State Service Commission).

SSC (State Service Commission) (1999d) *Integrated Service Delivery*. Occasional Paper No. 12, August (Wellington: State Service Commission).

State Service Commission (2000) *Crown Entity Reform: Overview* (Wellington: State Service Commission).

State Service Commission (2005) *State Structure 2005 – State Services and Wider State Sector*, 30 May (Wellington: State Service Commission).

Steering Group (1991) *Review of State Sector Reforms* (Wellington: State Service Commission).

Washington, S. (1998) *Pieces of the Puzzle: Machinery of Government and the Quality of Policy Advice*. State Service Commission Working Paper No. 4 (Wellington: State Service Commission).

Country Chapter: United Kingdom

6, Perri, D. Leat, K. Seltzet and G. Stoker (1999) *Governing in the Round: Strategies for Holistic Government* (London: Demos).

6, Perri, D. Leat, K. Seltzet and G. Stoker (2002) *Towards Holistic Governance: The New Reform Agenda* (Basingstoke: Palgrave)

Bellamy, C. (1999) 'Joining-up Government in the UK: Towards Public Services for an Information Age', *Australian Journal of Public Administration*, 58 (3), 89–96.

Blackstone, T. and W. Lowden (1988) *Inside the Think Tank: Advising the Cabinet 1971–1983* (London: Heinemann).

Blick, A. (2004) *People who Live in the Dark: The Special Adviser in British Politics* (London: Politico's).

Cabinet Office (1991) *The Citizen's Charter: Raising the Standards* (London: HMSO).

Cabinet Office (1999) *Modernising Government* (London: HMSO).

Cabinet Office (2000) *Wiring It Up: Whitehall's Management of Cross-cutting Policies and Services* (London: Performance and Innovation Unit).

Cabinet Office (2005) *Transformational Government: Enabled by Technology* (London: HMSO).

Coxall, B. and L. Robins (1998) *Contemporary British Politics* (3rd edn) (London: Macmillan).

Efficiency Unit (1988) *Improving Management in Government: The Next Steps* (London: HMSO).

Flinders, M. (2002) 'Governance in Whitehall', *Public Administration*, 80 (1), 51–75.

Fry, G. (1988) 'The Thatcher Government, the Financial Management Initiative, and the "New Civil Service"', *Public Administration*, 66 (1), 1–20.

Fry, G., A. Flynn, A. Gray, W. Jenkins and B. Rutherford (1988) 'Symposium on Improving Management in Government', *Public Administration*, 66, 429–45.

HM Treasury (1991) *Competing for Quality: Buying Better Public Services* (London: HMSO).

HM Treasury (1993) *Civil Service Management Code* (London: HM Treasury/ Cabinet Office).

HM Treasury (1999) *Modern Public Services for Britain: Investing in Reform: Comprehensive Spending Review: New Public Spending Plans 1999–2002* (London: The Stationery Office).

Hogwood, B. W. (1997) 'The Machinery of Government 1979–97', *Political Studies*, 45 (4), 704–15.

Hogwood, B. W., D. Judge and M. McVicar (1999) *Agencies, Ministers and Civil Servants in Britain*, available at: www.essex.ac.uk/ECPR/events/jointsessions/ paperarchive/mannheim/w1/hogwood.pdf.

Hood, C., O. James and C. Scott (2000) 'Regulation of Government: Has It Increased, Is It Increasing, Should It Be Diminished', *Public Administration*, 78 (2), 283–304.

House of Commons (1994) *Code of Practice on Access to Government Information* (London: HMSO).

James, O. (2003) *The Executive Agency in Whitehall: Public Interest Versus Bureau-shaping Perspectives* (Basingstoke: Palgrave Macmillan).

James, O. (2004a) 'Executive Agencies and Joined-up Government', in C. Pollitt and C. Talbot (eds), *Unbundled Government: A Critical Analysis of the Global Trend to Agencies, Quangos and Contractualisation* (New York: Routledge).

James, O. (2004b) 'The UK Core Executive's Use of Public Service Agreements as a Tool of Governance', *Public Administration*, 82 (2), 397–419.

Judge, D. (2005) *Political Institutions in the United Kingdom* (Oxford: Oxford University Press).

Kavanagh, D. and D. Richards (2003) 'Prime Ministers, Ministers and Civil Servants in Britain', *Comparative Sociology*, 2 (1), 175–95.

Klein, R. and W. Plowden (2005) 'JASO Meets JUG: Lessons of the 1975 Joint Approach to Social Policy for Joined-up Government', in V. Bogdanor (ed.), *Joined-up Government* (Oxford: The British Academy in association with Oxford University Press).

Le Grand, J. and W. Bartlett (1993) *Quasi-Markets and Social Policy* (London: Palgrave Macmillan).

Ling, T. (2002) 'Delivering Joined-up Government in the UK: Dimensions, Issues and Problems', *Public Administration*, 80 (4), 615–42.

Marsh, D. (1991) 'Privatisation under Mrs Thatcher: A Review of the Literature', *Public Administration*, 69 (4), 459–80.

Moran, M. (2005) *Politics and Governance in the UK* (Basingstoke: Palgrave Macmillan).

OECD (1999) *Strategic Review and Reform – The UK Perspective* (Paris: OECD).

Office of Public Service (1996) *Government.direct: A Prospectus for the Electronic Delivery of Government Services* (London: HMSO).

Peele, G. (1995) *Governing the UK*, 3rd edn (Oxford: Blackwell).

Pollitt, C. (2003) 'Joined-up Government: A Survey', *Political Studies Review*, 1 (1), 34–49.

Pollitt, C. and G. Bouckaert, (2004) *Public Management Reform: A Comparative Analysis*, 2nd edn (Oxford: Oxford University Press).

Pollitt, C., K. Bathgate, J. Caulfield, A. Smullen and C. Talbot (2001) 'Agency Fever? Analysis of an International Policy Fashion', *Journal of Comparative Policy Analysis*, 3 (3), 271–90.

Prime Minister and Minister for the Civil Service (1994) *The Civil Service: Continuity and Change* (London: HMSO).

Prime Minister and Minister for the Civil Service (1994) *The Civil Service: Taking Forward Continuity and Change* (London: HMSO).

Rhodes, R. A. W. (1996) 'The New Governance: Governing without Government', *Political Studies*, XLIV, 652–67.

Richardson, J. (1993) *Doing Less by Doing More: British Government 1979–1993*, EPPI Occasional Papers, No. 93/2, University of Warwick.

Seldon, A. (1990) 'The Cabinet Office and Coordination 1979–1987', *Public Administration*, 68 (1), 103–21.

Country Chapter: Sweden

Bouckaert, G., D. Ormond and B. G. Peters (2000) *A Potential Governance Agenda for Finland, Turning 90° in the Administration's Tasks and Functions* (Helsinki: Ministry of Finance).

Blöndal, J. R. (2001) 'Budgeting in Sweden', *OECD Journal on Budgeting*, 1 (1), 27–57.

Dahlberg, Lars (1993) 'The Swedish Experience of Decentralized Government through Agencies.' Paper presented at the 'Public Sector Reforms' Conference, Barcelona, 12 August.

Dahlberg, L. and C. Isaksson (1996) 'The Implementation of Benchmarking from a Swedish Perspective'. Paper presented at the 1996 Meeting of the Performance Management Network of the OECD's Public Management Service on Benchmarking, Evaluation and Strategic Management in the Public Sector.

Hinnfors, R. (1999) 'Stability Through Change: The Pervasiveness of Political Ideas', *Journal of Public Policy*, 19 (3), 293–312.

Hustedt, T. and J. Tiessen (2006) 'Central Government Coordination In Denmark, Germany and Sweden: An Institutional Policy Perspective', Forschungspapiere 'Regierungsorganisation in Westeuropa', 2 (Potsdam: Univ-Verlag).

Larsson, T. (1986) *Regeringen och dess kansli: samordning och byrakrati i maktens centrum* (Lund: Studentlitteratur).

Larsson, T. (1993) 'The Role and Position of the Minister of Finance', in J. Blondel and F. Müller-Rommel (eds), *Governing Together: The Extent and Limits of Joint Decision-Making in Western European Cabinets* (London: Macmillan).

Larsson, T. (1995) *Governing Sweden* (Stockholm: Swedish Agency for Administrative Development).

Larsson, T. and J. Trondal (2005) 'After Hierarchy? The Differentiated Impact of the European Commission and the Council of Ministers on Domestic Executive Governance.' Working Paper, Center for European Studies, University of Oslo, No. 22, August.

Mackie and B. Hogwood (eds) (1985) *Unlocking the Cabinet: Cabinet Structures in Comparative Perspective* (London and Beverly Hills: Sage).

Molander, P., J-E. Nilsson and A. Schick (2002) *Does Anyone Govern? The Relationship Between the Government Office and the Agencies in Sweden* (Stockholm: SNS).

Niklasson, L. (2004) 'Learning Networks for Regional Development: Evaluation as a Tool for Regional Governance.' Paper presented at the European Evaluation Society Sixth Conference, Berlin, 30 September–2 October.

OECD (1992) *Public Management Profiles: Sweden* (Paris: OECD–PUMA).

OECD (1998) *Information Technology as an Instrument of Public Management Reform: a Study of Five OECD Countries*. Unpublished paper, OECD–PUMA, Paris.

OECD (1999) *Management Developments in Sweden 1998* (Paris: OECD). Available at: www.oecd.fr/puma/gvrnance/surveys/pubs/report98/surv98swe.htm.

OECD (2001) *Issues and Developments in Public Management* (Paris: OECD–PUMA).

OECD (ed.) (2002), *Distributed Public Governance. Agencies, Authorities and Other Government Bodies*, chapter 'Sweden', by T. Larsson (Paris: OECD), 181–208.

OECD–PUMA (2000) 'Handout Sweden.' Presentation for the OECD Expert meeting on Management of Large Public Sector IT Projects Paris, 26–27 October. Available at: www.oecd.org/dataoecd/40/5/2023029.pdf dd.09092005.

OECD SWEDEN (2005) www.oecd.org/dataoecd/17/56/2005154.pdf dd. 09092005.

Pierre, J. (1993) 'Legitimacy, Institutional Change and the Politics of Public Administration in Sweden', *International Journal of Political Science*, 14 (4), 387–401.

Pollitt, C. and G. Bouckaert (2004) *Public Management Reform: A Comparative Analysis* (Oxford: Oxford University Press).

Regeringskansliet (1997) *The Swedish Government and the Government Offices* (Stockholm: Regeringskansliet).

Regeringskansliet (2000) *An Information Society for All* (Stockholm: Regeringskansliet).

Riksezvisionsverket (1997) *Report of the Auditor General to the Government 1997* (Stockholm: RRV).

Scheers, B. and G. Bouckaert (2003) *Internationale Trends in de Modernisering van de Overheidsboekhouding* (Leuven: Unpublished SBOV report).

SEMA (2004) *Improving Sweden's Emergency Management System – Summary in English*. Document no: 0931/2004.

Statskontoret (Swedish Agency for Administrative Development) (1998) *The Swedish Central Government in Transition* (Stockholm: Statskontoret).

Statskontoret (1999) *The Swedish Central Government in Transition* (Stockholm: Statskontoret).

Statskontoret (2000a) *Swedish Agency for Public Management. The 24/7 Agency. Criteria for 24/7 Agencies in the Networked Public Administration* (Stockholm: Statskontoret).

Statskontoret (2000b) *Analysis of Practical Aspects of Possible Later Participation in the Economic and Monetary Union (EMU)* (Stockholm: Statskontoret).

Statskontoret (2002) *Interconnected Government: A Proposal for Strengthening Central Co-ordination of E-Government Development Efforts* (Stockholm: Statskontoret).

Statskontoret (2003) *Financial Management Rating of Government Agencies in Sweden* (Stockholm: Statskontoret).

Statskontoret (2004a) *ICA (International Council for IT in Government Administrations) Country Report Sweden 2004* (Stockholm: Statskontoret).

Statskontoret (2004b) 'Public Administration in the E-society'. Unpublished memo, 11 November 2004, Statskontoret, Stockholm.

Swedish National Audit Bureau (SNAB) (1993) *Performance Auditing and the Swedish National Audit Bureau* (Stockholm: SNAB).

Country Chapter: The Netherlands

Algemene Rekenkamer (1995a) *Verslag 1994. Deel 3: Zelfstandige bestuursorganen en ministeriële verantwoordelijkheid.* Tweede Kamer, 1994–1995, 24 130, nr. 3.

Algemene Rekenkamer (1995b) *Herstel van het primaat van de politiek bij de aansturing van zelfstandige bestuursorganen.* Tweede Kamer, 1994–1995, 24 130, nr. 5.

Algemene Rekenkamer (2003) *Tussen beleid en uitvoering: lessen uit recent onderzoek.* Tweede Kamer, 2002–2003, 28 831, nr. 1.

Algemene Rekenkamer (2004). *Verantwoording en toezicht bij rechtspersonen met een wettelijke taak, deel 4.* Tweede Kamer. Vergaderjaar 2003–2004. 29 450, nrs. 1–2.

Algemene Rekenkamer (2004–2005) *Evaluatie VBTB.* Tweede Kamer, 2004–2005, 29 949, nr. 2.

Andeweg, R. (1985) 'The Netherlands: Cabinet Committees in a Coalition Cabinet', in T. Mackie and B. Hogwood (eds), *Unlocking the Cabinet: Cabinet Structures in Comparative Perspective* (London and Beverly Hills: Sage).

Andeweg, R. B. and W. Bakema (1994) 'The Netherlands: Ministers and Cabinet Policy', in M. Laver and K. A. Shepsle (eds), *Cabinet Ministers and Parliamentary Government* (Cambridge: Cambridge University Press), 56–72.

Bekke, A. J. G. M., R. D. Bekker and A. D. J. Verhoeven (1996) *Haagse bazen: een verkenning van de topstructuur van de ministeries* (Alphen aan den Rijn: Samson/ H. D. Tjeenk Willink).

Bergsma, E. N. and J. C. van den Brink (2002) 'De pre-marktfase in de sociale verzekeringen. Het gedrag van publieke organisaties nader bezien', *Bestuurskunde*, 11 (6), 235–42.

Bouckaert, G. and J. De Corte (1999) 'Contractmanagement en Management van Contracten', no. 3 in the series 'Overheidsmanagement' (Brugge: die Keure).

Bouckaert, G., K. Verhoest and A. Wauters (2000) 'Van effectiviteit van coordinatie naar coordinatie van effectiviteit'. no. 10 in the series 'Overheidsmanagement' (Brugge: die Keure).

Borghouts, H. C. J. L. (2002) 'Perspectieven voor effectiviteit en geloofwaardigheid', *Bestuurskunde*, 11 (3), 140–8.

Bovens, M. A. P. (2000) 'De vierde macht revisited' [Speech], Utrecht.

Breunese, J. N. and L. J. Roborgh (1992) *Ministeries van Algemeen Bestuur* (Leiden: SMD).

de Bruijn, J. A. and E. F. ten Heuvelhof (1991) *Sturingsinstrumenten voor de overheid: over complexe netwerken en een tweede generatie sturingsinstrumenten* (Leiden and Antwerp: Stenfert Kroese).

de Vries, J. and K. Yesilkagit (1999) 'Core Executives, Party Politics, and Privatisation in the Netherlands', *West European Politics*, 22 (1), 115–37.

Commissie Deetman (1991) *Bijzondere Commissie Vraagpunten. Eindrapportage. Staatkundige, bestuurlijke en staatsrechtelijke vernieuwing.* Tweede Kamer, vergaderingjaar 1990–1991, 21427, nr. 3.

Commissie Cohen (1997) *Eindrapport Werkgroep Markt en Overheid* (The Hague: Ministerie van Economische Zaken, Commissie MDW).

Commissie Deetman (1991) *Staatskundige en bestuurlijke vernieuwing. Eindrapport, Tweede Kamer – Kamerstukken 1990–1991,* The Hague.

Commissie Hoofdstructuur Rijksdienst (1981) *Eindadvies van de Commissie Hoofdstructuur Rijksdienst,* 's-Gravenhage.

Commissie Interdepartementale Taakverdeling en Coördinatie (1971) *Rapport van de Commissie Interdepartementale Taakverdeling en Coördinatie* (Commissie Van Veen), The Hague.

Commissie Kohnstamm (2004) *Rapport van de commissie Kohnstamm en de kabinetsreactie daarop. Tweede Kamer 2004–2005, Stuk 25 268, nr. 20,* The Hague.

Commissie Sint (1994) *Verantwoord verzelfstandigen,* The Hague.

Commissie Vonhoff (Commissie Hoofdstructuur Rijksdienst) (1980) *Elk kent de laan die derwaart gaat,* 's-Gravenhage.

Commissie Wiegel (1993) *Naar kerndepartementen, keizen voor een hoogwaardige en flexibele rijksdienst. Tweede Kamer, vergaderjaar 1992–1993, 21 427, nr. 51 TK,* The Hague.

Gemengde Commissie 'Sturing EU–aangelegenheden' (2005). Eindrapport, The Hague, 7 June.

't Hart, P. and A. Wille (eds). (2002) *Politiek-ambtelijke verhoudingen in beweging* (Amsterdam: Boom).

Hoogerwerf, A., (1982) *Overheidsbeleid,* 2nd edn (Alphen aan den Rijn, Samson).

Jongeneel, C. (2005) *Verzelfstandiging: stijl of trend? De stijlen van verzelfstandiging van de beleidssectoren van de Rijksoverheid; en hun consistentie met de institutionele context* [scriptie Bestuurskunde EUR], Rotterdam.

Kabinet (2003) *Actieprogramma Andere Overheid* (The Hague).

Kickert, W. J. M. (1998) *Aansturing van verzelfstandigde overheidsdiensten: over publiek management van hybride organisaties* (Alphen aan den Rijn: Samson).

Kickert, W. J. M (2005) *Lessen uit het verleden – Onderzoek naar veranderoperaties bij de overheid, In opdracht van het rijksbrede Programma Andere Overheid* (The Hague: Ministerie van Binnenlandse Zaken en Koninkrijksrelaties).

Kickert, W. J. M., J. Meines and K. Verdel (2005) *Lessen uit het verleden – Onderzoek naar veranderoperaties bij de overheid, In opdracht van het rijksbrede Programma Andere Overheid* (The Hague: Ministerie van Binnenlandse Zaken en Koninkrijksrelaties): See www.andereoverheid.nl.

Kickert, W. J. M. and R. in 't Veld (1995) 'National Government, Governance and Administration', in W. J. M. Kickert and F. van Vught (eds), *Public Policy and Administration Science in the Netherlands* (London: Prentice-Hall/Harvester Wheatsheaf).

Kooiman, J. (1971) 'Regeringsbeleid als proces', *Acta Politica,* 6, 388–99.

Koppenjan, J., J. de Bruijn and W. J. M. Kickert (1993) *Netwerkmanagement in het openbaar bestuur: over de mogelijkheden van overheidssturing in beleidsnetwerken* ('s-Gravenshage: VUGA).

Kottman, R. (1978) 'Horizontale taakverdeling en coördinatie (Hoofdstuk 19)', in A. Hoogerwerf (ed.), *Overheidsbeleid* (Alphen aan den Rijn: Samson).

Langenberg, P. J. and P. W. Tetteroo (2002) 'De toekomst van het grotestedenbeleid. Meer maatwerk, ontkokering en prestatiesturing', *Bestuurskunde,* 11 (8), 158–65.

Maarse, J. A. M. (2001) 'De hervorming van de gezondheidszorg. Enkele politieke aspecten', *Bestuurskunde,* 10 (5), 186–96.

Maarse, J. A. M and A. F. A. Korsten (2001), 'Gezondheidszorg: tussen continuïteit en verandering', *Bestuurskunde*, 10 (5), 182–5.

Ministerie van Binnenlandse Zaken en Ministerie van Financiën (1997) *Rapportage Doorlichting Zelfstandige Bestuursorganen* (The Hague: Ministerie van Binnenlandse Zaken en Ministerie van Financiën).

Minister voor Bestuurlijke Vernieuwing en Koninkrijksrelaties (2006) *Het resultaat is de maat. Een beter presterende rijksdienst*, The Hague.

Ministerie van Financiën (2005) 'Overview of Number of Agencies'. Available at: www.minfin.nl.

Nomden, K. (1999) *Interministerial coordination in the Netherlands*. Draft paper, EIPA, Maastricht.

Noordegraaf, M. (1995) 'Het bestuursraadmodel: individualisering van structuren', in M. Noordegraaf, A. B. Ringeling and F. J. M. Zwetsloot (eds), *De ambtenaar als publiek ondernemer* (Bussum: Coutinho), 127–40.

Programma team Andere Overheid (2006) *Voortgangsrapportage Programma Andere Overheid*, The Hague, Autumn 2006.

Rosenthal, U., M. P. C. M van Schendelen and G. H. Scholten (1975) *Ministers, ambtenaren en parlementariërs in Nederland* (Groningen: H. D. Tjeenk Willink).

Secretarissen-generaal (1993) *De organisatie en de werkwijze van de rijksdienst*, rapportage van de secretarissen-generaal, The Hague.

Smits, J. (1995) *Milieubeleid gestuurd?: Een onderzoek naar de invloed van het BUGM op het gemeentelijk milieubeleid in Noord-Brabant* (Amsterdam: Thesis Publishers).

Steur, B. F., P. J. M. de Goede and H. H. J. Schmeets (2004) 'Nationale coördinatie van Europees beleid, "best belangrijk"', *Bestuurskunde*, 13 (6), 255–62.

Van de Graaf, H. and R. Hoppe (1992) *Beleid en politiek: een inleiding tot de beleidswetenschap en de beleidskunde* (Muiderberg: Coutinho).

Van Dam, S., M. Esselbrugge and H. de Jong (2005) *Beter coördineren – Praktische analyse en aanbevelingen voor coördineren bij het Rijk*. Studie in opdracht van het Ministerie van BZK (Amersfoort: Lysias Advies BV).

Van der Aa, A. and T. P. J. Konijn (2001): *Ketens, ketenregisseurs en ketenontwikkeling. Het ontwikkelen van transparante en flexibele samenwerkingsverbanden in netwerken* (Utrecht: Lemma).

Van der Aa, A. and T. P. J. Konijn (2002) *Ruimte voor regie: Handreiking voor ketenregie in het openbaar bestuur* (The Hague: Ministerie van Binnenlandse Zaken).

Van der Knaap, P, C. J., A. M Termeer and M. J. W. van Twist (2002) 'Omwille van effectief toezicht – Reflecties op risico's van een hype', *Bestuurskunde*, 11 (3).

Van Duivenboden, H., M. van Twist, M. Veldhuizen and R. in 't Veld (eds) (2000) *Ketenmanagement in de Publieke Sector* (Utrecht: Lemma).

Van Klink, B. M. J. and W. J. Witteveen (2002) *De sociale rechtsstaat voorbij. Twee ontwerpen voor het huis van de rechtsstaat*, Voorstudies en achtergronden WRR, V 116 (The Hague: Sdu).

Van Oosteroom, R. and S. van Thiel (2004a) 'Agentschappen: kruiwagen voor modernisering?', *Bestuurskunde*, 13 (7), 292–300.

Van Oosteroom, R. and S. van Thiel (2004b) 'Nawoord', *Bestuurskunde*, 13 (7), 332–35.

Van Thiel, S. (2001) 'Kaderwet Zelfstandige Bestuursorganen; uniformiteit of verscheidenheid?', *Bestuurswetenschappen*, 55 (2), 189–193.

Van Thiel, S. (2008) 'The 'Empty Nest' Syndrome: Dutch Ministries after the Separation of Policy and Administration.' Paper presented at the Conference of International Research Symposium on Public Management, 26–28 March, Brisbane, Australia.

Van Thiel, S., F. L. Leeuw and H. D. Flap (1998) 'Quango-cratisering in Nederland?', *Beleid & Maatschappij*, XXV, 143–51.

Van Thiel, S. and C. Pollit (2007) 'The Management and Control of Executive Agencies: An Anglo-Dutch Comparison', in C. Pollitt, S. Van Thiel and V. Homburg (eds), *New Public Management in Europe: Adaptation and Alternatives* (Basingstoke: Palgrave Macmillan).

Van Thiel, S. and A. van Buuren (2001) 'Ontwikkeling van het aantal zelfstandige bestuursorganen tussen 1993 en 2000: zijn ZBOs uit de mode?', *Bestuurswetenschappen*, 55 (5), 386–404.

Van Twist, M. J. W. and R. J. in 't Veld (1993) *Over kerndepartementen, een vergelijkend onderzoek naar departementale veranderingsprocessen in Groot-Brittannië, Zweden, Noorwegen en Denemarken* (The Hague: Vuga).

Van Twist, M. J. W., R. Bagchus and F. O. M. Verhaak (1996) *Kerndepartementen op afstand? Een vergelijkend onderzoek naar departementele veranderingsprocessen binnen de Nederlandse rijksdienst* (Delft: Eburon).

Van Twist, M. and P. Plug (1998) 'Een moeizame verbinding: over de vormgeving en invulling van interfaces bij kerndepartementen', *Beleidsanalyse*, 27 (3), 15–22.

Verhoest, K. and S. van Thiel (2004) 'Herstel van het primaat van de politiek: een vergelijking van de ontwikkeling in het beleid rond verzelfstandigde organisaties in Nederland en Vlaanderen', *Beleid en Maatschappij*, 31 (1), 27–41.

WRR (1983) *Organen en rechtspersonen rondom de centrale overheid*, V35, parts 1–3. (The Hague: Sdu).

WRR (2000) *Het borgen van publiek belang*. WRR Rapporten aan de Regering nr. 56 (The Hague: Sdu).

Zalm, G. (2001) *Nota deelnemingenbeleid Rijksoverheid* (nr. FIN01–331). Nota aan de Voorzitter van de Tweede Kamer der Staten-Generaal, The Hague.

Country Chapter: France

Albertini, J-B. and J-L. Silicani (1997) *La déconcentration: l'administration territoriale dans la réforme de l'État.* Collection Collectivités territoriales. Série Droit (Paris: Economica).

Bodiguel, J-L. and L. Rouban (1991) *Le fonctionnaire détrôné? L'état au risque de la modernisation* (Paris: Presses de la Fondation nationale des sciences politiques).

Braun, G. (2001) *Le manque d'ambition du fonds pour la réforme de l'Etat: rapport d'information.* Les rapports du Sénat (383), Commission des finances, du contrôle budgétaire et des comptes économiques de la nation (Paris: Sénat).

Chaty, L. (1997) *L'administration face au management: projets de service et centres de responsabilité dans l'administration française.* Collection Logiques politiques (Paris: L'Harmattan).

Chevallier, J. and L. Rouban (2003) 'La réforme de l'Etat et la nouvelle gestion publique: mythes et réalités', *Revue française d'administration publique,* 105–106 (Paris : Ecole nationale d'administration).

Cour des comptes (2003) *La déconcentration des administrations et la réforme de l'Etat* (Paris: Documentation française).

Crozier, M. (1987) *État modeste, État moderne: stratégie pour un autre changement* (Paris: Fayard).

Crozier, M. and S. Trosa (1992) *La décentralisation. Réforme de l'état* (Boulogne: Editions Pouvoirs Locaux).

Direction générale de l'administration et de la fonction publique (1994) *Documents d'étude sur la modernisation de l'administration* (Paris: Documentation française).

Direction générale de l'administration et de la fonction publique (1990) *Renouveau du service public: les rencontres 1990: sélection des textes officiels* (Paris: Journaux officiels).

Documentation française (2006) *LOLF: ce qui change. Regards sur l'actualité* (n. 316 December 2005) (Paris: Documentation française).

Dupuy, F. and J-C. Thoenig (1985) *L'administration en miettes* (Paris: Fayard).

Fauroux, R., B. Spitz and N. Baverez (2000) *Notre Etat: le livre vérité de la fonction publique* (Paris: Laffont).

Gremion, C. and R. Fraissé (1996) *Le service public en recherche: quelle modernisation?* Commissariat général du plan, Secrétariat d'Etat à la recherche (Paris: Documentation française).

Hoffmann-Martinot, V. and H. Wollmann (eds) (2006) *State and Local Government Reforms in France and Germany: Divergence and Convergence* (Wiesbaden: Verlag für Sozialwissenschaften).

Institut de management public (2002) *Reconfigurer l'action publique: big bang ou réforme? Politiques et management public* (Paris: Institut de management public).

Institut international d'administration publique (1996) 'L'action extérieure de l'Etat: la réforme de l'Etat en France', *Revue française d'administration publique,* 77 (January–March).

Lasserre, B. and P. Chantepie (2000) *L'Etat et les technologies de l'information: vers une administration à accès pluriel.* Commissariat général du plan (Paris: Documentation française).

LOLF (2006) 'LOLF et gestion de la réforme publique', *Droit administratif*, 62 (10) (Paris: Moniteur, L'actualité juridique), 523–49.

Maisi, H., J-C. Thoenig and P. Bernard (eds) (1991) *Les nouvelles relations état collectivités locales* (Paris: Documentation française).

Muller, P. (1992) *L'administration française est-elle en crise?* Collection Logiques politiques, 4 (Paris: L'Harmattan).

Olivennes, D. and N. Baverez (1989) *L'impuissance publique l'État, c'est nous . . .* (Paris: Calmann-Lévy).

Rémond, B., J. Picq and L. Rouban (2002) *La décentralisation: réforme de l'Etat.* Pouvoirs locaux: les cahiers de la décentralisation (Boulogne Billancourt: Pouvoirs locaux).

Rouban, L. (2001) *Les fonctionnaires.* Idées reçues, 7 (Paris: Le Cavalier bleu).

Sapin, M. (2002) *L'état en mouvement* (Paris : Leprince).

Saunier-Seite, A. (1984) *Remettre l'état a sa place* (Paris: Plon).

Trosa, S. and Y. Cannac (2006) *Vers un management post bureaucratique: La réforme de l'Etat, une réforme de la société* (Paris: Harmattan).

Trosa, S. and Y. Cannac (2008) *La réforme de l'Etat* (Paris: Ellipses).

Trosa, S. and M. Crozier (2002) *Le guide de la gestion par programmes: vers une culture du résultat.* Collection service public (Paris: Editions d'organisation).

Winicki, P. and E. Pisani (2007) *Réussir une réforme publique* (Paris: Dunod).

X (2006) 'LOLF et gestion de la réforme publique. L'actualité juridique', *Droit administratif*, 62 (10) (Paris: Moniteur, L'actualité juridique), 523–49.

Country Chapter: Belgium

Berckx, P. (1993) 'De bestuurlijke vernieuwing en het Handvest van de Gebruiker van de openbare diensten', *Tijdschrift voor Bestuurswetenschappen en publiekrecht*, 5, 275–88.

Bouckaert, G. and T. Auwers (1999) *De modernisering van de Vlaamse Overheid* (Brugge: Die Keure).

Bouckaert, G. and A. François (1999) *Modernisering van de Overheidsinstellingen: onderzoeksvragen* (Brussels: DWTC).

Bouckaert, G. and A. Wauters (1999) *Moderniseringsinitiatieven binnen de federale overheid: organisatie* (Brussels: DWTC).

Bouckaert, G. (1993) 'Charters as Frameworks for Awarding Quality: The Belgian, British and French Experience'. Presentation at seminar on concepts and methods of quality awards in the public sector, Speyer, Germany.

Brans, M., C. Pelgrims and D. Hoet (2005) 'Politico-administrative Relations under Coalition Governments: The Case of Belgium', in B. G. Peters, T. Verheijen and L. Vass (eds), *Politico-administrative Relations under Coalition Governments* (Bratislava: NISPA), 206–37.

Collège des Secrétaires Généraux (1995) 'Actor I', Brussels, May 1995 (internal document).

De Borger, J. (1988) 'Depolitisering van het openbaar ambt, een must voor fatsoenlijke politiek', *Nieuw Tijdschrift voor Politiek*, 1988 (3), 53–87.

De Visscher, C. (2003) 'La relation entre autorité politique et haute fonction publique suite au plan copernic', in *Les Cahiers des sciences administratives* (Brussels: Haute Ecole Francesco Ferrer/Cefal), 51–70.

Depré, R. (1973) *De topambtenaren van de ministeries in België* (Leuven: KU Leuven, Faculteit Sociale Wetenschappen).

Depré, R., B. Mas and H. Van Hassel (1966) *Coördinatie van het overheidsbeleid in een evoluerende maatschappij* (Brussels: Instituut administratie-universiteit).

Franceus, F. and P. Staes (1997) 'De kwaliteitsbarometer: een federaal initiatief tot externe kwaliteitsbewaking in de administratie', *Vlaams Tijdschrift voor Overheidsmanagement*, 1997 (3), 22–8.

Franceus, F. (2004) 'Na Copernicus Keppler? De stand van de zon in het federaal openbaar ambt', *Tijdschrift voor Bestuurskunde en Publiek recht*, 2004 (1), 3–18.

François, A. and A. Molitor (1987) 'L'administration belge de 1970 à ce jour', *Administration Publique*, 99–123.

François, A. (1987) 'La modernisation de l'administration de l'Etat en Belgique', *Revue Internationale des Sciences Administratives*, 53 (3), 355–99.

François, A. (1998) *Histoire de la réforme administrative avant 1937* (Louvain-la-Neuve: AURA).

Hertecant, G. (1990) 'Een nieuwe structuur voor de Vlaamse administratie 1973–1983', in *Bouwstenen voor de Vlaamse autonomie, Vriendenboek Etienne de Ryck* (Tielt: Lannoo), 100–6.

Hondeghem, A. and R. Depré (2005) *De Copernicushervorming in perspectief: Veranderingsmanagement in de federale overheid* (Brugge: Vanden Broele).

Hondeghem, A. (1990) *De loopbaan van de ambtenaar. Tussen droom en werkelijkheid* (Leuven: VCOB).

Hondeghem, A. (2000) 'The National Civil Service in Belgium', in H. Bekke and F. Van der Meer (eds), *Civil Service Systems in Western Europe* (Cheltenham: Edward Elgar), 120–8.

Legrand, J-J. (1990) 'L'approche belge de la modernisation des administrations publiques: les cellules de modernisation comme outil stratégique de changement', *Administration Publique*, 1990, 2–3, 169–88.

Maes, R. (1994) 'De overheidsmanager in een veranderend politiek en juridisch systeem', in G. Bouckaert, A. Hondeghem and R. Maes (eds), *De overheidsmanager. Nieuwe ontwikkelingen in het overheidsmanagement* (Leuven: Acco), 21–42.

Maesschalck, J., A. Hondeghem and C. Pelgrims (2002) 'De evolutie naar een "Nieuwe Politieke Cultuur" in België: een beleidswetenschappelijke analyse', *Beleidswetenschap*, 16 (4), 295–317.

Molitor, A. (1974) *L'administration en Belgique* (Brussels: Institut belge de Science Politique/CRISP).

Nomden, K. (2000) 'De Copernicusnota: het mandaatsysteem voor federale topambtenaren bekeken vanuit een internationaal perspectief', *Vlaams Tijdschrift voor Overheidsmanagement*, 2000 (1), 4–15.

Parys, M. and A. Hondeghem (2005) 'Belgium: Staff Participation in the Copernic Reform', in D. Farnham, A. Hondeghem and S. Horton (eds), *Staff Participation and Public Management Reform. Some International Comparisons* (Basingstoke: Palgrave Macmillan), 100–13.

Parys, M. and N. Thijs (2003) *Business Process Reengineering; Or How to Enable Bottom-up Participation in a Top-down Reform Programme*. Paper presented at the European Group of Public Administration (EGPA) Study Group on Public Personnel Policies: 'Staff participation and involvement in European public services', Oeiras, Portugal, 3–6 September.

Parys, M. (2001) 'Het competentiedenken binnen de federale overheidsdiensten in België', *Vlaams tijdschrift voor overheidsmanagement*, 2001 (3), 10–18.

Pelgrims, C. (2001) *Ministeriële kabinetsleden en hun loopbaan. Tussen mythe en realiteit* (Brugge: Die Keure).

Pelgrims, C. (2002) 'Ministeriële kabinetten als flexibele brug tussen politiek en administratie. Een onderzoek naar de instroom in de ministeriële kabinetten', *Res Publica*, 4, 629–52.

Polet, R. (1999) *La Radioscopie des services publiques* (Brussels: DWTC).

Staes, P. (1992) 'De methodologie van de doorlichting', in M. De Mesmaeker (ed.), *Naar een beter en budgettair beheer in België. Nieuwe perspectieven vanuit de operatie Doorlichting* (Brussels: ABC).

Suetens, M. and S. Walgrave (1999) 'Leven en werk van de kabinetsleden. Wie zijn de mannen achter de minister en wat doen ze?', *Res Publica*, 4, 499–528.

Van de Walle, S., N. Thijs and G. Bouckaert (2005) 'A Tale of Two Charters: Political Crisis, Political Realignment and Administrative Reform in Belgium', *Public Management Review*, 7 (3), 367–90.

Van den Bossche, L. (2000) 'Het creëren van een veranderingsdynamiek bij de federale administratie', in *Jaarboek VVBB* (Brussels: VVBB), 55–63.

Van Hassel, H. (1974) *Het ministerieel cabinet. Peilen naar een sociologische duiding.* Doctoral dissertation, Katholieke Universiteit Leuven.

Van Hoorick, W. (1990) 'Een blauwdruk voor de Vlaamse administratie 1989-1990', in *Bouwstenen voor de Vlaamse autonomie, Vriendenboek Etienne de Ryck* (Tielt: Lannoo), 107–22.
Vancoppenolle, D. and A. Legrain (2003) 'Le new public management en Belgique: Comparaison des réformes en Flandres et en Wallonie', *Administration publique*, 2003 (2), 112–28.
Vermeulen, P. (1995) 'Kwaliteitszorg, prestatiegerichtheid en klantvriendelijkheid binnen het federaal openbaar ambt: een overzicht van de reeds genomen initiatieven', *Tijdschrift voor Bestuurswetenschappen en Publiek Recht,* 1995 (6), 297–303.

Country Chapter: United States

Aberbach, J. D. (1990) *Keeping a Watchful Eye: The Politics of Congressional Oversight* (Washington DC: Brookings Institution).

Aberbach, J. D. (1999) 'A Reinvented Government, or the Same Old Government?', in C. Campbell and B. A. Rockman (eds), *The Clinton Legacy* (New York; Chatham House).

Arnold, P. E. (2000) *Making the Managerial Presidency: Comprehensive Reorganization Planning* (Lawrence: University Press of Kansas).

Benda, P. M. and C. H. Levine (1988) 'Reagan and the Bureaucracy', in C. O. Jones (ed.), *The Reagan Legacy* (Chatham NJ: Chatham House).

Burke, J. P. (1992) *The Institutional President* (Baltimore: Johns Hopkins University Press).

Carpenter, D. P. (2001) *Forging Bureaucratic Autonomy* (Princeton: Princeton University Press).

Freeman, J. L. (1955) *The Political Process* (New York: Doubleday).

Gamkhar, S. (2002) *Federal Intergovernmental Grants and the States* (Cheltenham: Edward Elgar).

Hart, J. (1996) *The Presidential System*, 2nd edn (Chatham NJ: Chatham House).

Heclo, H. (1978) 'Issue Networks and the Executive Establishment', in A. King (ed.), *The New American Political System* (Washington DC: American Enterprise Institute).

Heclo, H. (1983) 'One Executive Branch or Many?', in A. King (ed.), *Both Ends of the Avenue* (Washington DC: American Enterprise Institute).

Kaboolian, L. (1998) 'The New Public Management: Challenging the Boundaries of the Management vs. Administration Debate', *Public Administration Review*, 58 (3), 189–97.

Kerwin, C. (2004) *Rulemaking*, 3rd edn (Washington DC: CQ Press).

Kettl, D. F. (2004) *System Under Stress: Homeland Security and American Politics* (Washington DC: CQ Press).

Kettl, D. F. and J. DiIulio (1995) *Inside the Reinvention Machine* (Washington DC: Brookings Institution).

Leeuw, F. L., R. C. Rist and R. C. Sonnichsen (1994) *Can Government Learn? Comparative Perspectives on Evaluation and Organizational Learning* (New Brunswick: Transaction Publishers).

Light, P. C. (1995) *Thickening Government* (Washington DC: Brookings Institution).

Maranto, R. (2005) *Beyond a Government of Strangers: How Career Executives and Political Appointees Can Turn Conflict into Cooperation* (Lanham: Lexington Books).

Mayhew, D. R. (1991) *Divided We Govern: Party Control, Lawmaking and Investigations 1946–90* (New Haven: Yale University Press).

Nicholson, S. P., G. M. Segura and N. D. Woods (2002) 'Presidential Approval and the Mixed Blessings of Divided Government', *The Journal of Politics*, 64 (3), 701–20.

Peters, B. G. (2001) *The Future of Governing*, 2nd edn (Lawrence: University Press of Kansas).

Peters, B. G. (2008) 'Political Advisors in the United States', in R. Shaw and C. Eichbaum, (eds), *The Role of Policy Advisors*.

Pollitt, C., C. Talbot, J. Caulfield and A. Smullen (2005) *Agencies: How Governments Do Things through Semi-autonomous Organizations* (Basingstoke: Palgrave Macmillan).

Polsby, N. W. (1975) 'Legislatures', in F. I. Greenstein and N. W. Polsby (eds), *Handbook of Political Science*, Vol. 5 (Reading MA: Addison-Wesley).

Porter, R. B. (1980) *Presidential Decision-Making: The Economic Policy Board* (Cambridge: Cambridge University Press).

Radin, B. S. (1998) 'The Government Performance and Results Act (GPRA): Hydra-Headed Monster or Flexible Management Tool?', *Public Administration Review*, 58 (4), 307–16.

Rose, R. (1976) *Managing Presidential Objectives* (New York: The Free Press).

Saldarini, K. (1999) 'Results Act Could Prevent Overlap, GAO Says', *GovExec, Daily Briefing*, 30 March. Available at: www.govexec.com/dailyfed/0399/

Samet, J. M. and T. A. Burke (2001) 'The Bush Administration, the Environment and Public Health – Warnings from the First 100 Days', *International Journal of Epidemiology*, 30, 658–60.

Savoie, D. J. (1994) *Reagan, Thatcher, Mulroney; The Search for a New Bureaucracy* (Pittsburgh: University of Pittsburgh Press).

Seidman, H. B. (1998) *Politics, Power and Position: The Dynamics of Federal Organizations*, 5th edn (New York: Oxford University Press).

Thompson, F. and L. R. Jones (1994) *Reinventing the Pentagon: How New Public Management Can Bring Institutional Renewal* (San Francisco: Jossey-Bass).

USGAO (United States General Accounting Office) (2000a) *Managing in the New Millennium* (Washington DC: USGAO, 29 March, GAO/T-OGC-00-9).

USGAO (United States General Accounting Office) (2000b) *Managing for Results: Barriers to Interagency Coordination* (Washington DC: USGAO, 29 March, GAO/GGD-00-106).

Walker, D. B. (2000) *The Rebirth of Federalism; Slouching Toward Washington* (New York: Chatham House).

Wolf, P. J. (1997) 'Why Must We Reinvent the Federal Government?: Putting Historical Developmental Claims to the Test', *Journal of Public Administration Research and Theory*, 7 (3), 353–88.

Wyszomirski, M. J. (1982) 'The De-Institutionalization of Presidential Staff Agencies', *Public Administration Review*, 42 (4), 448–58.

Notes

Chapter 2   Coordination: What Is It and Why Should We Have It?

1. Even at this stage of development of the State this ability to coordinate from the centre appears to involve some heroic assumptions. See, for example, S. E. Finer's descriptions in his *History of Government* (2007).
2. Offices such as the *intendants* in the ancien régime in France were responsible for ensuring something approaching uniformity. These officials evolved into the contemporary office of the *préfet*.
3. Some scholars have focused on 'policy integration' as one ultimate result or objective of coordination, and one with strong requirements on the participants. For example, Underdal (1980) argued that a perfectly integrated policy was one where '. . . all significant consequences of policy decisions are recognized as decision premises, where policy options are evaluated on the basis of their effects on some aggregate measure of utility, and where the different policy elements are consistent with each other'. In other words, policy integration requires that each policy choice take into account the effects of that choice on the full range of other organizations and programmes, and that as much consistency among the choices as possible be achieved. This is a difficult standard to achieve, but is facilitated by the development of comprehensive policy ideas that can guide the actions of a range of policy actors (Jacob 2004; Hertin and Berkhout 2003).
4. The 'coercion' here implies the use of hierarchical authority, whether between ministers and their officials, or between superiors and subordinates, within an organization. As such the major resource being used is authority rather than norms.
5. For 6 (2004) coordination refers to the development of ideas about joint and holistic working, joint information systems, planning and decision-making, whereas integration is concerned with the actual execution and implementation in the forms of common organizational structures and merged professional practices and interventions.
6. In particular the Conservative government created large numbers of executive agencies, disaggregating ministerial departments into quasi-autonomous organizations (Pollitt et al. 2004).
7. Perri 6 (2004) discerns the following levels of coordination: 1) policy formulation – policy coordination; 2) programme: coordination in relationships between programmes comprising clusters of more/less mutually supportive services; 3) service-providing organizations: coordination in relationships between services; and 4) services to the individual client: integration around the needs or preferences or deserts of individual clients.
8. According to Heffron (1989), horizontal differentiation in an intra-organizational context refers to the extent and type of job specialization within an organization, whereas vertical differentiation points to the nature and

depth of hierarchical structure. Together with spatial dispersion, these two elements form the three dimensions of organizational complexity.

9. An historical example is the separation of the ministry of environment from the ministry of health, as environmental policy was growing in importance.

10. That purpose for government organizations is often enshrined in law, and public managers tend to be very concerned with the need to pursue their legal mandates.

11. While desirable from a coordination perspective, this type of integration may encounter problems with privacy laws that prevent sharing of data across government departments. Those in the European Union present particular difficulties for this style of coordination.

12. That phrase has come to encapsulate coordination problems in intelligence and security in the United States.

13. These information asymmetries are central to many of the rational choice arguments about the deficiencies of the public bureaucracy and the difficulties of sponsors (meaning legislatures) in controlling those formal organizations. See Niskanen (1971).

14. For example, the Office of Management and Budget has developed a set of government-wide goals and performance indicators (OMB 2003).

Chapter 3   Resources, Mechanisms and Instruments for Coordination

1. Some scholars developed a slightly different typology, such as Peters (2003) discerning between market, networks, collaboration and hierarchy, or Hood (2005) differentiating between authority, architecture, mutual interaction, and market and price systems. We consider collaboration and mutual interaction as a more articulated form of networking with a greater willingness of the involved actors to cooperate (Peters 2003).

2. This relationship is inherent in the Weberian conception of public bureaucracy, as well as in other less formal versions of public bureaucracy.

3. Contracts can be a manifestation of coordination through markets, but they can serve coordination objectives by themselves. For example, Itoh (1992) discusses the possibilities for designing contracts within single organizations that can be used to reward agents for their contributions to collective outcomes, as well as to the outcomes of a more constrained agent providing a single product or service to the organization. The same logic may be applied to groups of organizations so that a 'grand contracting approach' can manipulate incentives to induce greater cooperation among the members of collectivities of organizations providing public services. Possible instruments for that purpose are generic objectives and standard contracts, shared indicators, cascading contracts downwards, screening and audits of contracts, or joining lead contractors.

4. In reality, the idea of equal contract partners does not match public sector reality fully, in which contractual relationships between ministers and agencies remain hierarchical and unequal to some extent.

5. Thus, this pattern of decision-making is analogous to satisficing or bounded rationality rather than optimizing behaviour (Williamson 1985).

6. We should note here that 'reframing' of policies, so that they cease to be conflicting, is a more political form of coordination that is not included in this book. In this approach to coordination, bargaining over the definition of a policy is the central element in deciding which organizations should be involved in providing the services, and in what way. This approach may be able to produce important levels of collaboration in problem solving, especially at lower levels of organizations (Bardach 1998). It also runs the risk of bargaining to a lowest common denominator with coordinated but poor-quality services.

7. This taxonomy of strategic management systems has been developed by Eva Beuselinck, to whom we are thankful for inspiring us.

Chapter 4   How To Map Coordination: Issues of Methodology

1. In this inital phase of analysis several collaborators at the Public Management Institute were involved: Amaury Legrain, An Wauters and Wim Pierlé. We are very grateful to them for their help.

Chapter 5   Coordination in New Zealand

1. In case that a ministry was funded out of more than one minister's portfolio, one minister was assigned responsibility for the department (Schick 1996: 29).

2. The State Sector Act gives the SSC an important role regarding coordination. First, the Commissioner was responsible for reviewing the machinery of government including 'the allocation of functions to and between departments; the desirability for the creation of new departments and the amalgamation or abolition of existing departments, as well as the coordination of the activities of departments' (SSC 1998: 11).

3. The five operating officials' committees were constrained in their capacity to act as 'strategically sensitive coordinating mechanisms' because of their preference for details, as well as their unclear informal role, that both make them easy to pass by. Problems in quality of policy advice prompted them to focus on quality control of the advice, rather than coordination itself. In addition, the ad hoc interdepartmental working committees had proved useful in some areas in order to improve links between departments as well as between policy and operations (although Crown Entities are not always included in them), but could be preoccupied with details. Thirdly, the mandated system for interdepartmental consultation enabled departments to comment on policy proposals from other departments and on their impacts on particular sectors and interests, but had the dangers of unclear ownership, of being mainly process-oriented and of resulting in inertia.

Chapter 6   Coordination in the United Kingdom

1. This chapter has been fully re-written and edited by Eva Beuselinck, to whom we are most thankful for this contribution.

2. It should be noted that until 1990, their existence was not formally acknowledged (Moran 2005: 121). The four principal cabinet committees, and the only ones officially admitted in the early 1980s, were Home and Social Affairs, Economic Affairs, Overseas and Defence, and Legislation (Seldon 1990: 113).
3. The British government consists of ministers of different levels and types. There are cabinet ministers and junior ministers. Cabinet ministers are also referred to as 'Secretary of State' when heading departments. Junior ministers can be ministers of state or parliamentary under-secretaries of state.

Chapter 9   Coordination in France

1. '*Département*' refers in the section to the territorial entity and not to central ministries (as in New Zealand), nor to parts of central ministries.

Chapter 11   Coordination in the United States

1. There really were no founding mothers in terms of involvement in decision-making about the Constitution.
2. In at least one case redundancy is designed into the administrative system with the existence of both the Federal Trade Commission and the independent regulatory agency, and the Antitrust Division of the Department of Justice, with each having some degree of jurisdiction over monopolistic practice.
3. The 'divided government' argument over the capacity to govern in the face of partisan differences is inconclusive (see Mayhew 1991; Nicholson, Segura and Woods 2002) but it does point clearly to the importance of this constitutional separation of powers.
4. For example, the state of North Dakota has ten state-wide elected officials plus several elected boards.
5. There are some indicators of this sort, but the dominant pattern continues to focus on the behaviour and outputs of individual organizations.
6. The personnel system has been, and remains, integrated across the federal government. There are several exceptions – the postal service, the Tennessee Valley Authority and the CIA, but most federal employees are either General Schedule or Wage Schedule, and managed from the Office of Personnel Management. This makes moving personnel easier, in principle, although the practice of hiring experts makes moving other than clerical staff more difficult.
7. The legislation was passed in 1978 but did not really begin to be implemented until the early 1980s and came to be known in some circles as 'Carter's gift to Reagan'.
8. In practice each administrative agency is overseen by at least four subcommittees: two functional subcommittees and two appropriations subcommittees, but all four tend to be composed of politicians whose constituents are served by the agency.
9. This act also merged the former Departments of the Army and the Navy to create the Department of Defense, another attempt at coordination that has yet to succeed in producing the type of integrated defence establishment envisaged by the writers of this legislation.

10. Until 2004 this was the General Accounting Office.
11. In particular the CBO was formed as part of the Congressional Budgeting and Impoundment Control Act that was a reaction to some of the budgetary excesses of the Nixon administration.
12. For example, in one week in 2005 the GAO published reports on coordination between various elements of the Department of Homeland Security, the Department of Veterans Affairs and the Department of Health and Human Services concerning medical services, and the coordination of a large number of programmes serving the elderly in a number of federal departments.
13. This discussion will focus on the early days of the Reagan administration. The government Reagan inherited in 1980–1 was described above, and the first few months represented an attempt by the administration to seize control of that existing structure.
14. The Senior Executive Service was thus described as 'Carter's gift to Reagan' because of its increased capacity to increase political appointments and political control over the bureaucracy (see Benda and Levine 1988).
15. Given the political power of individual agencies coordination within a department may be as important, and at times as difficult, as coordination across departments. For example, the Department of Defense still encounters substantial difficulties in controlling the four component armed services.
16. In the American context 'regulations' refers to secondary legislation issued by the bureaucracy through procedures defined by the Administrative Procedures Act of 1946.
17. For an excellent review of the Reagan administration and its impact on public management see Benda and Levine (1988).
18. Rather than passing a single expenditure act, Congress instead tends to pass approximately a dozen appropriations acts. Prior to the Congressional Budget Act there was no joint consideration of all those acts, and hence no means of coordinating public spending, and few financial means of coordinating the public programmes they funded.
19. Of course, the National Security Council remained in place for foreign and defence policy.
20. This effort has been mirrored in the GAO's ongoing research on 'high risk' issues, some of which do have coordination as a central element.
21. The Bush administration also made a major effort in e-government, but was relatively late in doing so. (American state and local governments have been way ahead of the federal government on these issues). Most ICT efforts have been monitored by the General Services Administration, although it is remarkable the extent to which common platforms have not been created. Also, privacy laws make sharing data for coordination extremely difficult.
22. Currently, the SES is still in place, although the lustre of the organization has largely dulled. The idea of there being a cadre of senior managers has been lost in large part because of the increasing politicization of the federal government.
23. The number of cabinet departments was stable until the creation of the Department of Homeland Security. There had been 14 until 2002.
24. The number of departments remained stable for most of the period. What has changed is the sub-departmental structure. The tendency has been

to reduce the number of agencies and offices in each department and to group them more under Assistant Secretaries (political appointees). Also the number of Independent Executive Agencies changed to some extent (for example, the Environmental Protection Agency), but compared to other countries this change is limited. One of the reasons is that service delivery is mainly done by state and local government, so agencification of service delivery tasks was not an issue to the extent that is has been in other countries (such as, for example, the UK and New Zealand).

25. As noted, the major attempt to create greater managerial autonomy came with the National Performance Review. Some organizations were designated Performance Based Organizations, and were made more autonomous, and self-funding. Most are now back where they started as components of the Cabinet departments. The best example of is process was the Patent and Trademark Office.

Chapter 12   Specialization and Coordination in Seven Countries: Findings and Discussion

1. The name of the coordinating structures for domestic policy have tended to change from administration to administration.

Index